STUDIES IN CARIBBEAN PUBLIC POLICY

Volume 2

Selected Issues and Problems in Social Policy

STUDIES IN CARIBBEAN PUBLIC POLICY

Volume 1   Evaluation, Learning and
            Caribbean Development
            Deryck R. Brown, ed.

Volume 2   Selected Issues and Problems
            in Social Policy
            Deryck R. Brown, ed.

Series Editor: Norman Girvan

Dedicated to the memory and work of Denis I.R. Dewar
(deceased October 1997)

Research by students at the Consortium Graduate School of Social Sciences has been supported by grants from the International Development Research Centre. The School's programme has also received support from the United Nations Development Programme, UNESCO, the Ford Foundation and the Commonwealth Fund for Technical Cooperation.
This publication was made possible by a grant from the United Nations Development Programme.

STUDIES IN CARIBBEAN PUBLIC POLICY

Volume 2

Selected Issues and Problems in Social Policy

edited by

DERYCK R. BROWN

Canoe Press
University of the West Indies

Barbados • Jamaica • Trinidad and Tobago

Canoe Press University of the West Indies
1A Aqueduct Flats Mona
Kingston 7 Jamaica W I

in association with

Consortium Graduate School of Social Sciences
The University of the West Indies
Mona Campus Kingston 7 Jamaica

ISSN 0799-0588
ISBN 976-8125-45-4

02 01 00 99 98   5 4 3 2 1

CATALOGUING IN PUBLICATION DATA

Selected issues and problems in social policy /
    Deryck R. Brown, editor

    p. cm.
    MSc. research papers, 1993/94 ; volume 2
    Includes bibliographical references.
    ISBN 976-8125-45-4
    1. Social sciences – Caribbean, English-speaking – Research.
    2. Caribbean, English-speaking – Economic conditions.
    3. University of the West Indies. Consortium Graduate School of
    Social Sciences – Dissertations. I. Brown, Deryck R.

    H62.5.C3E83 1998   300.4

Cover and book design by Robert Harris
Set in 10/14 Stone Informal x 27

Printed by Stephensons Litho Press Ltd, Kingston, Jamaica

Contents

Foreword

The publication of Volume 2 in the Studies in Caribbean Public Policy series, *Selected Issues and Problems in Social Policy*, edited by Deryck Brown, is a significant development for us at the Consortium Graduate School of Social Sciences. Together with those in Volume 1, these papers represent the first results of a programme of training in multidisciplinary policy-oriented research provided to graduate professionals from Caribbean countries through the MSc Development Studies degree. The degree combines courses in the theory of development and Caribbean society from a multidisciplinary perspective, with training in research methods and analytical techniques in specific areas of economic and social policy. The skills and insights acquired are further refined by the conduct of applied research on issues related to Caribbean development, the results of which are written up as short theses.

This volume makes a useful companion to the New Generation Series[1] of monographs, which are based on PhD and MPhil theses prepared at the Consortium Graduate School. Its publication at this time is meant to serve at least three objectives. First, the subject matter and findings are of intrinsic interest to policy-makers and the wider public, and we wish to make them more widely accessible. Second, the papers provide material of interest to other scholars, both for their substantive content and for the methods employed. Evaluating the "Evaluation research" itself is a useful exercise in its own right. To this end, Deryck Brown's Introduction locates this type of work in the context of the development of the Caribbean Social Sciences.

The papers also are an advertisement for the Consortium's multidisciplinary programme, which was set up to complement existing unidisciplinary graduate training in the Social Sciences. Hence the strengths, weaknesses and limitations of the programme can be assessed through an examination of its results by the wider community of scholars and policy-makers. This will contribute to the on-going dialogue and help us in the Consortium to plan for the continued improvement and strengthening of the programme.

We are particularly gratified to have as editor of volumes 1 and 2 one of the earliest graduates of the Consortium programme, Dr Deryck R. Brown. Dr Brown has also been a member of the Consortium adjunct faculty, and his present role as editor is a further indication of his sustained interest in the development of the programme and in the inclusion in it of a strongly policy- oriented component. To have edited each of these papers and weave them all into a coherent whole was itself no mean task, all the more so as Dr Brown was at the same time completing work on his doctoral thesis on Development Administration at Manchester University. I wish to thank him most sincerely for his ready agreement to undertake this responsibility, and for the high degree of professionalism which he brought to bear on it.

Norman Girvan
Professor of Development Studies and Director,
Consortium Graduate School of Social Sciences
Mona, May 1998

Note

1. Earlier titles in this series published by Canoe Press UWI for the Consortium Graduate School of Scoial Sciences include: (1) Ian Boxill, *Ideology and Caribbean Integration* (1993); (2) Girjanauth Boodraj, *Technological Behaviour Under Structural Adjustment: A case sudy* (1995); (3) Roslyn Lynch, *Gender Segregration in the Barbadian Labour Market*, 1946 and 1980 (1995); (4) Peter Adrien, *Metayage, Capitalism and Peasant Development in St Lucia 1840–1957* (1996).

Introduction

Selected Issues and Problems in Social Policy

Deryck R. Brown

This second volume in the Consortium Graduate School's series *Studies in Caribbean Public Policy* focuses on selected issues and problems in social policy. While the seven papers presented here are not easily grouped into a unifying theme, each is a case study which we believe offers fresh insights or radical reinterpretations of persistent problems in the region.

The first three papers focus on what are widely acknowledged to be vulnerable or marginal social groups: youths, women and the elderly. That these social groups bear certain distinct characteristics and present a unique set of considerations for policymakers is indisputable. Typically excluded from the formal, mainstream policy process, they have been identified, along with infants, as having suffered the severest negative impact of the structural adjustment programmes being implemented throughout the developing world since the early 1980s. Indeed, so-called social safety net programmes designed to mitigate the worst effects of structural adjustment are usually targeted at precisely these groups. Another measure of their marginal status – and their importance – is the number of special interest groups and NGOs set up specifically to tackle problems affecting them and to engage in policy advocacy at both national and regional levels.

Youth

We have witnessed the devastation wrought among the region's youth populations as a result of economic liberalization, broadly conceived, the reduction in employment opportunities and the drug culture which has spread to all parts of the world. Crime has become commonplace among large sections of the working class youth, particularly those from depressed urban areas. It is not surprising, therefore, that the label of delinquency has been attached to many young people. In policy terms, programmes to improve the situation among youths have tended to take the form of education, especially technical and vocational training, attitudinal development and entrepreneurial development activities, sometimes accompanied by credit programmes which provide small loans for youths who wish to start small, and microenterprises. The Human Employment and Resource Training (HEART) programme in Jamaica, the Barbados Youth Service and the Youth Training Employment Partnership Programme (YTEPP) in Trinidad and Tobago are examples of such programmes. They are heavily influenced and often assisted by international organizations such as the Commonwealth Youth Programme or the Organization of American States' Youth in Enterprise Programme.

Other programmes place greater emphasis on instilling discipline, often of the military variety, through the introduction of military-style national service programmes or boot camps where young offenders or potential offenders are exposed to military drills. Guyana has long had a national service programme; attempts to introduce one in Trinidad and Tobago in the late 1980s were frustrated by public outcries from ethnic and religious groups opposed to the idea.

Guy Hewitt's paper on "The Political Significance of the Working Class Youth Subculture in Barbados" challenges the basic premise of such programmes and offers an alternative to the delinquency label attached to youths in general, and working class youths in particular. Hewitt argues that the notable changes in values, attitudes and behaviour among these youths, far from being regarded as a manifestation of frustration, hopelessness and value erosion, ought to be seen as a form of antisystemic behaviour and political resistance directed at undermining the hegemony of the normative social order.

Using a phenomenological research design, Hewitt set out to observe the behaviour of working class youths from two communities in Barbados, a Caribbean island which is often characterized as being calm and stable, with no history of revolution or political upheaval. He finds that what is widely regarded as delinquency is part of a more far-reaching process of withdrawal from traditional forms of social, economic and political participation. This process is a subculture which affects attitudes towards family, politics, society, as well as choice of dress, music, economic activity, and even transportation. Far from being the unfortunate victims of a harsh economic system, Hewitt shows how these youths' lifestyles are the product of rational choices with their own internal logic. Consequently, policy interventions which do not recognize the endemic cynicism among youths and their desire to forge an entirely new model of social organization are simply 'more of the same' and are doomed to failure from the outset.

Women

In her paper on "Class, Race and Gender in the Lives of Three Caribbean Women" in Jamaica, Althea Perkins uses the life history method to gather data which are used to show how the factors class, race and gender operate together as interlocking forms of oppression. The findings generated from the study challenge the traditional feminisms which assume that women constitute a homogenous group. Indeed, their diversity based on social background creates different experiences of and resistance to their social realities.

This is not an insignificant point from a policy-making perspective. Too often when women's issues do receive the attention of policymakers, it is little more than tokenism which treats women as a social category without taking into account differences among women. More often than not, those who set the agenda by articulating the 'feminist position' on policy issues come from particular class and ethnic backgrounds. The question to be asked in gender planning is thus: Whose interests do these 'gendered' policies serve? Perhaps the most poignant lesson of Perkins' paper is that research which informs policy in this area must address itself to the lived experiences of 'ordinary' women. Moreover, the agencies which gather and analyze data on the situation of women and which formulate and implement social policy that impacts on women, need to be sensitized to the interplay of these structural factors instead of confining themselves to narrow categories which are not necessarily applicable.

The Elderly

The elderly are the third vulnerable group treated in this volume. Donneth Crooks examines the "Life Satisfaction among the Elderly in Urban Jamaica". While modern science and technology have been able to 'add years to life' with the result that life expectancy has risen substantially in most countries, what has not been determined is whether these added years have proved fulfilling. Crooks premises her study on the assumption that longer life span does not necessarily mean that people are more satisfied with their lives. She sets out to ascertain the level of life satisfaction among aged persons who live in residential-care homes in Kingston and to determine the factors contributing to satisfaction.

Care for the elderly is undeniably a major social policy issue for governments in the Caribbean and elsewhere. An aging population puts demands on the state for improved services, particularly health care, old-age pensions and other forms of public assistance. Structural adjustment has led to cutbacks in public spending, and the elderly have paid dearly in terms of loss of income, reductions in public assistance, elimination of benefits and the provision of services, in spite of the fact that at an earlier time they have contributed economically and, not least, to the public purse through their taxes. Yet they are often seen as a drain on public resources. For those who have no children on whom to rely, their twilight years could very well be spent in lonely isolation, ill-health and distress. Society has a moral responsibility to provide for their well-being. While Crooks' paper is valuable in pointing the way, its focus is primarily on elderly people in private residential-care homes. What of those less fortunate who must rely on state-funded care?

The paper concludes by calling for a national policy on the elderly in Jamaica, including appropriate legislation and the setting up of machinery for implementing, monitoring and evaluating such a policy. It suggests increased community participation and a public awareness programme, as well as locating institutions for the aged alongside custodial institutions for children. This is surely a proposal worth considering as it allows children without parental care to acquire an appreciation for the elderly and to benefit from their experience while, at the same time, providing the aged with an opportunity to feel needed and useful. Though not mentioned specifically, there is also a clear need, as part of a policy on the elderly, to provide some form of recognition and relief to carers of the elderly.

The remaining four papers in the volume touch on other equally crucial areas of social policy: education, crime and policing, rural to urban migration and labour relations. Though unrelated, each topic warrants in-depth study and consideration in its own right, and their treatment by the authors is nothing less than commendable.

Education

Sharon Kelly-Stair examines the role of secondary education in achieving economic competitiveness in Jamaica. The modern global economy is characterized by rapid technological change, the transformation of production processes, work methods, organizational systems, and enhanced trade and investment flows. The effective adoption, generation or adaptation of new technologies requires a completely new orientation and a high level of human resource development. Since the secondary education system produces the largest output for the labour market, the implications of this technological change for the system is vitally important.

This paper, "Human Development, Economic Competitiveness and Secondary Education in Jamaica", explores the impact of technological development and the requirements of economic competitiveness on that country's secondary education system. It identifies certain cognitive and affective skills including literacy, numeracy, creativity and critical thinking as vital for the development of the technological capability necessary if Jamaica is to be competitive. Using criterion referenced tests and other standardized instruments to determine current levels of proficiency in literacy and numeracy and to measure creativity and the capacity for critical thinking among secondary school students, the study points to severe structural impediments in the secondary school system which buttress the social inequities existing in the wider society. The author argues that these impediments inhibit the development of cognitive and other competencies among students, particularly those from lower socio-economic status. The study also shows significant differences in the relative performance of males and females.

Given the development imperatives confronting Jamaica and, indeed, the entire region, there is a clear need for urgent policy interventions aimed at improving the capacity of the secondary school system to respond effectively. Education reform, which is nothing new, must therefore receive high priority if the region in general is to advance in this brave new world of technology, economic competitiveness and efficiency. To that end, Kelly-Stair makes a series of recommendations for education policy in Jamaica which, with some modification, may well be applicable to other countries throughout the Caribbean.

Crime and Policing

Oral Khan's paper, "Community Protection in Inner-city Kingston", focuses on the methods employed at the community level to protect life and property. Crime in Jamaica has been the subject of many studies, seminars and policy debates. Much of the work has focused on the underlying causes of crime at the macro level. What distinguishes Khan's study from others is that it is an attempt at a micro level analysis of how two inner-city communities have actually sought to cope with crime and violence.

By selecting two particular communities, Hannah Town and Craig Town, Khan tries to determine why some communities in inner-city Kingston such as Hannah Town experience dangerously high levels of crime while others such as Craig Town enjoy relative peace and security. The study found that both communities rely primarily on the same informal methods of community protection and less on the local police who seemed unable to provide adequate security. Differing levels of vulnerability to crime and violence were explained by a few key variables, namely, internal cohesion, community reputation in relation to the reputations of its neighbours, and community leadership. The police, it found, were in many senses quite peripheral to efforts by local residents to reduce the level of criminal activity in their respective communities.

Among the more interesting findings is that the 'Don Man' system, in which one powerful figure comes to dominate the community and is looked to for protection, is in decline. The communities studied are searching for alternative means of protecting themselves, means through which they – as communities – play a greater role in establishing their own sense of security. From a policy standpoint, the important conclusion of Khan's paper is the need to introduce a system of community policing, in which the police work with local residents to rid the inner-city areas of crime and the stigma it brings.

Rural to Urban Migration

David Franklyn's paper on "Urban Bias and Livelihood Strategies in Grenada" explores the spatial aspects of the development process in this tiny island state. It examines the structure of the Grenada economy and shows how concentrated economic activity around the capital has led to an urban bias in the development process, with a consequent tendency towards rural to urban migration. Interestingly, the squatter communities which have sprung up around St George's are replicas of the rural villages from which the migrants are drawn. Alternatively put, migrant communities tend to be extensions of the villages from whence the migrants originated.

Franklyn's study draws attention to the often neglected spatial, social and equity aspects of national development efforts which tend to focus exclusively on macroeconomics. This is particularly serious in small island economies. The effects of urban bias on the agricultural sector, rural communities and, indeed, on the urban centres themselves are all important issues which are explored in this paper.

Labour Relations

The final paper in this volume is Kirk Meighoo's piece on 'The Left' in Trinidad and Tobago, entitled "Putting up a New Resistance: The OWTU and the Emergence of an Open, Plural and Democratic Left in Trinidad and Tobago". With the onset of structural adjustment, liberalization policies and technological change, efficiency has become the vital imperative of the industrial sector. 'Downsizing' and retrenchment have become the order of the day. As industry continues to discharge labour in large numbers and unemployment rates increase, the trade union movement is at risk of being marginalized permanently if it does not seek out and find new, novel and perhaps less confrontational ways of representing workers. Unions have a vested interest in employment generation and are challenged to change with the times to become part of the solution rather than part of the problem.

In this context, Meighoo traces the emergence and decline of the Left in Trinidad and Tobago and the Oilfields Workers Trade Union's (OWTU's) pivotal role in organizing the labour movement. The paper then identifies four likely "entry points" from which a 'New Left' may emerge. The paper is a useful historical account of popular resistance and sets an agenda for the future of the radical Left in the new world order.

These seven papers, not unlike those presented in the first volume,[1] are rich in methodological variation and theoretical insight. There is, perhaps, a lack of finality about them; they might best be conceived of as discussion papers and not as 'the final word' on the subjects they cover. It is hoped that they will be widely read and will inform ongoing debates on the range of policy issues dealt with, as well as providing the inspiration for further research.

Note

1. *Studies in Caribbean Public Policy*, Vol 1, *Evaluation, Learning and Caribbean Development*.

Abbreviations

ATSEFWTU	All Trinidad Sugar Estate and Factory Workers Trade Union	NJAC	National Joint Action Committee
ATSGWU	All Trinidad Sugar and General Workers Union	NSMs	New Social Movements
		NTUC	National Trade Union Congress
AWU	Amalgamated Workers' Union	NUFF	National Union of Freedom Fighters
CAFRA	Caribbean Association for Feminist Research and Action	NUFHB & AW	National Union of Food, Hotel, Beverage and Allied Workers
CEPAC	Churches for Ecumenical Planning and Action		
CLS	Committee for Labour Solidarity	NUGE	National Union of Government Employees
CNIRD	Caribbean Network of Integrated Rural Development	NUGFW	National Union of Government and Federated Workers
COLA	Cost of Living Allowance	OPEC	Organization of Petroleum Exporting Countries
COSSABO	Conference of Shop Stewards and Branch Officers		
CPTU	Council of Progressive Trade Unions	OWTU	Oilfields Workers Trade Union
		PAC	Political Action Committee
DEWD	Development and Environmental Works Division	PNP	Peoples National Party
		PRG	People's Revolutionary Government
ECLAC	Economic Commission for Latin America and the Caribbean	SACTF	Special Anti-Crime Task-Force
		SOPO	Summit of Peoples Organizations
HATT	Housewives Association of Trinidad and Tobago	SWU	Steel Workers Union
HEART	Human Employment and Resource Training	SWUTT	Steel Workers Union of Trinidad and Tobago
HDR	Human Development Report	TICFA	Trinidad Islandwide Cane Farmers Association
HSD	Human scale development		
ICFTU/ICTU	Islandwide Cane Farmers Trade Union	TIWU	Transport and Industrial Workers Union
IRA	Industrial Relations Act	TTLC	Trinidad and Tobago Labour Congress
ISA	Industrial Stablisation Act		
JTUM	Joint Trade Union Movement	TTT	Trinidad and Tobago Television
MMM	mass membership meeting	ULF	United Labour Front
MOTION	Movement for Social Transformation	UNC	United National Congress
		UNDP	United Nations Development Project
NAR	National Alliance for Reconstruction	UNESCO	United Nations Educational, Scientific and Cultural Organization
NATUC	National Trade Union Centre		
NFFA	National Foodcrop Farmers Association	WFP	Workers and Farmers Party
NFWU	National Farmers and Workers Union	WHO	World Health Organization
		WICP	Women in the Caribbean Project
NGOs	non-governmental organizations		

1

The Political Significance of the Working Class Youth Subculture in Barbados

Guy A.K. Hewitt

Introduction

There is a widely held perception based on the absence of ideological battles, practical struggles or political upheavals in the postindependence era, that Barbados is a calm and stable society with a calm political climate. This notion appears to be under threat. A fundamental challenge to the social structure has been issued by young people, primarily of working class origins. In essence, it questions the system's right to legitimacy and hegemony, and is articulated through the creation of a separate and distinct culture which challenges the authority of the major social institutions and the means of production.

The emergence of this youth subculture is significant when placed in the context of the sociopolitical development of Barbados. This current wave of antisystemic behaviour coincides with the recurring pattern of discontent emerging as a precursor to mass insurrection. Almost every sixty years to the year[1] the stable democratic process has been ruptured by a flood of accumulated frustration and dissatisfaction. When released against the existing sociopolitical structure, it has served to lay the foundation for the creation of a new social order.

The task of forecasting political upheaval is an ambitious but not an impossible one. Macmillan's (1938) accurate prediction of the 1930s mass insurrection indicates the possibility from a careful and thorough analysis of the sociopolitical climate. While an appeal to the concept of political cycles or waves, given the pattern of mass unrest in Barbados, could support an assertion of impending insurrection, for such a claim to receive credibility it would need to be grounded in observable phenomena identifiable as a precursor to the envisioned revolt.

This emerging youth culture, when linked to other major upheavals in the social, political and economic spheres within the global system, may be symptomatic domestically of what Alvin Toffler in his book, *The Third Wave*, describes as the impending "death of industrialism":

Looking at these violent changes, we can regard them as isolated evidences of instability, breakdown, and disaster. Yet if we stand back and take a longer view, several things will become apparent that will otherwise go unnoticed. To begin with, many of today's changes are not independent of each other. They are not random . . . They are in fact, part of a new phenomenon: . . . the rise of a new civilisation (Toffler 1980: 2).

The central hypothesis being advanced in this paper is that the changes in values, attitudes and behaviour among working class youth represent a form of political protest against systemic hegemony, and not a manifestation of delinquency or antisocial tendencies. Four related questions are pursued:

(a) What, broadly, are the main elements – that is, patterns, values, and behaviour – of the subculture?

(b) What broad form does each take; that is, what are their specific characteristics?

(c) Are they confined to the youth alone?

(d) How prevalent are these subcultural elements among the youth population as a whole?

Defining Youth as a Social Problem

Youth as a social group have increasingly come under attention. The Barbados government established a Commission on Youth and a Youth Desk, the university initiated a research project on youth, and the popular press has made youth a primary area of focus. All energies are directed towards countering the growing 'crisis' among 'Generation X', the fashionable term applied to symbolize the enigmatic quality of the youth today.

Hall, et al. (1978) assert that the definition of youth as a social problem reflects a country beset with 'moral anxiety' about changing social conditions, stemming from an inability to control the nature of the changes taking place. This perception of youth is simplistic. Absent is the recognition, already identified in current research on youth subcultures elsewhere, that these increasing manifestations of a 'delinquent' youth subculture – crime, drug use, indifference to work, and the accompanying value structure – are inherently political (Roberts, 1983: 193; Brake 1985: 192).

Government policy on youth has been premised on the view that youth have lost their social mooring and that, once restored, the escalation in what is considered to be merely delinquent behaviour will cease. The objectives of the Barbados Youth Service, established in 1991 as the hallmark of the government's policy on youth, reflects this orientation: "Its aim is to instill a sense of discipline, build confidence and heighten self-awareness . . . [based on] programmes geared towards attitudinal change" (Government of Barbados 1992: 122).

Such a policy, coupled with a nationwide campaign of family life education, increasing the role of the church, moral education in schools, family counselling, censorship of dress, films, and the media, is expected to contain and counteract the 'youth problem' in Barbados (Government of Barbados 1991: 14). While these policies might appear as practical short term solutions, they can also be interpreted as representative of a highly political agenda. Brake (1985: 196) and Roberts (1983: 126) conclude, based on an analysis of similar youth programmes, that the content of these programmes are intended to reinforce methods of social control, normally exercised through core institutions and agencies of socialization. They can be regarded as no more than an attempt by society to maintain the status quo.

The criticism that the youth policy in Barbados serves more as a means of propaganda is strengthened by the government's omission of measures directed towards addressing the existing structural imbalances which have led to the marginalization of youth in Barbados. In response to the levels of unemployment identified by the government as the primary cause of the youth problem, the Barbados Youth Service has amalgamated all the skills and vocational training programmes out of which "it is hoped that the training . . . would help produce citizens who are employable" (Government of Barbados 1992: 122). However, these are misplaced hopes, for as Kennedy (1989: 141) noted:

The expansion of technical-vocational education was unlikely to lead, on its own, to a reduction of unemployment among Barbadian youth . . . [as it was] noneducational variables which were the major determinants of unemployment.

In addition, Brathwaite (1985: 105), in his study of employment policies in Barbados, supports this conclusion. For instance, he states that "there are indications that the impact of such training is limited because of the difficulties experienced by trainees in locating employment". The programmes also fail to address the demands of youth in their employment pursuits. The Commonwealth Youth Programme (1987: 80) indicated that, apart from earning money, youth in the region want jobs which "develop their special abilities and creativity . . . are original and helpful to others . . . and provide a stable future".

The absence of such characteristics has resulted in the withdrawal of youth from participating in the government's youth programmes. The Barbados Youth Service, which was able to attract 800 applicants when established in 1991, is now underutilized, having received only 175 applications in 1993.

The overall indifference to the situation among youth is captured in the position taken by the then minister responsible for the establishment of the Youth Service who, in the 1994 budget debate, suggested as an alternative solution to youth unemployment that young people should be willing to "work for bus fare and lunch money".

The argument that youth are merely 'delinquent' also serves a political purpose. That is, in the name of 'law and order', the state is justified in using the law as an instrument of repression. Instead of adopting progressive rehabilitative and counselling policies in response to the increases in crimes committed by youth, the judicial system placed its emphasis on deterrence. There has been a marked increase in the incidence and the duration of incarceration, especially of persons under 30 years old. The prison population has increased by more than 50 percent between 1991 and 1994, and at present is nearly double the capacity of the facility.[2] The attempt to reintroduce the use of corporal punishment, contrary to the conventions of the Inter-American Human Rights Commission, indicates the extent of the focus on repression as a means of deterrence.[3]

The Barbadian police force has adopted a similar approach to crime. Indicative of this is that for the first time the wearing of side-arms is now standard in Bridgetown. A Crime Task Force – a mobilized unit of policemen armed with automatic weapons – has also been created. Deployed primarily to police the 'trouble spots' their informal objective, as a senior police official stated, is "to teach them vagabonds respect for the law".

The Public Order Act also seeks to control dress and behaviour. Youth have begun to complain that they are accosted, arrested and detained without charges "for no better reason than their 'unpleasant appearance' in the eyes of the police". There is a real danger, as has occurred elsewhere in the Caribbean, of the police becoming the agents for state sponsored terrorism, perceived simply as "a man who shoot you" (Edwards, 1981: 63).

The emphasis on deterrence and repression seems to have received popular support. Indicative of this is both the passionate lobbying through the media for the reintroduction of corporal punishment and the popularity of a particular calypso entitled "Fighting Back". The chorus of this song warns:

> We fighting fire with fire
> We fighting 'till them surrender
> Arm the police (pow, pow)
> De violence will cease . . .
>   (Mighty Gabby 1993)

Youth and Politics in the Caribbean

Working class youth subculture in Barbados, to be understood, requires redefinition. This is necessary not only for policy redirection but for the more fundamental reason that the delinquent label is unable to evaluate the political elements within the subculture.

Treating nonconformist youth as delinquent is inconsistent with the reality that Third World youth have invariably been politicized. Pick (1964) described youths in Latin American and African countries as being highly involved, and in many cases as being a critical factor in the politics of these developing and newly independent nations. Relatedly, Fishman and Solomon (1972: 248) argue that: "What is not usually obvious is the fact that the directions and pace of social change may be heavily influenced if not instigated by the activities of these young people".

The politicization among Caribbean youth today emerged during the independence era, with the increase in political interests and social aspirations coinciding with the growth, development and consolidation of the nation-state (Rubin and Zavalloni 1969: 69). The acute political awareness of Caribbean youth has taken them onto centre stage in the many social and political movements which evolved in the post-independence era – Rastafarianism, decolonization and anti-imperialism, the Black Power struggle, and contemporarily, the gender and environmental movement.

The political interests among youth have been traditionally recognized as an important factor for the successful management of the Caribbean state. Regardless of ideological orientation, Caribbean governments have sought to implement policies and programmes directed at actively harnessing and maintaining the support of the youth in the society. Increased marginalization has tended to catalyse the politicization of the region's youth. As a primary group affected by the sociopolitical and economic crisis which has emerged in the region,[4] they have begun to respond. As James-Bryan (1986: 19) states:

Vanquished by negative prospects for the future and governments which seem to see the young as part of the problem rather than part of the solution, these young displaced take to the streets daring society to see the reflection of unsuccessful development policies in their hopelessness. It is not only the unemployment, unavailable housing, inadequate health facilities, drug addiction, nor irrelevant education and training. It is the despair that comes from seeing no hope on the horizon, and a lack of credibility in those empowered to trigger that hope and turn it into optimism and a tangible contribution to society. Perhaps the real despair comes in seeing the fickleness of the independence of which the elders boasted, accompanied by corruption, mismanagement, and blatant bureaucratic bungling by those elected to lead them to the glory of nationhood.

What we are witnessing among youth is a protest against the system by their simultaneous withdrawal from the major social and political institutions, and the construction of a "distinct form of political expression" (Edwards, 1981: 178).

Youth and Crime: Changing Political Responses

The dramatic increase in crime among youth (Table 1), has been highlighted mainly as an area of youth delinquency. The perception of and responses to it exemplify this misconception of youth in Barbados and the need for clarification and redefinition.

Studies on unemployment do not confirm a direct correlation between unemployment and crime (Commonwealth Secretariat 1987: 32; Girvan,

Table 1.1   Persons Found Guilty of Crimes (All Courts)
in Barbados 1985 and 1989*

Selected Category	1985	1989	% Increase
Crimes against person	5	4	-20.0
Crime against property with violence	66	157	137.8
Crime against property without violence	144	285	97.9
Malicious injury to property	12	16	33.3
Drugs and other crimes	121	172	42.1
Minor assault, breaches of the peace	114	199	74.5

* Statistics for persons aged 16–30 years

Source: Commissioner of Police Report

et al. 1973: 267). Yet the recent escalation in crime in Barbados has been attributed by the ministry responsible for youth affairs to the rapid growth in unemployment (Government of Barbados, 1991: 49). This view is consistent with recent research on youth in the Caribbean. Academia has drawn on a plethora of theories to explain youth crime ranging from concepts of alienation, anomie and aggression to social pathological explanations of breakdown in socializing agencies: father absence, community erosion, and inadequate child-rearing practices (Carter 1992; Degazon-Johnson 1982; Demas 1977; Goodridge 1986; Stokes 1984). Like the government, they infer that the increase in crime among youth is an aggregation of individual reactions to worsening socioeconomic conditions, a combination of survival strategies and widespread delinquency created by frustration.

Critical criminologists, in seeking to reinterpret the meaning of crime, are revealing that vandals and hooligans are not mindless as the press, politicians and mainstream society have assumed (Roberts 1983: 125). Delinquency cannot be wholly 'explained away' in terms of inadequate socialization in broken homes and disorganized neighbourhoods, or departures from consensual values. Rather, it reflects the contradictions deeply rooted in the class structure.

It has been further shown that this illegal behaviour is not simply due to 'alienation', 'status frustration' or meeting material needs (Downes 1966: 257), but are part and parcel of a misunderstood burgeoning youth culture, which itself is a political response to a consciousness of the situation facing youth as a group (Frith 1984: 42, 63). Research into the nature and causes of crime among youth in the Caribbean has begun to highlight the political component (Dodd and Parris 1976: 1; James-Bryan 1986: 7), revealing "an objective, intrinsically subversive meaning and an incarnate embryonic revolutionary ideology" (Gramsci; quoted in Femia 1981: 46).

The dismissal of crime by youth as mere 'delinquency' can be attributed to the failure by youth to adhere to the accepted forms of political struggle and agitation. Beckles' (1987) response to the objection that the term 'politics' should not be applied to the slave struggle because of an absence of "sophisticated and intellectually conscious action", is relevant here. The political component of their action he states:

. . . is not difficult to defend, since workers, even in socially backward slave societies of the region, made definite political analyses of the power structure they fought against, and use almost every natural and human force available in that struggle – cultural, linguistic, military and psychological (Beckles 1987: 2).

The use of crime as a form of political protest is documented throughout the history of the Caribbean. What researchers have generally failed to consider in their analysis of the increasing crime among youth, is that most of the crime is directed predominantly against private property (see Table 1.1). For instance, in his study on Trinidad, Trotman (1986: 101) noted:

Crimes against property are useful indicators not only of the effect of economic conditions but also the extent of social discontent and disorder. Discontented citizens may vent their feeling against property as the only tangible symbol of the source of their discontent.

Since the slave era, in Barbados as in other islands, the destruction of property and praedial larceny were used as avenues of resistance and, more importantly, accepted as legitimate means of resisting oppression (Beckles 1987: 138). This tradition of crime, primarily property damage, as a response to oppression, continued in the postemancipation era. The history of mass struggle is marked by larceny, looting, burning and other forms of property destruction (Belle 1993; Craton 1993; Rodney 1993). The masses recognized it was the holders of property who were the main beneficiaries of their exploitation. Beckles (1993: 531) points out that in Barbados "in the 1816 rebellion, the masses burnt the sugar plantations, in 1937 they were smashing the financial and commercial plantations".

While historical evidence supports the claim that increased crime against property and the propertied class can be a representation of an alternative form of radical political action by this new group of socioeconomically dispossessed, the politics of the 'lumpen' – "the most self-consciously dispossessed of the urban strata" – indicates that this form of rebelliousness expressed outside of systematic and coherent patterns of mass political organizations still exists. Stone (1973: 157) concluded from his analysis of the 'lumpen' in urban Jamaica, that their contemporary criminal activities contain "a high level of class antagonism towards the affluent and often expresses a self-conscious class militancy".

The decision to study working class youth thus stems from three interrelated factors. Firstly, the working class in the Caribbean has historically been the class that has been most involved in the struggle for political change. Secondly, cultural politics and cultural resistance have been the domain of subordinate groups. Thirdly and most importantly, as existing research on youth has already shown, youth subcultural style is part of the working class experience. It is an adaption by the youth to a similar class experience that is occurring within a different historical context.

Methodology

The study was based on two densely concentrated working class communities: Bay Land and Deacons Farm which are located in the urban parish of St Michael, near the capital Bridgetown. Apart from their working class character, the choice of research sites was a consequence of the ability to gain entry and acceptance into the youth section of these districts.

Definition of youth

The term youth has become so generic that it requires some clarification. The United Nations has defined youth as all persons belonging to the age category of 18 to 24 years. The definition is currently under review, a consequence of much criticism levelled against the acultural bio-psycho-logical criteria which informs it. As critics have pointed out, youth is in fact a social category and must therefore correspond to the sociocultural practices within the specific context.

For the purpose of this study, youth is defined as all persons belonging to the age category of 16 to 27 years of age. The lowering of the age occurred because, as 16 is the official school leaving age, it is for many young people, especially in this study, a period of transition. The increase in the upper limit reflects the increasing marginalization of many young people. As the current economic climate continues to diminish the ability to attain some level of independence, individuals in their late 20s find themselves facing the same socioeconomic situation of those in their early 20s, and reflect a similar perspective of their life situation.

Constructing a framework for stylistic analysis

The style of the working class youth subculture can be regarded as a text inspired by their consciousness and compiled as a means of articulating their resistance to and protest of the existing social order. Because these political responses are coded, the message must be sought "at a level beyond the verbal through the patterns of styles, argot and appearances" (Brake 1985: 68).

Hall, et al. (1978: 203) note that "the primary act of analysis is an act of decoding this text", to uncover the meanings attached to its constituent elements and the relations between them. Using qualitative research researchers, apart from subcultural theorists, have proven capable of going beyond "the overtly committed content" of political struggle, to decipher the meanings of cultural politics and resistance (Gilroy 1987; Scott 1990).

The analysis of the nature and meaning of youth subcultural style has two components. The first is to identify the elements of the style itself. Subcultural theorists identify four modes for the generation of subcultural style: dress, music, ritual, and argot (subcultural slang). The term ritual refers to the "ordered and repeated expression of a particular collective behaviour" (O'Donnell 1985: 45). The second is to identify how this style serves a political purpose. Brake (1985: 68) suggests that to understand the political dimension of the subculture's style, we need to examine the "contest for hegemony", how the subculture wins "space" held by "what Althusser calls ideological state apparatuses – social, cultural, educational and legal institutions".

Findings and Analysis

The attitude to mainstream politics

The Democratic Labour Party (DLP) held a meeting in Independence Square for the official "presentation of candidates". The meeting began with a performance by "Krosfyah", one of the more popular live-bands in the islands. The crowd enjoyed the performance, dancing, and singing with the music, but were anxiously awaiting the political segment to begin, a quiet falling over the crowd as the chairman took the podium to introduce the first speaker. This was the point of departure for our posse, we had heard what we came for – the entertainment.

The impending general elections demonstrated the aversion by the youth under study to all forms of political participation. They refused to support candidates, attend meetings, involve themselves in discussions, or follow televised debates. This is consistent with the findings of the ISER (1992) survey on youth in Barbados, which indicated a high level of a disaffection with the political system.[5] This disaffection should not be interpreted as a lack of politicization, but of a change in form and expression. The political dimension of the working class youth subculture exists beyond an overtly oppositional content, as the resistance employed is produced by and in response to the particular experiences facing youth as a group.

Every political candidate passing through the area was enthusiastically greeted and guaranteed absolute support in the election. During this politicking youths would ask the candidate to "furnish" them with a little "blens". Although skeptical as to their sincerity, the candidate would oblige. Ten or twenty dollars would be offered and accepted with accompanying expressions of gratitude, "you is the only one for we", "you can't lose". There was never any actual intention to vote, far less support the candidate. This performance was all part of gaining easy money. The farce of stating political allegiance reverses the traditional power relations in the political process allowing the youth to manipulate it for their own ends.[6] It was remarked thus: "dem does give we 'blens' to vote for dem, but we know dem is all the same, no blasted use. I wouldn't vote for none ah dem, but dat dhon stop me from tekking dem money."

The significance of this process is not only that it emphasizes the attitude of youth to politics but that it exemplifies the orientation of the subculture's politics and resistance, to invert the power structure and relations within society.

Challenging hegemony: the values of the subculture

The youth subcultural challenge to the dominant hegemony was manifested in the structure of their daily life, their attitudes to work, leisure,
fashion, music, sex, violence and education. There seemed to be a general
undercurrent of ambivalence to life running through the youth in these
areas, as the vast majority of them, although unemployed, made no
attempt to ameliorate their marginalization through trying to find a job
or learning a skill as a means of increasing their marketability. They
simply allowed their fixed future and limited life chances to perpetuate
themselves. The structure of their daily lives conveyed this sense of futility.
There was never a format to the day; no prior agreement on where to meet,
at what time, nor any indication of what was to happen. At first, this was
taken as a reflection of despondency about the situation they found themselves in, but this inference proved inaccurate as those youth who were either
employed or in school manifested a similar disinterest with the passing of
life. The response of Lisa-Marie, a department store sales clerk, is instruc-
tive: "I get paid to go to work so I go, I need the money. I do what them
tell me, or what I got to, then I gone". She was later fired for tardiness.

This indifference among the youth has been criticized by the government and employers as a lack of direction and ambition, but this is
precisely its intention. Living for the moment challenges the widespread
acceptance of the notion of deferred gratification, that each day should
be an investment in the future. The position adopted by the youth goes
beyond simple alienation, a rejection of the commodification of human
labour. It is not the quality of work being questioned but the purpose of
work itself and its accompanying lifestyle.

Whereas their parents have sought to improve their quality of life
within the existing social relations through economy, their children are
rejecting them. The lifestyle of these youth has redefined the hierarchial
order of ontological needs placing the pursuit of pleasure above the
routinization of the daily survival exercise. As Peter, an unemployed youth
from the Bay Land, forcefully asserted: "My mudder work hard all she
life, then she dead, for wha? See me, I gon live an have fun, to hell with
work!"

It was during the unfolding of the day's activities that the dynamics of
the subculture began to emerge. Daily events centred around leisure
activities, which were directed both at enjoyment and excitement, and

affirming their rejection of their parents' lifestyle. Excitement always surrounded the decision whether to go to the beach, 'chill' on the 'block', 'hang' in the city, or 'lime' in the maxi-taxi stand. The choices for daily excitement may appear repetitious, restrained by limited funds, but they were always treated as if novel and innovative. Like children planning a school outing, the final selection was usually based on the amount of enthusiasm expressed for each alternative choice. The most striking feature of these activities was their location in public places. The beaches chosen were the more popular ones in the island, the local meeting point was usually at busy intersections.[7] In the city, Broad Street, the main street was the popular place to 'hang', and the maxi-taxi stand was the busiest public transport facility.

Being in public provided the opportunity for interaction with "everyday life" which, by its very nature, was a source of mockery. Ordinary events and occurrences, such as an accident or traffic jam, people rushing somewhere, looks of exhaustion or anger, or someone 'cussing' – any arbitrary event that reflected the frustrations of everyday life – provided amusement and entertainment. They laughed at what they considered a futile pursuit of the 'almighty dollar'.

Public locations also had a strategic purpose. They provided the genesis of autonomy, a feeling of being in control of one's situation. Being at home or in the neighbourhood was always avoided as it provided an opportunity for confrontation with parents or relatives over their adopted lifestyle. "We would just sit around doing nothing, lined off like birds on a fence, but it was never dull." It could not be monotonous because the "idleness" signified a choice to be free, a rejection of all the responsibilities the agencies of socialization sought to instil were necessary to be a productive and full member of society. Public places, considered to "belong to we", were treated as such. They were part of a process of territorial conquest, where individuals outside the subculture are reluctant or unwilling to enter the domain of "these young vagabonds". Boisterous conversations, conducted with gesticulations as if in a heated debate, displays of aggression, and intimidating stares at passers-by, created invisible fences around the youth as they congregated.

These events also put the subculture on display. Their situation, perceived by others as hopeless or pitiful, was carried with pride, a self-confidence derived from the control they have over their lives. It was this pride that stirred reaction in people as they looked upon the group. The stares, the judgement and condemnation from passers-by as the youth gathered in open defiance of the normative values could be felt. This defiance occasionally led to confrontation with the police as they tried to break up the 'loitering'. There is no fear or apprehension among the youth, only contempt as they challenge the police to "do someting . . . lock we up!"

A characteristic feature of these activities was their spontaneity. As quickly as they began they could end; very often they would be "chilling" somewhere, and someone would simply say "leh we leff", and with that the group would dissolve with a few possibly staying on. The difficulty it created in planning an observation schedule was part of ensuring that their life was never routinized but, more importantly, the constant movement served as a barrier, protecting against infiltration from outsiders.

This pursuit of pleasure can be traced in the less public activities pursued by the youth. The preferred activities in these situations were: watching videos, drinking, smoking marijuana or trying to 'score'. The videotape rental industry is heavily patronized by youth. There is a noticeable bias within the subculture away from comedies and dramas, in favour of action-adventures and thrillers. The aversion to dramas with their depiction of 'reality' was understandable, as the reality was not theirs but the reality of the middle class. The dislike of comedies, however, given their humour and light-heartedness, seemed paradoxical. It was explained during one of the complex selection processes by Larry, one of the more vocal and a de facto leader of the 'posse' from Deacons Farm. His reasoning was simple yet profound: "Dem so [comedies] does try to mek [ordinary] life look funny, but it ain't! . . . You see anyone out here happy [?] . . . not even de children". This revelation allowed for a more complete understanding of their preference for action-adventures and thrillers. The excitement derived from the plots was a significant factor that influenced selection as the youth would become part of the movie, criticizing, advising, directing, narrating. But it went beyond that. The youth saw in the sex, violence, twisting plots and unexpected endings, their own life patterns. This was the reality they could identify with, as much as the 'drama' reflected the reality of the middle class.

Drinking alcohol has always been a popular social activity in the region, used for celebrating special occasions, and especially for the working class as a means of relaxation from the stress of work. For the subculture, entering a 'cemetery' has one sole purpose – to get 'bent'. All the social conventions were discarded; it was not restricted to weekends, to evenings or to special occasions. It happened when money was available to drink. The atmosphere was similar to what one would expect when sailors come to shore after months at sea. The air was overflowing with noise, restrained only by a pause to go "bottoms-up". Onlookers are amazed by this festive atmosphere, aware as they are that there is nothing to celebrate, but they were celebrating. As one youth put it: "We're drinking because we can". They were simply celebrating life.

The use of marijuana was also prolific, used like alcohol as a form of personal freedom. But unlike drinking alcohol, smoking marijuana was a sombre affair, everyone sitting smoking, talking under their breath as if participating in some religious ritual, as if in anticipation of something wondrous. Having observed this process a number of times, the expectation became understandable. It came from the attainment of a greater degree of freedom and autonomy, not only from everyday life, but from one's physical self. It was as if Nirvana had been reached, expressed in the vivid descriptions of what life meant to them: "to be free as a bird", "living to have fun", "to enjoy life no matter what", "to forget reality, it is only pain and suffering". The absence of addiction was significant. It highlighted the fact that drugs did not serve as a means of escape, which creates the dependency that leads to addiction. Addicts or 'paros' were scorned because they lost control over their lives which, paradoxically, was considered similar to the situation their parents faced being forced to work just to survive.

The pursuit of pleasure by youth, generally perceived by society as a manifestation of delinquency, allows them to live on the margins of the dominant social order without threat. But this subculture is a threat, for pleasure is not an end in itself; it is the subculture's means of resistance.

To capture the essence of the working class youth subculture, it has to be traced through the 'bram'. It acts like Alice's 'looking-glass', through which one can see and understand their world. The 'bram' is not just a club or somewhere to party, but the forum for complete expression of the subculture's politics and elements of resistance.

In the 'bram' the entire process of production and consumption and its accompanying social relations are turned outwards; no longer a private, passive or individual process, it becomes a procedure of collective affirmation and protest in which a new authentic public sphere is brought into being – it is here hegemony is placed under contest. The first striking factor about the 'bram' is the ambiance. Traditional clubs radiate bright, hypnotizing light and frequent excited contact, which for the working class facilitated, based on a recognition of a common suffering, a means for collective release. The 'bram' does not radiate, it absorbs. The atmosphere, deep pulsating lights, a repetitive bass-line, and lyrics which vocalize the life of the youth, assimilates the struggle by youth against the normative order, processes it and transforms it into power. It carries a force similar to the slave festivals – collective identity and empowerment, the genesis of resistance.

This nocturnal culture has been identified by sociologists as the key causal factor behind what they consider to be the erosion of the values among the youth due to "poor role models" and the "perverse behaviour", which are part of this environment (Carter 1992: 120). The significant impact of the subculture on these values has not been through the process of erosion, however, but through supplantation. The subculture's choice of an alternative value system is not a reactionary but a conscious position transcending rebelliousness or alienation. It is their way of attempting to undermine social structure.

Fashion

"Glamorous and glitterous" is how you would best describe their 'get-up'. Covering the spectrum of the rainbow, the colours of their attire pierce the murkiness of the night. The men in their multi-coloured denim suits or NBA T-shirts line the walls, leaning up as if unable to bear the weight of the gold chains that adorn their necks. The female apparel is by far more spectacular: chunk heeled shoes; ultra short dresses, spandex bottoms, and B-riders, combined with skin tight blouses exposing the midriff and cleavage or a bra-top for the more daring. They are as outrageous as they are sensational. Mainstream society cannot avoid noticing them, regarding the 'glamour and glitter' as evidence of the "slackness, immorality, and decadence" of the subculture's lifestyle.

The fashion is the uniform for the subculture, its most vivid form of expression, in the most direct and obvious ways. The reordering of society's dress code, creating this festive apparel is not just 'style' but on a deeper level reflects and negotiates an identity. The coarse materialism found in the ostentatious jewellery, the expensive hairstyles, the 'Toni Braxton', crunch and finger wave, the numerous outfits and the imported accessories are all signs of money, with no visible income present. It demonstrates the ability of the youth to maintain themselves outside a system which stresses wage labour as a prerequisite for survival. Wearing dazzling colours at night instead of the socially prescribed subdued tones also reinforces their statement that darkness is not a period of relaxation but celebration.

The incorporation of the black North American 'home-boy' style of wearing athletic 'gear' is part of a common celebration of the ability of the black race, as black athletes have, through the successful development of their talents, made sports a part of their ethno-cultural domain.[8] As with the synthesis of 'rap' and 'Caribbean-beat', it also reveals a transnational consciousness as West Indian youth, through music and films, recognize a common plight with black urban America. As one youth exclaimed during *Malcom X*: "I keep hearing bout how great Amer'ca is, but by Christ, is de same shite happening down dere".

Language

The depth of the antagonism can be glimpsed in the ways that language is itself used in the pattern of cultural struggle. It is possible, for example, to interpret the screams, wails, grunts, scatting and wordless singing that appears in the subculture as both indicative of a struggle to extend communication beyond words and as a commentary on the inadequacy of the existing language as a means of expressing certain truths.

Youth have used language with a great deal of diversity. Interwoven in the speech form is the use of an ever-changing usage of phrases, clichés and slang words accompanied by some creative onomatopoeia and dramatic gesticulations, complete with its particular style of walk and facial expressions. This vernacular symbolizes for the youth a certain amount of fraternal camaraderie within the ranks of the peer group, while at the same time providing an effective screen against outsiders.

The language style and expression of these youth convey a certain cavalier sense of defiance sufficient to make it distinctive from that practised elsewhere. This exceptional quality is in part responsible for a reinforced self-acceptance among the youth, and in this respect converted a socially despised life and talking style into almost a fashion statement.

Music

Inna party she ah bogle dancer, but inna me pad she nuh have character
She jump up and a bump, and posey, posey, but in me bedroom she favour duppy
Criss little browning outta country, no other gal ah test from inna de city
After she dance, da gal ah vex me, she chaan do a ting although she sexy
She Got De Stamina, Ah, Ha, Inna De Dance, But Not De Bedroom, Oh No

She Got De Stamina, Ah, Ha, Inna De Dance, But Not De Bedroom, Imagine
She Doin' The Bogle So Nice, She Doin' The Armstrong Nice
She Doin' Everything So Nice, But Not The Bedroom, No.
[Splashband]

Black music in the Americas has always been linked to a consciousness of our history in an alien world where social divisions of class are further complicated by the added dimension of the cultural division by race. The music of the subculture has been criticized for breaching this tradition, replacing consciousness with 'slackness'. Yassus Afari, a leading Jamaican dub poet, challenges this depiction, seeing it instead as an "evolutionary process". Speaking in a Jamaican context, but relevant to Barbados, he states:

Dancehall plays a role in the evolution of the Jamaican musical experience, as a place where people gather and celebrate music and dance. This happened in different phases of evolution, ska, rocksteady, you name it. We know the link between language and people's experience, geography and history and the role which music plays in all of this (Afari 1994: 8).

To understand the music of the subculture, reggae and calypso (social commentary), it must be placed in a sociohistorical context. The 'consciousness' of the latter two musical orientations flourished within the era of the 'New World Order', when it was believed that capitalism could be reformed for the benefit of those historically exploited by this system. The music of the subculture grew out of the failures of this era and the current free market trends within the world system. Listening to the music of the subculture with an inner ear, one can hear the echos of protest and affirmation in the best of all these new musical creations. It has begun by projecting a 'vulgar' message that generates a hostile or fearful reaction, which in itself is political.

The blatant emphasis on 'sexuality' is part of the politics of 'self' which has blossomed out of the atomization of societies, as globalization erodes traditional forms of collective resistance at all levels: class, race, locality and family. Sexuality stands therefore not only as an area of conflict in its own right, but as a symbol of freedom. Sex is taken out of the closet and treated as something positive and wholesome.

To understand the full meaning of the music we must examine the relations among musicians, audiences and the layers of social context within which they live, "for the production of overall meaning occurs at the intersection between the works musicians produce and the uses and interpretations individual audience members have for those works, an interaction that can only occur within the layers of surrounding social context" (Robinson, et al. 1991: 15).

Musicians can defy conventions of form and sound, and users can violate social norms on how music should be experienced. For example, highly ritualized exchanges between the DJs and the crowd that convey appreciation of a particular rhythm or style frequently involves the systematic corruption of standard English words into new forms of public speech. 'Massive', 'safe', 'settle' and 'worries' are all words which are playfully endowed with meanings unrelated to those invested in them within the dominant discourse. In this context, the subversive potential in the ability to switch between the language of the oppressor and oppressed is appreciated (Gilroy 1987: 194). It is the autonomy of the creation and dissemination of music, its relative independence from hegemonic control, which is in itself political, that allows this music to act as a means of empowerment. Denied access to formal music training, instruments and technology, the music evolved out of the subculture as they transformed the record player from consumption technology to literally an instrument for production, becoming the basic tool in the complex processes of creative improvisation.

The content of the music acts as a political text as the DJs, organic intellectuals, transmit and affirm the values of the subculture. These young performers have become role models and de facto educators for members of the subculture. The impact of this music on the youth is recognized outside the subculture as DJs, while being criticized for their style and music, are simultaneously sought to write music to convey messages against violence, promiscuity and the like.

Sexuality

We were chatting when this girl walked in. She wore a skintight black spandex. I couldn't believe someone so big, so enormous, could fit into something so small, everything was overflowing. Apparently she knew some of the girls in the crowd, because she walked up and spoke briefly. I couldn't hide my amusement. One of the other girls looked me cold in the eye, 'wha de ass wrong with you?' I said nothing. She didn't see anything funny. Interestingly, none of the other fellas appeared to either.

The female 'get-up' is not restricted to 'X-rated' expressions. Linen suits, jeans suits, poet and peasant blouses with laces and frills are also worn. All of these can be a part of the 'bram' fashion "depending on the jewellery, shoes and handbag worn". The important feature is that women dress as they want to, no adherence to social or gender conventions exists. Accused of contributing to gender exploitation, paradoxically, this 'X-ratedness' serves as an organic form of feminism's 'sexual politics'.

These women have reclaimed possession of their bodies and their identity. Their dress is not determined by male expectations but by their free choice from a diversity of options. They have redefined the meaning of 'looking sexy', as women of all shapes and sizes dress in similar 'get-ups' neither uncomfortable nor self-conscious. Men appear to respect this new self-definition, as no matter how scantily clad and regardless of their conduct, women are generally free from harassment and molestation.

Violence

Up to now I'm not sure what caused the fight tonight. That was not the issue for the 'fellas', all they were aware of that Mango was in trouble, that appeared to be enough. Within seconds a 'war' had erupted between the Bay Land posse and the posse for the Pinelands housing area. Mango never explained why the fight started nor did he thank the 'fellas' for stepping in, he just took it for granted they would back him up.

The rejection by youth of their parents' traditional means of political agitation through the trade union, political party and the electoral process has been compensated for by utilizing informal forms of solidarity and collective action.

The fluidity of these forms of solidarity is a reflection of the existence the subculture has adopted. Survival strategies based on informal economic activity and the development of resistance by challenging hegemony through individual lifestyle choices is antithetical to institutionalized forms of politicization. Solidarity among members of the subculture follows a grass roots orientation similar to the working class of the pre 1930s. It is directed towards specific focal concerns of the youth, in the same way that Friendly Societies emerged to provide economic security and the Land Ship for social cohesion for the masses prior to the social revolution of the 1930s.

Violence as a response to insults or physical threats, while appearing irrational, is a microcosm of the wider subculture's attempt to win space for itself. Violence signifies territorial preservation on the individual or group level. Having defined their life as a political statement, youth perceive aggression against self as a threat to their autonomy or independence, reacting in a similar manner expected by society if the sovereignty of the state was under threat. It is from this willingness among members to fight for autonomy when aggregated, that the subculture finds its strength to resist collectively the normative order, just as the willingness by workers of the region in the 1930s to risk their security and strike was the strength behind the social revolution which followed.

Parenting and partying

Whenever we go to the 'backyard', Simone and Shaquira are always there. We know them because they too are from the Bayland. They are constantly harassed for being out partying instead of staying home with the children. It's not that their children are not of concern, but Simone has a child for Mango, one of the fellas, and she won't let him check another woman in peace. The 'bram', far from being the exclusive domain of men, is ardently supported by women, who return night after night to these subcultural assemblies. What is perturbing is that many of these women are single parents, who appear willing to abandon their children in the pursuit of fun and excitement. It's not that these young mothers don't know where their children are, for they are usually with an aunt, mother or grandmother, but that the responsibility for the nurturing of the child has been given to some relative. It would be so much simpler if they avoided getting pregnant.

The child rearing practices of these young women appear consistent with traditional theories on the working class family, based on a correlation between the role of the extended family in nurturing and their socioeconomic status (Clarke 1957). Careful analysis reveals a divergence between theory and practice. It is not, as is stressed in the literature, their economic conditions which require them to leave their children in the care of relatives while they work, as many of these women are unemployed, but their subcultural leisure lifestyle.

The high level of unemployment, continued delinquency in child support payments among the young males in Barbados (Barbados Family Planning Association 1990), and the increased knowledge and use of contraceptives (Ellis, et al. 1990) negate further suggestions that recurring single parenthood among these young women is attributable to their economic situation, through attempts to gain financial security (Commonwealth Secretariat 1987; Jagdeo 1984) or inadequate knowledge of or the unavailability of contraceptives (Jagdeo 1984).

Young parenthood is part of the political resistance of the subculture, and finds its historical roots in slavery. The issue of childbirth was critical to the amelioration of work policies and the economic conditions women faced under slavery (Beckles 1987: 90–110) and has remained as a political issue as working class women resisted family planning on the grounds that it was devised for social control through a reduction in the size of the working class (Brody 1981: 84).

The meaning of parenthood within the subculture is that it signifies to the individual members that their lifestyle is both acceptable and reproducible. To set restrictions on having children due to the socioeconomic marginalization these young people face is to negate the high valuation placed on the subculture as an alternative lifestyle and means of resistance. The adornment of their children in fashions consistent with that of the subcultures; the sanctioning of recreational activities – television and videos, games, going shopping, or to the beach – with a concomitant de-emphasis on education; and the absence of instruction in civic behaviour are all indicative of the parents' affirmation of the value and virtues of the life that they have chosen.

The most direct challenge to the hegemonic order is the location, organization and orientation of the 'bram'. Located on the periphery of the city centre, the heart of economic activity, and ironically scattered around 'Independence Square', the alternative lifestyle of leisure to work is literally juxtaposed, as if deliberately demanding a choice. The youth do choose this lifestyle. The choice is made as they abandon all thought of the negative consequences that being out all night has for work in the morning. The choice is made when they defy their parents' emphasis on studying hard to secure themselves a future. It is made when they put on their 'gear' which costs more than their parents earn in a week. It is made when they spend all their money without a care about how they will survive tomorrow.

Resistance to the hegemonic order occurs through the high degree of participation given to leisure when compared to productive activity. The nature of these activities, lasting through the night and occurring throughout the entire week, renders any productive activity worthless. The selection of this nocturnal lifestyle directly resists the normative order's demand for a high daily output of human power necessary for the reproduction of capital.

Economic activity and education

The organization of the 'bram', part of the so-called informal sector, the unrecognized part of our development process, offers the youth a part in breaking the oligarchic control of the economy by the large conglomerates. They are able to influence directly the redirection of surplus accumulation through supporting the economic enfranchisement of the small business sector. As a youth stated outside one 'bram', "he [ie, the owner] could get my money anytime, he is one ah we!"

The patronage by youth of small enterprises, identified as connected to the lifestyle of the subculture, has been influential in the economic development of certain small business sectors. This is evident in the expansion of the video industry in many working class areas, through nearly exclusive rental of action-adventures and thrillers; the collapse of the state-run transport board owing to the competitive popularity of minibuses, minivans, and maxi-taxis whose expansion grew out of a marketing strategy of speed, dub-music, and stylish automotive trimmings; and the successful growth of street vendors and ICIs selling fashionable clothing and accessories.

In contradistinction to the operation of other sectors of the economy, these young 'consumers' have a direct control over the type of product offered by the music component of the entertainment industry. Changes in the 'sound system', in the 'live-bands', in layout or prices, is subject to the response of these 'consumers', and this power is carefully protected. To overlook this fact is to face financial ruin, as the operator of the popular 'September Nightclub' realized during a boycott caused by his attempted price increase. He forgot that "him don't control we, we control he". The prices were subsequently reduced.

To travel by maxi-taxi, especially at night to a 'big bram', is to experience first hand the influence of the youth on the products and services. The youth only patronize certain maxis – "their maxis" – and their preferences will determine the type of service offered. "Their maxis" are generally brightly painted, two-tone, with chrome trim. The drivers are usually under thirty, and part of the subculture. They drive fast and dangerously, pausing only to off-load. The music systems on board are very powerful despite being illegal.

Hegemony is challenged through the effect of the subculture on labour, an essential element for the continued functioning of capitalism. The reorientation of outlook is caused by the influence of the subculture's value structure away from the hegemonic definition of life as a mere ingredient for capitalist production, which threatens the required guarantee of an availability of future labour reserves.

Recurring stories of parents being called to schools and of employers issuing warning letters to youths unable to concentrate on their work, are communicated with an air of pride and amusement, as it indicates their commitment to the values of the subculture. On the few occasions where individuals were either fired from their jobs or expelled from school for their indolence, all feelings of regret or remorse were absent. Buddy, a 23-year-old supermarket worker, declared on the day he lost his job: "Boy, I really glad. I hated that job. I was only there because my mudder get it for me". He reacted in amazement to questions about whether he planned to look for another job: "I look like I want work?" If one takes account of his gold chain, L.A. Gear shoes and Bugle Boy suit which, incidentally, his salary could not afford, it is clear that his job meant little to him.

Education

Is not that I don't like what they teach in school. It is that they can't teach me nutting. They talk 'bout getting the most out of life. Getting $250.00 when the week come is life? That is what they want to teach we! And we are supposed to learn dat?

Two boys, Jimmy and Spade, around the age of 15, came out with us tonight. Their parents were unaware, understandably, as it was a school night, not that they would have been given permission otherwise. They had the time of their lives, drinking beer, dancing, trying to 'chat-up' older girls. On the way home they expressed an indifference to being caught by their parents or staying awake at school in the morning. I know they'll be back out with us soon. The subculture had just recruited two new members.

Prior to the rise of the youth subculture, the educational system, although unable to fulfil the aspirations of working class youth in Barbados, was still accepted due to the uncontested legitimacy of the official school ideology. Students sought to gain some benefits from the system despite the pervasive recognition of its sterility, and its incapacity due to increasing labour market segmentation to meet its stated objective of offering a means for social mobility (Anderson and Gordon 1989: 187; Baksh 1986: 23).

The impact of the subculture is manifested in the reversal of this trend of pursuing the limited benefits available from the education system. This

Table 1.2   CXC Results – Basic Proficiency[9]

Year	1985	1986	1987	1988	1989	1990	1991
% Passes	48.7	49.2	45.4	44.0	41.7	42.3	39.7

Source: Ministry of Education Annual Report

is reflected in recent examination results of the Caribbean Examinations Council (CXC) (see Table 1.2).

The 18.5 percent reduction in academic performance, and the accompanying "negative trend in technical and vocational skills training" (Government of Barbados 1991: 6), is part of the growing antischool culture. Truancy and 'fooling around' in class are no longer the primary means of protesting the system's uselessness (Baksh, 1986: 37); the mere acceptance of the subculture's alternative value system resists through its negation of the entire orientation of the educational system. This collective volition of self-exclusion from education, given the importance of this primary agency of socialization, is detrimental to the stability of the normative order. Education has never acted simply as a means for transferring knowledge. Figueroa and Persaud (1976: 23) identify as the salient functions of the education system: "system maintenance; the transmission of society's culture; social, occupational and academic selection, and socialization".

From its inception in the early postemancipation period, education has been directly linked to the economy. Gordon (1968: 107) informs us that the 1875 Mitcheson Report recommended elementary education for ex-slaves in Barbados in order "to make ex-slaves better labourers than would be the case without school training in the habits of obedience, order, punctuality, honesty and the like". The rejection of education undermines the very foundation of the social relations required for capitalism to continue.

It is not that young people are unwilling to work; it is that they reject the dominant work culture. The subculture serves as a critique of productivism: work, the labour process and the division of labour under capitalism. With the aggregate unemployment figures for those aged 15–24 moving from 37.35 percent in 1991 to 47.1 percent in 1992 during the first year of the IMF programme,[10] the youth continue to reject opportunities to do menial and poorly paid work.

Many of the youths are aware of how they will survive. The refinement of their daily activities to inexpensive activities, liming or hanging-out in public places and the supply of food and shelter from family members meet their daily needs. Accepting temporary work, whether legal or illegal, small loans from friends, remittances or parcels from abroad provide the resources for meeting any extraordinary expenses.

It is in the 'informal economy' that the subculture finds its economic base, where the financial resources are found for the subculture with no obvious source of income to reproduce or maintain itself. Very often these youth have intermittent involvement in informal commercial importation (ICI), the entertainment industry, maxi-taxi operators, fishing and small craft, petty larceny, or drug dealing.

It is not exclusively their socioeconomic circumstances that influence their involvement with the underground economy. The very character of the underground economy – hustling – reflects their world. It is exciting and dramatic, and outside the dreary world of wage labour. In this economic world they are in control. They decide when, how, and under what conditions they work. To endure the abuse when negotiating prices with ICIs for the latest 'gear', which is a complete reverse of the buyer-seller relationship, is to understand the autonomy and empowerment that these marginal economic activities permit.

Conclusion

The unidisciplinary methodological approach of researching and inter-preting phenomena within the social sciences has restricted the ability to capture in a holistic manner, the multifaceted character of social reality. This has resulted in a limited and sometimes inaccurate portrayal of the phenomena under investigation.

The political dimension of the youth subculture which has developed among working class youths in Barbados has been neglected because of this unidisciplinary approach to researching social reality. Failing to conform to the established criteria of political resistance and agitation, the dynamics of the youth subculture have been ignored by political science, leaving sociologists to research this burgeoning social movement. The consequence is that the antisystemic tendencies within the subculture have been interpreted as a manifestation of societal breakdown rather than as part of a struggle for sociopolitical change.

The rise in political resistance can be attributed to the increasing marginalization of youth in Caribbean society, youth now seen as a social problem rather than a future resource, and a growing recognition that the legitimacy crisis of the political and economic systems cannot be resolved within the existing political and economic framework.

The working class youth subculture is a response to this crisis, as youth have not only created an alternative value system and lifestyle, but have been able to use it as a means of political resistance by using the elements of the subculture to challenge the hegemony of the normative order. The success by the members of the subculture not only to maintain this alternative existence but also, in the process, recruit new members is now receiving growing attention from the traditional elites. They are able to identify the potential threat to the stability of the social order, but incapable of accepting the subculture as a progressive force, a natural response to eroding economic democracy and mass participation. Repression has become the primary tool of response.

Physical coercion has historically served as an effective mechanism for containing social explosions. These measures are inappropriate, however, when applied to the youth subculture. The youth subculture is not following the traditional path of mass mobilization which can be repressed through force, but through its values, attitudes and behaviour, undermines the social fabric, encouraging social implosion. Force cannot deter this.

To counteract the growing subculture, policy formulation must incorporate working class youth into the development programme of Barbados. Policies aimed at attitudinal change and skills development are inappropriate as they are geared towards managing the marginal situation among working class youth rather than towards alleviation.

In respect of this, the following suggestions are being advanced for the consideration of policymakers:

1. Employment and training programmes must be developed which allow for the economic enfranchisement of these young people, including entrepreneurial skills development, available financing for microenterprise, and marketing assistance for product development and distribution.

2. The orientation of the economic development policies will need to be adjusted, as the existing liberalization thrust is antithetical to government expanding its role in the economy, and giving short-term protection to such an enterprise.

3. Incentives should be offered to the private sector to encourage them to invest in employment and training of the youth in Barbados. Tax credits for employing young people or deductions for training programmes could increase the marketability of young people who, in the current economic situation, are competing with skilled persons on the job market.

4. The education system should be evaluated and reconsidered to determine how it could best equip young people to develop to their full

human potential. The current grammar school orientation is out-dated.

5. Government departments that maintain a youth focus or component – schools, courts, police and probation, welfare services, and community development – require training to develop an awareness to the fact that the situation among youth is not a manifestation of delinquency but of the marginalization of youth within the overall development of Barbados.

Notes

1. These include the 1816 slave rebellion, the 1876 Confederation revolt and the 1937 riots.
2. Due to the unavailability of official statistics this information was gathered from the Public Relations Office of the Royal Barbados Police Force.
3. The sentencing of persons to be flogged was overturned by the Court of Appeal in 1993, on the grounds that no statutory provision existed which accorded to any individual the authority to administer a flogging on another person.
4. In the national survey of Youth in Barbados conducted by the Institute of Social and Economic Research, UWI, 75 percent of those surveyed felt life is worse today than five years ago, with 70 percent holding the opinion that it will become even worse over the next five years (ISER 1992).
5. Sixty six percent of the sample expressed a negative view of the political process, stating the process was either corrupt, inefficient or irrelevant to their needs or situation (ISER 1992).
6. This could explain the incongruity between the actual disinclination among youth to participate in politics and the low amount of youth articulating this opinion on voting in the September 1994 pre-election polls (Emmanuel 1994).
7. In both the Bay Land and Deacons Farm, the youth congregate by the local recreational parks adjoining the roads used by motorists and public transport.
8. Research at the UWI has begun to focus, primarily through cricket, on the link between sports and the development of race consciousness and cultural nationalism.
9. The basic proficiency level is geared towards students in the newer secondary school, who are almost exclusively working class.
10. Although official statistics are unavailable for 1993 or 1994, this figure is estimated to have increased significantly as the total unemployed population increased for 21, 000 persons in 1991 to a current total of approximately 30,000 persons. *Source:* Ministry of Labour and Community Development.

Glossary

beast	Member of the police force
bent	To get drunk
blens	Money
block	Local meeting point
bram	A pay party open to the public, held in nightclubs or assembly halls, catering to the tastes of working class youth
breed	To make or become pregnant
cemetery	A rum shop, the place where spirits are found
chill	A loose gathering of individuals within a certain area
crop	Supply (usually of marijuana)
cussing	The use of profanity
dan	A well-liked man, renowned for his popularity with women
deal	To be involved with in an intimate relationship
fellas	A group of friends
front-house	Living room
furnishing	The lending of money
gear	Clothing
get-up	Fashion
glamour girls	Well-groomed and well-dressed women
hang(ing)	An assembly of individuals with no specific purpose
higgler	A small trader
hobbie-class	Free entry
liming	A spontaneous get-together
operator	Owner or host of the bram
paro	A drug addict
posse	A collection of individuals, usually friends from one area
pounding	Very loud (music)
scene	Area or locality
score	To have sex
spar	A friend
spring	To pay for

2

Issues of Class, Race and Gender in the Lives of Three Caribbean Women

Althea Perkins

Introduction

Caribbean research on women originally served the purpose of ensuring that women's experiences were recorded. The methodologies used, for the most part, added women to the existing data instead of providing a theoretical framework within which the experiences of women in the Caribbean could be examined. The experience of women in the Caribbean and other parts of the world has proven to be theoretically beyond the limits of grand theories which have guided scholarship in the past. This has resulted largely from the lack of a feminist perspective in these paradigms. Sandra Harding (1987) notes this about the use by feminist scholars of conventional theoretical frameworks:

[They] have stretched the intended domains of these theories, reinterpreted their central claims or borrowed their concepts and categories to make visible women's lives . . . After our labours these theories often do not resemble what their non feminist creators or users had in mind, to put the point mildly . . . it has never been women's experiences that have provided the grounding for any of the theories from which we borrow. It is not women's experiences that have generated the problems these theories attempt to resolve, nor have women's experiences served as the test of the adequacy of these theories (cited in Aptheker 1989: 10).

These attempts to add women to already existing theories have yielded theories which have proved inadequate in providing an understanding of the diversity and difference in the experiences of black women and those from other ethnic groups. This is so largely because their formulation has been carried out by white middle class feminists, mainly from North America and Europe, whose theorizing has been confined to their own experiences, and who have presented these experiences as though they are representative of all women. Clearly, these experiences cannot explain those of women of other classes, races, ethnicities and cultures. The life of a woman cannot be assessed or theorized in isolation. It needs to be located in the context of her life experiences, and these differ over space and time. As Elsa Barkley-Brown (1992: 298) notes:

. . . we need to recognize differences and the relational nature of these differences. Middle class women live the way they do because working class women live the lives they do.

Illustrative of this is the situation facing the average middle class woman. She can relieve herself of the primary responsibility of the home and children because working class women working as domestic helpers take on this responsibility. The same argument can be put forward in respect of race or colour differences. In the Jamaican context, a black skinned woman may experience feelings of inferiority when she sees from year to year that her features are neither represented in beauty contests nor do they appear in advertisements or magazines. In other words, the black skinned woman does not fit that concept of beauty which has been defined and accepted by the society at large. Issues of race, class, and culture thus are important considerations when theorizing based on the experiences of women.

It may be argued that consideration of racial, class and cultural dynamics in attempts to understand the experiences of women may result, in fact, in the fragmentation of the feminist movement and perhaps its eventual demise. Aptheker (1989) does not share this view. She notes, rather, that women, despite their differences, have a consciousness of social reality which is distinct from that of men. While all women do not have the same consciousness, they are similar to the extent that they are subjected to the sexual division of labour and are institutionally subordinated to men. This is reflected in employment, violence against women, education, religious and cultural practices. Of course, this consciousness is expressed in different ways in different cultures. Thus, only an examination of the circumstances of the specific culture can lead to an understanding of the particular consciousness of women in that culture.

No theorizing about women would be meaningful, then, unless it examined issues of women's strategies of resistance and survival, as well as the ways in which they shape their lives and define their existence, not only in terms of their relationship to males but also on their own terms. The need is to transcend the boundaries which examine women's lives only as supplementary or, in reaction to a male paradigm, and seek to understand society from a female perspective.

The experiences of women in the Caribbean did not become the main focus of analyses until the 1970s. Even though the works offered some semblance of a feminist perspective, they have not yet produced a relevant theoretical framework which would provide a more holistic assessment of women's experiences and acceptance or resistance to their subordination. The Caribbean thus needs a feminist theoretical framework which will allow for a deeper understanding of social reality than has been provided to date.

Research Problem and Objectives

Since race, class and gender continue to be the three most powerful forms of oppression in the Caribbean, the main objective of this paper is to assess their interrelation in the lives of three women. Relatedly, one examines how the three forms of oppression interact to create different experiences and forms of resistance for women despite their female consciousness. Additionally, based on the data obtained, the paper develops and offers some preliminary thoughts on a feminist theory which is more applicable to the Caribbean.

Theoretical Framework

Women's subordinate status and their struggle for human rights led to the origin of the feminist movement. The movement developed as a reflection of the experiences of women in different contexts which has resulted in different feminisms, namely, Liberal, Marxist, Radical, Social-ist, Postmodern, Black and other indigenous feminisms. These analytical approaches to women's issues were developed within a context which either assumed the homogeneity of women as a group, or lacked a perspective which took into account the experiences of women outside the context of the white middle class perspective from which they originated.

The lack of a perspective which takes into account the struggles of women instead of seeing them as mere victims of patriarchy or capitalism, has rendered these works inadequate to deal with the differences experienced by women in different contexts and the particularity of their struggles.

Postmodern feminism came as a challenge to the abovementioned approaches. Works such as that of Irigaray (1985) acknowledged a more rounded and holistic vision of the female. Here, woman is not seen merely as an object, that is to say, a victim, but as a subject struggling to change her life within and in spite of her environment. The postmodern approach, therefore, allows for the recognition of oppression of females while, at the same time, paying attention to plurality and difference in their lives.

In response to contextual demands the postmodern approach has influenced several indigenous feminist critiques and theoretical formulations from Asia, Native America, Africa and the diaspora, lesbians, and Latin America. Reflective of such works is Moraga and Anzaldúa (1983) which provides a challenge to traditional analyses, research and experimentation and puts forward a "theory of the flesh". This is described as one in which:

the physical realities of our lives – our skin colour, the land or concrete we grew up on, our sexual longings – all fuse to create a politic born out of necessity. Here, we attempt to bridge the contradictions in our experience:

we are coloured in a white feminist movement

we are feminist among the people of our culture

we are often the lesbians among the straight

we do this bridging by naming ourselves and by
telling stories in our own words. (Maraga and Anzaldúa 1983)

Many of the works have drawn largely on personal experiences to show the ways in which one's particular context or culture serves to create different experiences for different individuals and groups, and sometimes different experiences for the same individuals across space and time.

The Black Feminist Critique

The conceptualization of race, class and gender as interlocking forms of oppression and exploitation of black women and men and those of other ethnic and racial groups has been expressed in black feminism. The works of Davis (1981), Hooks (1981; 1988), Lorde (1984), and Hill-Collins (1991), among others, have located the struggles of black women within a wider struggle.

These studies challenge the universalist claims of the theoretical frameworks developed by white middle class feminists. Black feminism argues that white middle class feminism has not only served to present a false history of non-white women and men, but has also failed to address feminist issues as they relate to non-white women. Of course, dominant feminist theories have been an important base for the development of the feminist movement. Yet they have had to be broadened to take into account the experiences of women other than those which may be coming from the white middle class.

Quite obviously, the black feminist critique has to be used guardedly. This is so because, despite the common experience of slavery, the United States and the Caribbean have different realities. Thus, unlike the United States where racism is more institutionalized and the social structure more definitively demarcated into black and white, in the Caribbean, social segments are more fragmented on the basis of skin colour. There is, in effect, a colour spectrum ranging from black through shades of brown to whites, with the whites being the privileged minority at the top of the social ladder.

The critique is important for the Caribbean because it represents a reconceptualization of feminism which sees patriarchal domination as sharing ideological foundations with other forms of oppression. Hooks (1989) defines this as the "politic of domination". She states that rather than sex alone, it is sex, race and class which, as interlocking systems of domination, determine the nature of the woman's status and identity, the extent to which she will either dominate or be dominated. In short, systems of domination interact to provide the context and experiences in the lives of women. And it is only through an analysis of all systems collectively that diversity and the complexities of the female experience can be adequately explored and analyzed.

Hill-Collins (1991) shows that black feminist thought challenges the two prevailing conceptions in the understanding of the consciousness of oppressed groups. The first relates to the Marxist-influenced approach which holds that subordinate groups identify with the powerful group and have no independent interpretation of their reality. The second relates to the position which assumes that the oppressed are less capable of expressing their standpoint. Both perspectives thus see oppressed groups' consciousness directly as a result of that of the oppressors, implying that the oppressed are incapable of political activism. This challenge to the lack of autonomy of oppressed groups, and in particular women, suggests that they have also been integrally involved in the process of determining their realities. Implied in this capability of political activism are strategies of resistance and coping which are employed by these groups as an active process in determining their life experiences.

Resistance and Strategies of Coping

Rather than accepting the concept of resistance in its traditional sense and in this way linking it to progress achieved through political social movements, resistance is here seen as acts involving individuals or small groups which, even though they may not challenge the social system, serve to influence the realities of those performing the acts. Thus oppressed groups, based on race, class or gender are capable of an autonomous consciousness which, through small acts and strategies, resist domination. Scott (1990: 188) refers to these acts as hidden transcripts which are not only "behind-the-scenes griping and grumbling"; they are, he argues, also "enacted in a host of down-to-earth, low profile stratagems designed to minimize appropriation". The informal, as opposed to an organized political context in which these acts of resistance are carried out suggest that they are largely confined to informal networks of family and community, and are also expressed at the individual level.

A gender perspective will undoubtedly enhance the differences in these forms of resistance as they are performed by women compared to men. Women's responsibility for the domestic sphere would suggest that there are identifiable ways in which acts peculiar to females are carried out in this context. Aptheker (1989) refers to this form of resistance as expressed in "the dailiness of women's lives". She states:

By the dailiness of women's lives I mean the patterns women create and the meanings women invent each day and over time as a result of their labours and in the context of their subordinated status to men. The point is not to describe every aspect of daily life or to represent a schedule of priorities in which some activities are more important or accorded more status than others. The point is to suggest a way of knowing from the meanings women give to their labours. The search for dailiness is a method of work that allows us to take patterns women create and the meanings women invent and learn from them. If we map what we learn, connecting one meaning or invention to another, we begin to lay out a different way of seeing reality. This way of seeing is what I refer to as woman's standpoint. (Aptheker 1989: 39)

The discussion of black feminism and resistance has served to show the importance of an analysis which uses women's experience and their context as valuable sources of research and theorizing. As members of an oppressed group where the sexual division of labour and institutional subordination have facilitated a consciousness, this experience should not be assumed to be homogenous. Difference and diversity need to be accounted for in any analysis which seeks to describe social realities adequately. Hence, class, race and gender need to be viewed as interlocking categories of analysis to show the interlocking systems of domination as they exist in society. It is only in this way that a holistic picture can be created instead of a variety of scenes that are parts of the whole.

The Caribbean and Gender Analysis

Caribbean social structure has its grounding in the period of slavery which was characterized by antagonistic social relations between the white planters at the top and the black slaves at the bottom of the social ladder. The coercive and consensual sexual relations between the female slaves and white planters produced a coloured class which was to be superior to the blacks but inferior to the whites, and enjoyed a status of freedom by virtue of manumission granted by planters. They would act as a kind of mediator between both classes. An analysis of *Lady Nugent's Journal of Her Residence in Jamaica* by Mohammed (1994) shows how the social realities based on the social structure with the white as ideal has been reinforced materially and psychologically. Concepts of ugliness and beauty correlated with race, the ideal of beauty being the white. The patriarchal order was based on white male domination and even white women suffered under this system. Mohammed also found that ideas of masculinity and femininity differed based on race and class. White women were constructed as frail, while black women could work hard.

Both black women and men occupied a position of inferiority based on their race and their socioeconomic status. As Mathurin-Mair (1975) noted, slaves were "equal under the whip". Female slaves, however, were not only dehumanized as were males, but also defeminized as a result of rape and sexual abuse, and the redefinition of their reproductive roles from mothers to suppliers of the labour force. Thus, while the slavery experience had the effect of levelling the sexes to the extent that both males and females underwent similar treatment in the fields and in terms of punishment, there were different experiences, subtle and effective resistance based on the sexually determined roles of female slaves. Rather than collaboration with the system, female slaves risked their lives to resist slavery. Beckles (1986) notes:

Women fought, ran away, committed suicide and murder, became mistresses and prostitutes to their oppressors, terminated the lives of their infants as well as raised large, emotionally cohesive families . . . these actions and decisions suggest [women] sought to do the best for themselves in the only way that seemed possible. The overwhelming impression that springs from the data is that women were seriously concerned with the survival and improvement of their own and their kin's conditions and did whatever was necessary to attain these ends. (cited in Barriteau-Foster 1992: 32)

We see, therefore, that although they were all African slaves who experienced a similar kind of oppression, gender inequalities existed to the extent that the sexually defined role of women resulted in abuse and resistance peculiar to this role.

The informal networks of family and kin were therefore important in the expression of the resistance by female slaves. In addition, the female slave was largely responsible for the survival of the African heritage which can be identified as another form of resistance against a system which sought to destroy these traditions. It was the female slave who, despite all odds, was often successful in maintaining these ties of kinship and family. The survival of family traditions would become influential as a motivation for women in their participation in labour riots in the 1930s in the Caribbean. Reddock (1994) notes that Caribbean women's responsibility for their own welfare, their children and their relatives motivated their participation.

Emancipation transformed the slave plantation society into a capitalist economy where the majority of slaves who were not able to buy land and become part of the peasantry became wage workers. But the social structure continued to be differentiated based on race and ethnicity. It was at this time that the society was transformed to include a brown middle class comprising those born during slavery, as well as Jews and Lebanese traders from the Middle East who constituted a merchant class. It is this merchant class that would eventually become the ruling class of Jamaican society when the white Europeans migrated. With this change in the social composition of the ruling class the concept of 'white' also changed. White no longer meant only those of European ancestry but now included the Jewish and Lebanese itinerant traders who were now "socially or Jamaica white". Indian and Chinese indentured labourers were brought in to supply the plantations with cheap labour, thus adding to the black working class base of the society. The status of the Chinese improved immensely when a new wave of emigrants came in the early twentieth century and established grocery shops.

This capitalist system introduced the sexual division of labour which further transformed gender relations on the plantation where males, who eventually controlled most of the jobs on the estates, were better paid. This experience resulted in the displacement of black women from work on the estates to subsistence agriculture and domestic work.

Adding Women to the Agenda

The Women in the Caribbean Project (WICP) undertook an in-depth study of women in the region from 1979 to 1982. The multidisciplinary study provided a more woman-centred approach since the experiences of women were central to the project. However, as Barriteau-Foster (1992: 8) points out, the project missed important dimensions of women's experiences because of its use of traditional methodologies which are not equipped to provide an understanding of the complexities of Caribbean women's realities.

Despite the lack of a framework which seeks to analyse the interrelationship between the factors of race, class and gender in shaping Caribbean realities, the project did provide information which attests to the diversity and differences which exist among and between women of the Caribbean. The findings showed that women were economically vulnerable and insecure, displayed high levels of female self-contempt, deferred decision making to male partners and recognized that they must accept male domination. But at the same time they were seen as resourceful, decisive and self-assertive, dominating decision making in the household, and between 82 percent and 92 percent felt that gender differences made no difference to personal development (Barriteau-Foster 1992: 9). Other works have added to the knowledge base in areas of social mobility and the labour market (Hart 1989), socialization, home and family life (Senior 1991), women in public life, and rural and urban employment (Momsen 1993), but, like the WICP, the works offer no theoretical framework.

The works of the WICP and Senior (1991) are important for their insight into lives of Caribbean women and the ways in which their resistance is carried out daily. Despite increasing living costs and declining living standards, Caribbean women have struggled and resisted their circumstances to 'make do' in order to maintain their survival.

The work of Sistren and Honor Ford Smith (1987) is one of the earliest accounts of women's experiences using the method of life histories for expressing the resistance of women in their daily lives. A reading of the stories show the interplay of race, class and gender in the lives of the women and together provide an important knowledge base which can be analysed and used in Caribbean feminist theorizing.

In recent years, the concept of gender has been transformed from a descriptive category into an analytic tool in Caribbean scholarship. Reddock (1993) remarks that by 1983 the concept had begun to be tentatively recognized. For instance, it was noted that the social role of women in the Caribbean necessitated a theoretical synthesis of sex with race and class, which was seen to be feasible without "sacrificing the notion of the primacy of class relations in social development" (Reddock 1993: 44).

Since independence in the Caribbean, the colour distinctions may have become less clearly demarcated, but class and gender relations have become more distinct (Wiltshire-Brodber 1988). Economic control continues to be largely in the hands of the "whites" but increasingly, the coloureds and blacks are moving up the socioeconomic scale. The class and race/colour structures were and continue to be integrally related in Caribbean society and continue to be reinforced ideologically and institutionally, though informally rather than by legal sanction. Thus, while no one can be legally discriminated against because of class or colour, there is an ascriptive social code which Patterson (1967: 99) captures succinctly when he wrote: "You can sum up Jamaica, my Brothers, in three little lines. If you white, you all right; if you brown, stick around; if you black, stand back".

In a much earlier study, Miller (1969) shows the social divisions among women based on different skin colour. In his study, Jamaican school girls were asked about their perceptions of beauty and self-worth. The majority saw the beautiful girl as having long hair, straight nose and fair skin while the handsome boy would have straight hair, straight nose and fair skin. This was in contrast to their own dark skins, kinky hair and African features. This ideal is reinforced by media houses and beauty contests, which portray caucasian features as being more admirable than the African features in an individual. That a particular physical feature is preferred even amongst girls without these features, suggests that there are differences between women based on colour and also points to the negative implications for females with strong African features who would be seen as inferior to the female with caucasian features.

The result has been societies clearly demarcated in terms of class and colour, and the meanings of these groupings change, when gender is included as a critical category of analysis of the social structure. Barriteau-Foster 1992) suggests that Caribbean women are affected by class, race and sexual identity differently in different social contexts. The possible range of interactions based on these three forms of oppression are "fluid and constantly changing" (Barriteau-Foster 1992: 21). In all situations the woman is a gendered woman but differences based on class and colour will result in different experiences.

Notwithstanding their constraints, women in the Caribbean have been making steady advances in the labour force since independence. For instance, Gordon's (1987) study for Jamaica shows that the upward mobility of women doubled between 1943 and 1984 from 36 percent of the labour force to 45 percent. There has also been an increase in the proportion of women in higher managerial and professional jobs from 4 percent of the labour force to 32 percent between 1943 and 1984. During this period also, the clerical positions which were originally male dominated, became feminized by 1984 with 72 percent of that labour force being female compared to 24 percent in 1943.

Miller (1986), in his work dealing with the marginalization of the black male, developed his marginalization thesis within the context of the rise of women in the teaching profession and confirms the sexual division of labour faced by Caribbean women by showing that the ruling male minority have maintained their position in the system to ensure their privileged status through institutionalized sexist and racist policies. However, in a subsequent work Miller (1991), argues that the rise of women has been allowed by the white elite at the top of the social ladder as a means of challenging the rise of the black male to positions of power in the society. Women's increasing successes and upward mobility, however, are only allowed to go as far as it does not challenge white male power. While the work offers an interesting viewpoint, especially in its analysis of race, class and gender in the formulation of his theory, Miller has fallen into the trap of not providing women as a group with some degree of responsibility for their successes. His thesis regarding their upward mobility denies women their struggles and their role as active players in their quest for advancement. He therefore recognizes that women continue to be subordinated despite significant advances.

In both the private and public sectors women's subordinate position in society continues to be institutionally and ideologically reinforced. The upward mobility of women in education and the labour force serves to mask the sexist orientation which continues to be perpetuated. This is explained by Gordon (1987), who shows that despite the improvements, compared to men, there has been no real change in the societal structure since men continue to dominate top positions across classes. Women continue to be concentrated in lower status professions like teaching, nursing and clerical positions, while men continue to dominate higher managerial, professional and lower managerial levels (Gordon 1987: 78).

In many cases, even where the women have high status jobs the work ethic is still based on a male paradigm and men continue to be influential in the decision-making process. Women also continue to experience the double burden of work outside the home and domestic work which is accorded extremely low status. The subordinate status of women continues to be sanctioned both overtly and covertly in the education system, government policies, religious institutions, through the media and in cultural practices. It could be argued that the sexual division of labour and institutional subordination experienced by women in the Caribbean has resulted in a female consciousness. This consciousness, however, is experienced and accepted or resisted differently by women based on their class position and race/colour. In other words, as Mohammed (1993: 209) states:

. . . while they may be born into a certain set of arrangements not of their choice, their lives can be viewed in terms of how they use these arrangements to get the best out of them; to fight against them or to be defeated by them; how they may use parts and reject others.

This division based on colour and class among women was forcefully articulated in a recent personal experience with a female higgler selling fruits and vegetables in Liguanea. When approached to make a purchase and asked if a box nearby was for garbage, she angrily told me that I should keep my own garbage – "all unu brown class people waan do is throw unu garbage pan wi". She went on to say that she is black but she "alright" and I didn't even have to buy from her. Despite the embarrassment and pain which I felt, I realized that this woman, in her own way, was resisting domination based on colour and class which had relegated her to an inferior position. I was seen to represent the brown middle class oppressor, while she represented the black oppressed working class. The experience, in my view, supports the claim of the inadequacy of traditional feminisms which view women as a homogenous group, and the related preference for a theoretical framework which takes cognizance of their differentiation, and the reality of female oppression of females.

It is important to note that the social constructs of race, gender and class are not merely descriptive categories of oppression or domination but they constitute arenas of relational differences. Hence, in the experience with the higgler in Liguanea, her perceived inferior status based on her colour and class is informed by the related perception that being brown and middle class made me superior. The relational position is further reinforced by her very friendly interactions with her peers of the same colour and class at the time of the incident. She could be described as being two persons at the same time: one in relation to an oppressor and one in relation to equals. The possibility exists that she could have reacted differently to a black middle class woman. In this case the overriding identification of oppression would have been based on colour rather than on class, though class differences will be influential but not at the same level, at the particular time. It thus depends on the social context and the time of the interaction or incident. As Barriteau-Foster (1992) points out, the Caribbean woman may occupy different spaces at different times: thus at one point her working class position may be the most dominant, while in another her colour may be. There are situations where more than one form of identity serves to interact at the same time. The point is that all three forms of oppression operate simultaneously but may have different levels of influence based on the particular circumstance.

Thus, the gendered woman's experiences of social relationships differ and change over time and women are instrumental in these changes over time. In other words women are not purely victims and, in fact, may be oppressor and oppressed at the same time. This is illustrated by the example of interactions between a middle class black woman and her working class black domestic helper which will be influenced by their class positions. In another setting, with strong racial prejudices, the two women may receive similar treatment (Barriteau-Foster, 1992: 24).

Louise Bennett, in her poetry, captures the social distance between women based on class position. Her poem, based on the launching of the Jamaica Federation of Women early in the twentieth century, portrays the resistance met by a lower class woman attempting to get to the centre of the function by the middle class women in attendance:

> Me was a dead fi go inside
> But when me start fe try
> Ooman queeze me, ooman push me,
> Ooman frown and cut dem y'eye.
>   (cited in Cooper 1988: 50)

The paradox is that, even in the women's movement, the issues of class and colour have served to divide women. Even though the movement in the Caribbean advocates an end to sexist oppression of women, very often they have not addressed inequalities based on class or colour, that is, the larger context in which sexist oppression takes place. Thus, even though all women in the Caribbean experience sexist oppression, the black lower class woman is subjected to victimizations not experienced by the brown middle class and fair or white upper class woman.

In some cases, the dominant ideologies and values which are shared by middle and upper class women, usually the heads of these organizations, are viewed as correct and thus were instrumental in shaping the orientation and structure of the women's movement. For instance, Bennett refers to the imposition of legal unions on the unmarried working class women in her poem:

> Dat lady Mrs Married Knibbs
> She is a real Godsen
> For every man now mus' tun husban'
> Dem kean noh mo' bwoy frien'
>
> An she meck nine-toe Berty
> Wed kraas eye Sue you know?
> An she force awn Mary Fowl Head
> Pan Mis Biddy cousin Joe
>
> So fine a good man dat yuh hooda
> Like fi stan up beside,
> Den see Miss Knibbs an yuh will be
> Mongs de nex mass wedden brides.

Relatedly, traditional feminists also share the largely middle class derived assumption that the nuclear family, based on the male bread winner model, is the norm or ideal family form. Black feminists have challenged this assumption which has been contradicted by the fact that several family forms have been shown to coexist in the Caribbean. For instance, McKenzie (1993: 76) has shown that of the women who have had unions, 48 percent were married, while 20 percent were in consensual unions not legally sanctioned. In addition, in many cases, persons live with kin rather than in an independent household, even when they are married. Generally, the union type can be correlated to class positions. Economic and social factors play a role in the unstable conjugal relationships which are largely found among the lower class. Whilst the middle and upper classes tend to emulate the western-nuclear family, there is increasing evidence to suggest that this pattern is changing. McKenzie (1993) suggests that the well educated and high status women are tending towards the matrifocal organization of the lower class. In addition, Douglass (1992), in her study of the Jamaican family elite and McKenzie (1993) suggest that among this group kinship linkages are as important as support networks.

Class oppression and identity may take precedence over gender relations depending on the context. This, however, does not deny gender oppression which may take place at another level. In Jamaica, for example, the inequalities in the social structure and the continued harassment of inner-city youths by the police are largely seen by all, including the women in the communities, as a violation of their rights as human beings. News reports invariably show the women in the communities taking the side of the male victims who are wanted for criminal activities by the police. The women's position in this situation needs to be addressed in the larger context as a class and consequently colour issue where, as a group, they are being 'downtrodden' by the system. In many cases the support of a 'don' (big man) in the community may directly relate to the economic support which families, and importantly the women, gain from these men.

Gender relations are played out at a different level within the same community. It is highly likely that these same women who protect the men actually live in abusive relationships with their male partners. We thus can identify two levels of interaction and resistance: one against a system which oppresses the lower class regardless of gender, and one at a more personal level based on gender relations. The women in this context have a class consciousness which informs their resistance strategy that involves their male class counterparts. Their resistance in terms of their gender relations will be played out against the same "man" who they protected but at a more personal level.

The important point that needs to be made is that men are also discriminated against based on class background. The poverty experienced by this class as a whole influences gender relations. As Rohlehr (1989: 235) states:

We are never far away from the context of hunger, unemployment, economic depression, worker militancy, desperation, struggle and sheer survivalism out of which fictions of the 1930s were shaped. This context provides the frame for the domestic encounter of male and female.

In the same way, the black lower class woman experiences oppression at two levels, from her male partner based on gender and from her middle class female employer for whom she works as a domestic helper. She may therefore find it difficult to cooperate with her middle class employer in the name of the struggle against male domination, including that of her husband, when her life experience dictates that she ought to be struggling against her female employer also.

Notwithstanding the peculiarity of the female condition, a female perspective is still lacking in the Caribbean in light of the dominance of the male paradigm in the society. As a related consequence, the dominant discourse renders many acts of resistance which do not fall into the dominant perception of resistance as, at best, insignificant. For instance, Barriteau-Foster (1992: 26) shows that the conclusions of the WICP survey, which stated that women are not actively involved in political activity in the region, is based on a measurement using male standards of participation as universal norms. She states that there is "no sense of gendered women affecting race or class to overcome constraints and pursue their political interests". If the issue is examined from a female perspective, then it becomes clear that even in the same study women were, in fact, involved in political activities. What needs to be considered in the analysis is that the female perspective of political participation is different from the dominant male perspective and, without this consideration, women's participation is interpreted as passive and marginal to the political process. In this respect it was noted that:

If women failed to participate at the same rate and in the same ways as men, this was considered proof of their inadequacies rather than of sexist bias in the definition of what was political, or evidence that there remained material obstacles to the full participation of women as a group. (cited in Barriteau-Foster 1992: 26)

This brings us back to female understandings and female resistance which are different from those of the dominant paradigm. In this case, because women are not actively involved in high profile positions which may, for example, be measured by number of seats filled by women in a political party or in parliament, their participation is not seen as politically active. However, we see that even in their political strategies, women's political activities have served to satisfy their psychological, emotional, economic and political needs (Barriteau-Foster 1992: 27). By placing Caribbean women at the centre of the analysis the concept of political participation takes on new meanings and can be recognized as political activities where their family, community and everyday struggles serve to guide their participation. Thus Reddock (1993) argues for the radical rethinking of race and class structures in the Caribbean using the insights of Western feminist scholarship, but being careful not to lose sight of differences in the Caribbean.

Methodology

The study employed the life history method and was based on the lives of three women. The latter were selected based on three major criteria:
(a) they had to be between 35 and 45 years of age;
(b) similar maternal and maternal status/experience;
(c) they had to be representative of the three major class groupings in the society and the major colour/racial cleavages.

Of the three respondents, one served as my domestic helper (Phyllis), one was an acquaintance of middle class status (Jackie), while the third was of upper class origin (Ana). While the first two were selected based on the extent of their familiarity with the author, the third person was selected based on a newspaper feature on her. In relation to their marital status, while Phyllis had never been married, Ana and Jackie were both divorced/separated. They were all single mothers. In terms of their colour/racial characteristics, Phyllis was black, Jackie was brown, while Ana was "almost white".

The life history method and feminist research

Feminist research values the experiences of women from which researchers can generate indicators of the realities against which hypotheses can be tested (Harding 1987: 17). Duelli Klein (1983) argues for new feminist methods which will go beyond traditional scientific methods where hypotheses are tested by isolating variables:

We should recognize that to keep variables constant, or to choose which one is the dependent and which one the independent variable reflects our need to categorize rather than trying to convey a holistic picture of the problem researched. (cited in Shields and Derwin 1993: 66)

Conventional methods have not provided a focus on gender differences which would provide a more holistic and accurate picture of society. Feminist standpoint theorists argue that knowledge – opinions and beliefs – are socially constructed, and by using women's experiences and making use of the differences in the situations of men and women, feminist researchers provide valuable resources that have not been traditionally considered (Harding 1991: 120–21). In other words, the distortion and obscurity of women's lives by male paradigms is challenged by using women's lives and experiences as valuable to the research process and may, in fact, lead to the decrease in the distortions and inaccuracies which have been produced by the natural and social sciences.

Women's experience is valuable for the research process because, as Harding (1991: 124) points out, their "marginalized" position as outsiders to the dominant culture makes for a "combination of nearness and remoteness, concern and indifference, that are central to maximising objectivity". Additionally, their experience as an oppressed group means that, compared to men, they have less interest in maintaining the status quo and thus are more equipped to distance themselves from the social order which increases further their potential for providing new and critical insights.

A large portion of the work on women in the Caribbean has been carried out using quantitative methods which have been very helpful in providing empirical data on women in the region. Theses have added to the data base and have shown up the differences which exist amongst these women. However, these traditional research methodologies have largely been carried out with preconceived notions, with the subjects being seen as numbers providing empirical evidence rather than as human beings, with feelings, living in a particular context. It is strongly believed that the empirical data need to be reinforced with methodologies which allow for the input of the views of women within their context and experiences. Such a strategy will allow for in depth research of participants which will give deeper insight into their lives.

It is important to point out that the aim of this type of research is not to make generalizations, but to supplement and critique generalizations which have been made on the basis of quantitative research. As Barriteau-Foster (1992) points out, there is a difference between research on women and feminist research. Research on women which has been extensively carried out in the region adds information on women to the literature, and produces a more complete and statistical profile of women. What is needed now is a method of which the starting point is "where there is society there is gender" (cited in Barriteau-Foster 1992: 6).

Chandra Mohanty and her colleagues note that testimonies, life stories and oral histories are a significant means of remembering and recording experiences and struggles. As a feminist methodology, it serves as a corrective to historical gaps and the neglect of women's voices as a result of hegemonic masculinist history. They argue further that the practice of remembering and rewriting leads to the formation of politicized consciousness and self-identity (Mohanty, et al. 1991: 33–34).

As noted earlier, one critique of the white middle class orientation of traditional feminist theories is based on the exclusion of women of different ethnic, racial and class backgrounds. Life histories, as a means of articulating and locating the struggles of women, represent an effective way of breaking the silence. According to Behar (1990: 225):

Rather than looking at social and cultural systems solely as they impinge on a life, shape it, and turn it into an object, a life history should allow one to see how an actor makes culturally meaningful history, how history is produced in action and in the actor's retrospective reflections on that action. A life history should allow one to see the subjective mapping of experience, the working out of a culture and a social system that is often obscured in a typified account.

This viewpoint challenges the position of women as passive victims and places them in an active role. Mohanty sees it as a means of challenging universal images of the "Third World woman" as the veiled woman, the powerful mother, the chaste virgin, the obedient wife (Mohanty, cited in Behar 1990: 231).

The location of women's experiences as theoretical resources results in the challenge to the "universal man". Harding describes the result of this process as culturally different men and women who have different experiences of race, class and cultures across which the definition of femininity and masculinity may differ. Class, race and culture are also seen as categories within gender since women's and men's experiences differ depending on these categories (Harding 1987: 7).

Unlike the traditional scientific methodologies which seek an 'unbiased' result, feminist research recognizes the input of the researcher as part of the research process. It is important that the researcher is consciously aware of her background, race, class and culture in relation to that of the woman being interviewed. Harding (1987: 9) notes that: ". . . the researcher appears not as an invisible, anonymous, disembodied voice of authority, but as a real historical individual with concrete, specific desires and interests".

Undoubtedly, I was active and at times very involved in the conversations. I felt it necessary to share some of my experiences which sometimes served to fill gaps when the respondent had spoken for a long time and obviously needed a break; sometimes simply because it was a conversation between two persons, and sometimes because I wanted to encourage the respondent to continue when I sensed uncertainty about continuing, perhaps because the issue was particularly painful. I used an audiotape and took notes manually as well in the interview sessions and in sessions which were not actually scheduled. At times, I would accidentally or purposely meet one of the participants but with no intention of interviewing. Sometimes the conversation would actually be about the research project; sometimes it was just general conversation. Invariably I would begin to make notes at the same time or try to remember the conversation to make a note of it when I got home.

Findings and Analysis

The examination of the life history of each woman will be first dealt with separately and structured around three major related themes: significant life events, interpersonal relationships and strategies of resistance or coping. Subsequently, their histories will be compared to highlight the combined workings of race, class and gender and the implications for feminist theory and research in the Caribbean.

Life history no.1: Phyllis

Phyllis was born in Clarendon to farming parents. Her siblings – two sisters and three brothers – all resided at the home. Phyllis' experience as the eldest female child resulted in a limited education up to fourth grade at the Wilbury General School. At the age of thirteen she left school to take on the full-time domestic responsibility in the home. Chores included washing the clothes, cleaning the house and looking after the younger children and helping out in the field, usually reaping peas. At the age of fourteen she had her first child and at the age of seventeen, her second. Soon after giving birth to her second child she left home for employment as a cook for cane cutters. This, however, did not last for a long time as the condition of her sickly mother had worsened and she had to return home. A deteriorating home life, largely a result of an abusive mother and the physical exhaustion from too much housework, resulted in her running away to live with her grandfather who would become very influential in her life. She eventually left for Kingston to seek a better life which, according to her, "mi still a look fi it but at least mi still alive".

Initially she left her children in the country and when she could afford to, she sent for them. Life was almost unbearable initially, sleeping on old clothes and cardboard on the concrete floor and eating the bare minimum. Through her hard work, despite the circumstances, she has been able to purchase some furniture and send her three children to school. Phyllis continues to do domestic work and live in a tenement yard in the Barbican area of Kingston with her two daughters, two of her grandsons, the father of her daughter's baby father who does not reside there permanently and her male friend.

Significant life events. Phyllis resents the fact that she had to give up her education to take over full-time domestic responsibilities of her parents home:

Me neva get much schooling . . . me feel bad sey me did have to give it up especially now that me other brothers and sisters no have no respect for me. Dem no too bad off yu nuh . . . dem can help themselves. But them did get the chance dat me never get.

This has resulted in a resolution to ensure that her children obtain at least a secondary education. Her two eldest children have completed their education, but her daughter who is unemployed continues to live with her.

Apart from the excessive housework, Phyllis was beaten constantly by her mother. Both led to her running away to live with her grandfather, also a farmer and higgler. He provided her with a fairly stable home until he died.

Despite the abuse as a child, in retrospect, Phyllis feels it was for her own good and treats her youngest daughter the same way:

My mother used to beat me, yu know, fi mek sure dat me turn inna somebody and a so me haf fi beat him fi she turn inna somebody . . . Cause my mother use me an hear him nuh – me a beat yu yu know girl so yu no tek youself plaster ya so, plaster de so and yu name call, call, call, call. Me need fi know seh you can cook and wash and iron. A no everybody have education, some have to do domestic work, some have to do babysitting and some have to look after old people.

This position articulated by her mother is very similar to that expressed by Phyllis to her youngest daughter. Phyllis suspects that because she has done badly in school, she will have to resort to domestic work just as she had to herself. While she does not see this as an ideal situation, she figures that there is no way out. In fact,

If me mek it a do domestic work then she can mek it too . . . But she so stubborn sometimes . . . A sick she sick yu noa . . . She have internal bleeding sometimes and she cyaan learn anything . . . all she do is sleep at school.

Her experience of the sexual division of labour with almost total responsibility for the domestic sphere has reinforced her perception of the female's responsibility for this sphere. In an incident at my home where she asked her daughter to wash the dishes, I explained that it was alright and that I would wash them, but Phyllis retorted: "A no bwoy pickney, a gal pickney, him fi wuk".

However, one can clearly see that this was an element of class differences at play because the alternative dishwasher would not have been a male, but myself, a female. One could perhaps speculate that had the visiting child been a son or a grandson Phyllis might herself have decided to do the dishes, thus maintaining class distance and the sexual division of labour.

The men in Phyllis' life have had a significant impact on her. Her grandfather whom she ran away to live with and her father have been most influential. Her grandfather, for a time, provided for her and made a very difficult life that much easier. Her experience with men has led her to conclude that men have more opportunities than women:

If me did born a man me wouldn't have it so hard . . . me would have three trade and me wouldn't be wanting for anything. As a woman to borrow money is difficult and you can't make it fast enough to pay back.

In addition, she feels that if her daughter had been born a boy, she would have been better off. This relates to her life chances as well as the added burden Phyllis sees in bringing up a female child compared to a male child. In this regard she commented: "Me neva want her because me did know seh is a gal pickney an mi neva want no gal pickney". When questioned further, she responded:

Me no have time fi watch her . . . People will talk 'bout you when trouble tek you pickney . . . Dem talk some tings you neva know. Sometimes you go a work an you come home an you feel so good but when you reach home she inna pure war with di pickney dem . . .

Phyllis' experience as a working class woman has shown her that her working class male counterparts are better off than the females even if females like herself have to provide some support to them sometimes.

Interpersonal relationships. Phyllis' first two children were born in Clarendon. She lived for some time with the father of her child in a very rocky relationship, filled with fighting and tension, until she packed and left one day when he was out. Of this man, she remarked: "Him was too wild . . Him go out inna de evening an no come in till all hours".

Phyllis was asked if she saw herself as being an abused woman, and responded thus: "Well I guess if him lick me me abuse but dat mean seh him abuse too because me nah jus stan up an tek no lick me a fight back and him get some lick too".

Phyllis' outlook on relationships and marriage engenders her independence. To begin with, she decided from early in her life that she would not get married because she likes to be in charge of her own life and do things her own way. This does not mean that she does not have relationships with men. Her position is: "Me is a person – mi no have Dick and have Harry . . . if a one mi jus stay with the one until me feel fi leave mi jus leave – yu know dem way deh . . . "

This outlook has influenced her position regarding her status in the household. She considers herself the head, largely because the lease is in her name and she provides most of the money for the running of the household. This position goes against the traditional conception which tends to assume the resident male as head. In Phyllis' case there have been times when she has had to provide financially for her mate, a construction worker, due largely to the seasonal nature of his occupation. Phyllis speaks very highly of him as helping out whenever he can afford to, especially since she has no children with him. She sees his role as primarily an economic one.

Phyllis' conversations regarding one of her employers are reflective of the entrenchment of the dominant values regarding the definition of beauty in terms of caucasian features. An episode involving the employer's organization and actual coordination of a birthday party for one of Phyllis' grandsons reflects this. Phyllis explained with pride how "Ms

Carlton" bought the ice cream and cake and even came to help her at the party:

Ms Carlton share out dem ice cream and when dem get it dem wouldn't eat it because them jus a stare pan her. Is not no bwoyfrien' ting you know . . . Is jus her colour an how she look . . .

Phyllis obviously thinks very highly of brown skin and straight hair, especially in contrast to her own features and that of her children, grandchildren and the others who live in the yard.

The scene of the birthday party with Ms Carlton handing out the goodies evokes in one's mind a scenario of the patronizing brown middle class woman in relation to her 'less fortunate' black helper. Such a patronizing relationship encourages a dependence on the part of Phyllis and ensures a level of loyalty even at the expense of her own (Phyllis') family. Ms Carlton's high profile' presence at the party rather than just 'behind the scenes' assistance ensures an integral and physical presence in Phyllis' and her family's life which is rewarded by considerable loyalty.

One needs to be careful, however, not to view the scenario outlined above as the total picture. My interviews and relationship with Phyllis, also as an employer, suggest that she makes the best of her situation. Thus, despite a subordinate status in relation to her employer, she is not merely a victim; she actively ensures that she also gains from the relationships. Phyllis, in a very astute way, has recognized that she can elicit sympathy from her employers and receives this help in the form of financial assistance as extra money or loans, help with schooling her children, and clothing or food. In addition, there are the non-material benefits of having a more pleasant environment compared to the yard in which she lives, where she can spend extended periods even after work hours, and where she can also take her children and grandchildren, especially her youngest daughter, whom she prefers to have with her rather than have her stay in the 'yard' all day.

Strategies of coping and resistance. Phyllis' daily life activities centre around the survival of her family. She ensures that her family has food to eat, though it may not be the best at all times:

Mi struggle hard to help mi family . . . mi try in every way to help them. Me all beat cane joint fi boil porridge to give the children.

Sometimes mi no have enough money fi buy food but mi nah borrow from the people inna di yard because mi no want dem fi know mi business. Me prefer fi borrow from Ms Carlton. She will always lend. You know you can get some tings at a cheaper price and still mek a nice meal out of it but sometimes it nah go taste so good but dem know dat another time it will better.

At the same time that Phyllis insists on bringing up her children in the right way, which has similarities to the way in which her mother treated her, there have been some changes in Phyllis' expression of motherhood. This is expressed largely in the increased freedom with which she has allowed her children to express themselves, especially her female children whom she now allows to go out, but with the behaviour that is expected of them and knowledge of the consequences for behaving otherwise. Scarce resources sometimes necessitate sacrifice on the part of Phyllis. In respect of appearance, Phyllis remarked: "If me a go out me a go want fi look good so me jus haf fi mek up mi mind and mek she (Annie) look good and me stay home".

Looking good, however, is not confined to Phyllis' person but also her surroundings. Phyllis related an incident where she spent her own money to purchase a shower curtain for the communal shower so that it could look nice.

Life history no. 2: Ana

Ana was born in Chicago in 1953 of Jamaican parents. Her father was a member of the United States airforce and her mother did not work outside of the home. Her earliest memories of a home is of that of her maternal grandmother, a two-storey apartment in the South Side of Chicago.

Much of the family wealth came from the efforts of her grandparents. Her grandfather studied accounting and became one of the first non-Europeans in the United States to become involved in real estate. At the breakup of her mother's relationship, her grandmother brought herself and her mother to Jamaica. Ana therefore spent the early years of her life in Jamaica where she attended Priory School and was taken care of largely by nannies and cooks. Her mother was extremely uncomfortable with her divorced status and this had the effect of making her sickly and withdrawn. She later remarried and had another daughter. Ana's relationship with her mother, which was already strained, only worsened after the second marriage. At the age of eleven, a visit from her grandparents who were concerned about the unhealthy family life to which she was exposed, resulted in her attendance at boarding school in England.

Boarding school, where she encountered other girls from different parts of the world, made visits to their homes and received constant visits from her grandmother, made for an exciting and fulfilling experience in England. After school in England, she attended Stanford University in California where she studied anthropology. She returned to Jamaica in the 1970s where she worked at the University of the West Indies and the Institute of Jamaica. Her relationship with an American boyfriend, who had come to Jamaica with her, did not work out so he left while she stayed on and worked.

She returned to the United States to undertake graduate studies, got pregnant and had her daughter Sue. This period was extremely difficult; as a single parent she was forced to accept welfare. When Sue was one year old, she went back to graduate school and, ten years later, finished her degree based on research in the area of malnutrition in children and women in Nicaragua.

In Nicaragua she met and married a white English journalist, adopted a Mesquito Indian and then gave birth to another son. The marriage did not last. Ana has now returned to Jamaica where she works as a research assistant at the University of the West Indies and lives in a middle class neighbourhood in St Andrew with her two sons. Her teenage daughter continues to live in the United States with her boyfriend. Ana recognizes that the lack of attention which she received has resulted in her deviant behaviour. She continues to be extremely concerned about the conditions of Sue.

Significant Life Events. The divorce of her parents led to a distant relationship between Ana and her mother, which became even more distant when she remarried. Ana related:

After she married Neville and had my stepsister she was even more removed from me and I started being designated the problem child in the family and everything. I was very, very skinny as a child and I wasn't very athletic. I was very sickly and she would always ridicule me.

At a very early age Ana realized that in Jamaican society the lighter one's skin colour and the straighter one's hair, then the better was one's status. Even within the same class, in her case, in comparison to her mother, these qualities improved one's status:

She would ridicule my skin colour – she was very slightly fairer than me. She was obsessed with me not going into the sun and not getting dark. And there was an obsession with my hair because hers was straighter than mine – again just slightly – more of an American Indian type of hair.

It was while at boarding school in England meeting people from other parts of the world, some darker and some lighter, and travelling home with friends to Africa, that Ana's self-esteem with respect to colour and gender increased:

So my self-image soared – and my image of myself as a female vastly improved and I no longer felt you had to be blond with straight hair. Going to Africa had a tremendous impact . . . you see that there are black people with their own cultures and civilization and ethnic groups and class and it is not everybody who is black is poor.

In terms of gender at that school, it was a girl's school. The headmistress was a brilliant woman, all the teachers were intelligent and I never felt that being a woman I couldn't do anything.

Only persons from extremely rich families, especially those coming from the colonies, could have afforded to attend boarding school in England in the early 1960s. One could therefore argue that even if there existed inequalities based on colour these would have been extremely subtle since all students, regardless of colour, would have had similar socioeconomic backgrounds and would have been treated accordingly. Ana's identity problem resurfaced in North America:

I tried to be black American and that didn't work . . . I didn't want to be white American and I wasn't totally American Indian so there was this whole identity thing and What am I?

The black guy said I was black enough to be with him and the black woman said I was too light to be with him.

I even wore an afro wig for one year at Stanford and the black guys would comment "But you have good hair".

She was thus faced with the issues of her skin colour where she was accepted by the black men, but rejected by black women of darker skin colour. Her identity crisis at this point was solved with the help of a professor at Stanford for whom she had the greatest respect. According to Ana: "He let me see that all the different parts of me could fit together".

Her time spent in Jamaica in the 1970s could be described as a rebellious period when she defied the norms of her upper middle class status by becoming very involved in the Rastafari movement and the music industry; even travelling with Bob Marley to Trench Town. After her rebellious period in Jamaica, she returned to graduate school in the United States when she immediately got pregnant at the age of 24. It was a carry over from the rebel period in Jamaica when she was highly influenced by the Rastafari religion which encouraged the subordinate status of women. She states:

I was totally brainwashed. You must breed for the dread and be his babymother. At twenty-four if you had not had a child yet then you were ready for the old folks home.

So I had my daughter, Sue. That was a very rough period because he (the baby's father) was very unstable . . . we broke up all the time, he didn't help me with the baby. I was on welfare in the States . . . begging for crumbs and all this kind of stuff.

At this point then, Ana's upper middle class status changed but with the help of friends, she was able to get back on her feet. Her experience of the feminist movement where she sought support during her crisis is very relevant, especially regarding the need for a feminism which accounts for differences among women. The differences based on class background or sexual orientation were not taken into consideration in the early women's movement, and thus Ana's presence with a baby was seen as a distraction:

There were a lot of women's organizations – support for women. However, I found that the orientation was towards white professional women. So, I would go to meetings of these feminist groups and I would have people say could I please leave . . . I was breastfeeding. Imagine these people, just the presence of the baby. Many were gay and thought you shouldn't have children to tie you to a domestic role and I thought: "Why can't you be a brilliant executive and have children?" I didn't see why it had to be unilinear . . . so I got little support from the movement because the black feminism hadn't started yet.

The experience in North America, where there is an even more clearly demarcated social stratification based on race, meant that Ana's privileged status based on colour and class which she would have enjoyed in Jamaican society had changed. In one incident at Berkeley University when she sought extra time for a research paper, she received an insensitive retort from her white female professor who thought that as a strong black woman she should have been able to manage. Ana's retort reinforces her social distance from the lower class and confirms the differences among women in Jamaican society:

Well, you know, I don't know what you mean by that but my cultural background in which I grew up in Jamaica was quite a privileged background . . . I was in training being a single mother so nothing in my background prepared me for this.

After the experience of the United States, Jamaica provided a more stable and acceptable environment:

Things are calmer now in my life than they have ever been. At least I have a regular job. As a woman, and a non-white woman I feel that Jamaica is really a good place to be. As a professional divorced woman there is a niche for me here.

Interpersonal relationships. Ana's experience with her stepfather encouraged an early awareness of the reduction of the female to sexual attributes. She remembers clearly that:

His message was that women were sexual objects. He was very abusive. Even as a little girl he looked at me as a sexual object – whenever I would talk to my mother about it she would blame me . . . Something I will never understand. Why would I make that up? So she didn't really protect me from him at all. He didn't actually rape me but he would try to do inappropriate things. Luckily the marriage didn't last too long – two years of screaming, yelling, bottles flying, other women . . . I never saw a happy marriage.

She also remembers the attempt at an imposition of the sexual division of labour with her stepfather when he asked her: "So you want to be a teacher or a nurse?" To this she responded:

No. I don't like teaching and I don't like being around sick people or blood . . . Of course these are things a woman should do (said with sarcasm). I am interested in lots of things.

Referring to the newspaper article in which she was featured, she stated further: "I hope he saw the article in the Sunday paper to see that I didn't become a teacher or a nurse".

Her relationship and marriage in the early stages was happy but, with her increasing independence, resentment on the part of her husband started to build up and

he became emotionally and physically abusive and wasn't as supportive as he used to be and once I got my doctorate he has been totally absent from my life. It was painfully clear that he was threatened in every way. But I stuck it out until I got a job, was economically independent then I talked to a lawyer about a divorce.

In an effort to gain some insight into her relationship with women from the lower class I asked Ana about her relationship with her domestic helper: "I try to be nice and they totally walk over me and treat me bad and things disappear. Now I have adopted a businesslike approach. I realize there is a thin line between being unfair and being a pushover".

Strategies of coping and resistance. Ana's method of coping is largely informed by her interest in securing a decent life for her children materially and emotionally. This involves nutritious meals and spending quality time with the children. I wanted to know how Ana managed from day to day as a single parent. She related the incident of one month when the children's father had not sent the child support cheque. That month, she had to borrow from friends until her problem had been sorted out. She also tries to ensure that her surroundings are kept beautiful. During one visit to her home, she was in the process of organizing the landscaping of her yard.

Life history no. 3: Jackie

Jackie was born in Trinidad. At the time of her birth her mother was sixteen and her father was twenty-two. Her parents got married during the pregnancy. They were not able to have any more children. Her father began working at the age of thirteen as an apprentice plumber; her mother never worked outside the home. The family occupied one room in the home of her maternal grandparents which also housed the other nine children of these grandparents.

Jackie attended the Tunapuna Government School then went on to Bishop's High School, one of the prestigious schools in Trinidad, when she passed her final examinations at primary school. Despite economic difficulties, her education was seen as priority and her parents ensured that she always had what was necessary for a successful education. This provision included relief from domestic chores. She was thus able to spend much of her time reading. She completed secretarial and typing studies in a commercial institution after high school, then attended the University of the West Indies where she completed a degree in economics.

While at university she got married. Shortly after the birth of her first child she went to England to pursue a postgraduate degree. By this time, her marriage was failing, though it survived her absence and produced a second child. However, her marriage worsened and resulted in her relocation from Trinidad to Jamaica with her son and daughter. She currently works in a senior administrative position at the University of the West Indies and lives in a middle class neighbourhood in St Andrew. She has lived in Jamaica for four years.

Significant Life Events. Jackie's life has been spent in a close-knit family whose sacrifice and hard work laid the foundation for her success in life. Despite the relative poverty in which the family lived Jackie remembers that:

I never wanted for anything . . . Whatever I needed I would get. So I never felt deprived or that I was poor or never had enough. I have always had the best shoes to go to school and always had the best clothes . . .

Jackie learned very early in her life that education was very important. According to her, her parents made her realize that:

School was very important . . . They always used to tell me that education was the way out of the poverty . . . So she (her mother) spent a lot of time helping me with my homework . . . we didn't have electricity so we used lamps . . .

It was Jackie's mother who did all the housework and ensured that Jackie could devote all her time to her education:

School work was so important that Mummy made sure that she did everything so that I could do my schoolwork. Mummy would comb my hair every morning until I was in fourth form, iron my clothes and Daddy would clean my shoes . . . I never had chores.

Jackie remembers her grandmother being concerned about her lack of domesticity when she explained that "My grandmother used to tell them they were spoiling me and I wouldn't be able to do anything and I wouldn't get a husband." Thus, at an early age, Jackie was introduced to the woman's role in the household through the total dedication of her mother to this sphere. In addition, from the views of her grandmother, this role was promoted as guaranteeing a husband in one's life.

When Jackie was asked if she thought that her parents, especially her father, may have wanted a boy rather than a girl, especially since her mother was able to have only one child, she responded: "Never . . . I was always the best thing in his life . . . He was always telling me and mummy how much he loved us and anything we wanted we would get."

The influence of her uncles, some of whom were close to her age, resulted in her growing up like a tomboy:

I grew up with a lot of uncles . . . I spent more time with my uncles because they were more my age. So I grew up like a tomboy . . . lots of picking mangoes and climbing trees. I grew up in pants. Mummy had a hard time getting me into a dress. I never had dolls, never played with dolls . . . I played with cars and so.

Her close identity with her uncles resulted in her seeing herself as a strong person who would fight boys but never girls. Jackie, therefore, despite being female, developed a perception of females being the weaker sex, but felt herself at an advantage based on the strength she derived from her association with her male uncles. The inferiority of the female sex was also reinforced at school when she fought and beat up a boy. The principal's response to the boy was: "You mek a little girl like this beat you . . . You just to get some more licks." Her closer association with males has also resulted in the tendency for her to have male rather than female friends. In this respect she stated: "Because I spent so much time with them I get along better with men than I do with women. I feel more comfortable with men."

Jackie's experience of her father as economic provider has influenced her perception of the male as main provider, leader and protector while the female provides a supportive role. When I asked why she felt this way she responded:

The relationship of my parents has reinforced it. My father fits the role of man in the house. Not perfectly, but as near a model as I have seen.

Interpersonal relations. Jackie's self-concept began to assume a more female as opposed to male orientation when she met her first boyfriend at high school. She was thus no longer the protector but expected to be protected. Physical abuse was no longer seen as an activity between equals regardless of gender, but as violence against women:

One day David decide to hit me . . . Can you imagine! We went out and I decide to dance with one of his friends and coming up the road after the party he hit me . . . Well that was it – we remained good friends but no boyfriend, girlfriend.

Her relationship with her husband began because he was associated with Jackie's perception of the economic role of provider which a man ought to play in a relationship, for she stated: "Joe was my first man. He represented manhood to me. He had many cars and his own construction company."

Her marriage, like that of her parents, was largely a result of her becoming pregnant. Things took a turn for the worse and the marriage became an emotionally and physically abusive one:

I felt like an oppressed woman in the marriage. I wasn't free to express myself . . . The whole thing was a pretence. I pretended emotions that were not while I was dying inside, emotionally drained and had nothing more to give. The real me inside wanted to get out, be free and be true to myself . . . free to be.

Her method of dealing with the abuse took many forms:

I tried to be a wife then I just stopped. When I changed I think he realized that he could not dominate me anymore. I started going to my parents for meals and spent less and less time with him. I got a British Commonwealth scholarship and left Jomo (her first child) with Mummy and went to England. I met someone there and I felt free and loved. I had no child, no husband . . . I felt whole. There were no demands and no pretense.

For the first time I enjoyed sex. I didn't have to give in and pretend pleasure and an orgasm as I had with Joe to get him in a good mood.

The values of Jackie's father's were expressed clearly to her despite the abuse which she had gone through and this would be instrumental in her decision to try again, to rescue her marriage, an effort which proved futile. Her father told her: "A wife's place is with her husband."

I was interested in Jackie's relationship with members of the lower class since she was from a similar background herself. I therefore asked her about her relationship with her helper, to which she replied:

I don't see her much because I am usually at work while she is working . . . we usually talk on the phone. I think the relationship is a good one because coming from a similar background, my grandmother having been a domestic helper herself, I understand her.

I have always found it easier to relate to people from that background. You see . . . my thinking has not really changed even though I can now afford to live in a nice house and drive a car . . .

With regard to her physical features, I wanted to know whether Jackie had found her complexion to have had any significant impact on her life chances. She replied in the negative but then stated:

I sometimes wondered why certain people wouldn't check me. Darker men, for example . . . Now I think about it, it was perhaps my colour and them feeling that I was better than them. The fairer ones never checked me either. Usually it was Indians or men of my complexion.

Strategies of Coping and Resistance. Jackie realized, even before the end of the marriage while living with her husband, that the marriage had ended. In order to survive she closed off herself emotionally. She stopped trying to be a wife. With the change he realized that his domination was less effective. She spent less and less time with him, going to her parents home every day for meals.

With regard to caring for her two children as a single parent, she outlined her strategies thus: "Prayer and trusting in the Lord; prioritizing needs; separating needs from wants; understanding what is important; practising patience."

Jackie also ensures that her home is attractively decorated with potted plants, coordinated furnishings and accessories.

Phyllis, Ana and Jackie compared

Despite the similarities of being female and single parents, the life stories show that the experiences of all three women have varied as a result of the different situations in which they were born. Phyllis was born into poverty with the responsibility of her family at an early age; Ana, despite a traumatic childhood, was born to wealthy parents, and Jackie was born in Trinidad in a working class environment, where, unlike Phyllis' situation, she was the only child and the limited resources could be shared more easily, thus allowing her a more prosperous childhood and increased chances of a better life.

In the lives of the three women we see that traditional gender roles and the sexual division of labour were instilled either through enforcing the actual carrying out of the duties, as in the case of Phyllis, or through expectations of and examples set by parents or relatives. Phyllis began at an early age to take on domestic responsibilities. Ana was asked by her stepfather whether she would be a teacher or a nurse and Jackie was told by her grandmother that she would never find a husband because she did not know how to help herself around the house. Despite a patriarchal ideology which permeates Caribbean society one could argue that, in the case of these women, colour background has resulted in different experiences of the ideology. Their backgrounds enabled Ana and Jackie to overcome what they considered to be low status occupations. While Jackie did come from a lower class background, her childhood experiences suggest that middle class values were promoted in her home. For instance, not only was she given full support towards academic achievement materially and emotionally, but she always had whatever was necessary in terms of the best shoes and clothes and never felt deprived of anything. She was also steeped in the middle class value of legal marriage rather than a consensual union.

The experiences of the three women show a change in gender roles between generations, if not so much in ideology, certainly in practice. The mothers of all three respondents were responsible for the domestic sphere and none worked for wages outside the home. The circumstances which led to these conditions were, however, different. Phyllis' mother helped on the farm close to home as well as carrying out the household chores which she had to discontinue due to ill-health. Ana's mother stayed home but her class position allowed her to hire the necessary help which relieved her of physically carrying out household tasks though she remained at home. Jackie's mother took on the full responsibility of her household. Their socioeconomic status meant they could not afford to hire help and the ideology which pervaded the household was that of the male as provider and the female as support.

The question must be posed: Why was Jackie able to move upward out of her working class position whereas Phyllis has been unable to? Their different experiences based on the employment status of their parents provide a possible explanation. Phyllis' parents were small farmers which, in Jamaica and in the Caribbean generally, means unstable employment for which the returns have hardly been above subsistence levels. On the other hand, Jackie's father's skills as a plumber provided more regular employment and income which allowed for a more stable environment and a quality of life during her childhood which ensured her high level of education and upward mobility. It could also be suggested, based on the fact that she was kept away from school to care younger siblings, that in Phyllis' family the value placed on education was not as high as in the case of Jackie's family.

Phyllis' conviction that, had she been a man and her daughter a male child, things would have been better, suggests that Phyllis has, in her own way, analysed her society as being patriarchal. She, however, helps to maintain the status quo; she does not go against expectations in terms of gender roles or in the expectations she has for and transmits to her daughter. It is only if she had been male that she would have been able to enjoy the more lucrative forms of employment. Phyllis also recognizes that society has played its part in making sure that women become institutionally subordinated when she says that "As a woman to borrow money it difficult and you can't make it fast to pay back".

The values based on class background and family life experiences have provided a basis for the interpretation of male/female relationships of the three women. All three women experienced physical abuse by male partners but have reacted differently. Phyllis' background did not instil a 'proper' code of behaviour and conducting oneself as a 'lady' and thus, in fights, she retaliated and defended herself effectively. She therefore does not feel any sense of inferiority in physical confrontation with a man but claims that "him abuse too". Her perception of a male partner is largely to provide an economic support though there are many times when she has had to provide for him also. The sense of independence in Phyllis' life has engendered an approach to relationships which may be short or long-term depending on the conditions, which is why she has not opted for marriage but prefers some sense of control over her participation in the relationship – where she can leave when she feels like it. Her consensual union status is reflective of one of the dominant types of unions in the Caribbean which is experienced based on choice.

Ana's experience of the unsuccessful marriage of her parents and herself, as well as physical and emotional abuse from her husband and other sexual partners, has resulted in a high level of independence as a single parent and very strict criteria for choosing male partners. Despite her reality, her upper middle class values of the nuclear family and a stable family life are still dominant in her outlook. She believes that the ideal is for children to be reared in a situation where there is a male/female partnership, if even to provide the children with a male/female balance. At the time that her marriage became abusive, Ana did not leave immediately, largely because of her need to establish her financial independence and ensure that she would have been able to provide adequately for her children.

Jackie's life was stable until the time of her marriage, which was emotionally and physically abusive. The norms of a nuclear family have been instilled in her by the values of her grandparents and parents, and she thus feels a sense of being incomplete without a male partner in her life. Her values of family life and gender roles have been deeply entrenched based on her early experiences and, despite her lived reality of providing financially throughout the marriage, and now as a single parent, she feels that the male role ought to be one of main economic provider, while the female plays a supportive role.

All three women in the study have left their homes for work outside the home thus challenging the gender roles defined by their mothers. Ana and Jackie's education and class positions allow them to hire domestic helpers to take care of their households while they work to provide for their families. Phyllis, who has not transcended her lower class status, continues to work in the domestic sphere of someone else's household.

Phyllis' experience and difference from the other two respondents can be expressed in relation to the fact that Phyllis represents that group of women who also work in other women's households as domestic helpers. Based on class differences, Phyllis would relate to Ana and Jackie in a manner that is different to how the latter would relate to each other.

The difference in women across class was highlighted in the response of both Ana and Jackie to their domestic helpers. It is noticeable that the class origins of both respondents were influential in their attitudes across class boundaries. Ana, who originated from the upper middle class, has difficulties relating to her helper and has given up trying to be nice (a position which could have bordered on being patronizing) for a more businesslike approach; while Jackie, on the other hand, with lower class origins herself, is able to identify more with her domestic helper and enjoys a more comfortable working relationship.

As single parents, Phyllis and Jackie have gone against the traditional roles of their mothers who remained in marriages until they died. In Ana's case, her mother was divorced but her embarrassment at this status probably rushed her into an unhappy second marriage, and also contributed to the apathy which characterized her existence in later life. Despite being divorced she still maintained that it would have been better to be married.

The three women have accepted the societal value of education as a means of social mobility. This acceptance has come to Ana and Jackie through the advantages which they received via education, while in Phyllis' case the lack of a proper education has reduced her life chances significantly. This has led to her decision as a parent to ensure that all her children are educated. Class background may be an influential element in determining what each woman considers an adequate education.

The lives of all three women focus around the survival and development of their children. They have all sought to ensure a full life for their children which they all see as providing an adequate education, making sure that they are properly fed and that quality time is spent with them. Again class background and, by extension, the spending power of each mother will determine how and to what extent these activities are carried out, but the important thing is that they all share the same sentiments regarding their children. In the case of Phyllis, the sentiment may be the same but at times may be expressed in very different ways compared to Ana and Jackie. The value of abusive discipline instilled in her from childhood by her mother is still largely used by her with her children, especially her youngest daughter, which is intended to serve the purpose of making sure that "she turn inna somebody".

Ana's experience of life in North America shows how her prestigious position based on gender, class and skin colour in Jamaica shifted when she changed location. Her upper middle class and almost white status was totally eroded to that of being a minority. Apart from the personal problems of being a single mother and being on welfare, the reactions of white male and female Americans eroded this position. There she was seen as a black woman and was expected to conform to the stereotype of the black female. On returning to Jamaica, Ana has found that the society is more accommodating than North America. Of course this may be due largely to the fact that in Jamaican society she resumes membership in the prestigious social group based on class and skin colour, and would therefore live a more comfortable life than that in North America where her position changes to one of lower status.

Despite the experiences of all three women which confirm their development in a patriarchal society and hence their institutional subordination as women, they have not merely been victims and accepted these positions. All three women have struggled and now head their households, and are taking care of their children.

Strategies of resistance. It has been shown that the lives of all three women have been characterized by a multiplicity of roles which require their responsiveness to change and adaptability to new environments, all rooted in the survival of their families. The sexual division of labour and their consequent responsibility of the household as well as careers or work outside the home, require different strategies for satisfying needs which have to be accommodated on a daily basis. The resistance of the three women can be seen in their struggles to sustain and change their lives even with regard to issues outside of their control. Their creation of conditions necessary for life and, hence, resistance, of course, differs across class and racial boundaries.

The women have also in their own ways dealt with their abusive relationships. It would be easy to analyse on the surface and argue that all women were mere victims in the situations. However, all have clearly expressed their acts of resistance in the abusive situations. Phyllis reacts violently and leaves when she feels like it. Her independence is guaranteed by the status of her union, which is itself resistance against the ideal of marriage, and which does not require legal input for its termination. Jackie spent as long as she could hoping for some meaning and fulfilment in her marriage, but at the same time, though she did not fight back physically, she faked orgasms to end, even in the short term, what might have become a more abusive situation. Jackie maintained her marital status, despite abuse, until it was financially convenient for her to leave the union with her children. In the case of Ana and Jackie, it was they who had the final say in the termination of their marriages. Jackie took her children and left Trinidad for Jamaica and Ana filed for a divorce and returned from the United States to Jamaica. All three women in their acts of resistance in the face of domestic violence have challenged the passive role of women in these relations.

In addition, they have not merely experienced, but they have learnt from their experiences which has resulted in strict criteria for future relationships. Thus, to have a man in their lives is not enough, though in the earlier phases of their lives it perhaps was.

Their act of living as single parents – though this is not the ideal situation for Ana and Jackie – can also be interpreted as acts of resistance. Society today accords more status to the married woman compared to the single. In fact, it is not surprising to hear of the married woman who becomes upset and quickly makes the correction if she is referred to as Miss rather than Mrs.

Part of the daily lives of women in which resistance can be identified comes from the act of making their homes and surroundings beautiful, even in the face of poverty. For Ana and Jackie, with their access to financial resources, this act is easier to achieve compared with Phyllis. Both spend their time in landscaping and decorating their homes with care. Phyllis, who has less resources available to her, spent her own money on a nice shower curtain for a communal shower. In this act we see the effort at creating beauty even in the face of adversity.

Resistance and coping strategies are also identified in the reactions of and to domestic helpers. Unlike other forms of employment where job descriptions tend to be more clearly stated, the personal level at which the domestic helper works requires an understanding at a more emotional level. Undoubtedly, Phyllis has developed an understanding of her employers so that her work will be satisfactory and mutually beneficial. One could argue that she has, perhaps, recognized her value to her employer and uses this to her advantage. Similarly, the employers, who are usually female, also need to develop an understanding of their helpers to ensure that good work relations are maintained. Ana speaks of her need to change her relations when she suspected that her initial one was not providing the best results. Jackie, being at an advantage in having shared a similar background to the domestic helper, was better able to understand the feelings and needs of her domestic helper and thus has always had a good working relationship.

The role of family and community networks in acts of resistance amongst women is very powerful. In the lives of all three women, their efforts at securing better lives for themselves and their families have been accommodated by family and friends. Phyllis' parents took on the task of caring for her children when she went to Kingston to seek a better life for her family. Jackie's parents kept her son while she studied in England to increase her chances of a more financially stable life, and Ana's friends in the United States provided the support she needed to survive the birth and care of her first child and her re-enrollment into graduate school.

Preliminary Thoughts on a Caribbean Feminist Theory

The life histories of the three women show that they are not homogenous. In fact, there are vast differences based on the conditions into which they were born and hence the different factors which constituted their life experiences. The life histories show the need for a theoretical position which will account for these differences and for an analysis which demonstrates the value of the individual experience. Barriteau-Foster's (1992) call for a postmodernist feminist approach would be one approach in the Caribbean which sufficiently takes into account the differences as experienced by various men and women in these societies. In addition, the outline of an Afrocentric feminist epistemology given by Hill-Collins (1991) provides a useful framework for developing preliminary thoughts on Caribbean feminism. She argues that the combination of an Afrocentric standpoint consisting of Afrocentric values which pervade the black family and community, as well as the female standpoint which produces a female consciousness outside of race and class differences, provide a basis from which to analyse the experiences of women. In the Caribbean today, though some features of the African value systems have survived the horrors of slavery, there are also other value systems which have been observed, accepted and incorporated over time. As has been shown here, there are many cultural elements which coexist in the Caribbean which will eventually need to be incorporated into the analysis.

Hill-Collins (1992) identifies certain dimensions of an Afrocentric epistemology, viz.: concrete experience as a criterion of meaning, the use of dialogue in assessing knowledge claims, the ethic of caring and the ethic of personal accountability.

The recounting of experiences of the three women and the impact which these experiences have had on their lives has vividly given meaning to the development of their gender identity and resistance. Unlike the methodologies which utilized traditional theories, we were able to develop a more in-depth and holistic picture of the lives of the three women and hence a deeper understanding of their acts which might otherwise have gone unnoticed or misunderstood. The fact that the women have lived lives with the everyday experiences of race, class and gender oppression suggests that their related concrete experiences must be a powerful source of knowledge.

The life histories show that Caribbean feminist theory would be very limited and inadequate if it takes the traditional dichotomous position of defining woman as 'not man', which implies that women are a homogenous group. Women therefore need to be seen not only in relation to man, but as a gendered woman who interacts with and is acted upon by her environment (Barriteau-Foster 1992). There is need for an understanding of the fluid and changing nature of gender relations which are affected by race and class but are not overdetermined by them. Thus, depending on the circumstances or the particular context, gendered relations may change when they react with class and race.

Moreover, while class, race and gender are the three most powerful forms of oppression in the Caribbean, those who have experienced varying forms of oppression have not simply accepted their lot with a sense of inevitability. Rather, most women in their daily lives, while they may face inhibitions as a result of these forces, carve out niches within the system in which they can become empowered and actually be influential in the events in their lives. Their actions serve to challenge gendered relations. Phyllis' life circumstances resulted in a life as a domestic helper; while recognizing that this is not an ideal, she works to make sure that she can make the best out of her situation. Barriteau-Foster (1992) comments on the importance of the fluidity of any theoretical model so as to recognize that women's gendered experiences of social relations change over time; in some cases the women themselves, through reflection, may alter their behaviour. The three women have sought to transform the nature of their social relations with male partners based on their experiences with former partners.

The Afrocentric tradition of dialogue based on the strong oral tradition has many meanings and uses. Apart from the passing of cultures through generations, it serves as a means of connectedness which encourages the holistic nature of African traditions compared to the fragmented tradition of Western culture. Dialogue becomes a very important means of assessing knowledge claims based largely on the humanizing element of this type of speech. It offers resistance to domination which can take many forms. For example, dialogue provided a means of living through crises in the lives of all three women interviewed. It was based on Phyllis' storytelling that she became one of the subjects for the study. Her constant relating of her experiences provided a means of focusing on her situation as well as receiving advice. The actual conduct of this research also reinforces the use of dialogue. There were, undoubtedly, times when the process was used as a means of resistance even in the act of talking about particular issues. An example, for instance, is when Ana expressed the hope that her stepfather had seen the newspaper article, so that he would know that she had not conformed to his traditional expectations.

The ethic of caring places value on individual expression, emotions of the speaker and the capacity for empathy. Because the experience of the individual is considered important and unique from the Afrocentric and female standpoints, the emotions in dialogue serve as a means of identifying the conviction of the speaker to what she is saying and hence a means of validating the knowledge being passed on. The capacity for empathy is another female tradition which serves the process of opening up to others, thus facilitating the process of dialogue, connectedness and sharing, which in turn facilitates the relating of life experiences and generation of support which may be outside of the dominant institutions. Invariably, such institutions limit the expression of the average black female.

As well as passing on and showing concern for knowledge claims, persons are expected to be personally accountable for their claims. Unlike the Eurocentric tradition which rejects probing into the personal viewpoints, this aspect of the Afrocentric female epistemology considers the personal experiences and viewpoints as central to the knowledge validation process. Thus views which have been put forward by the three women in their life histories are considered valid and their personal accountability is measured by their personal experiences which resulted in their knowledge claims. The female and Afrocentric derived epistemology serves to critique conventional truths and theories which have served to guide thinking on social reality. In this way personal female experiences offer a valid accounting of truth based on the concrete experiences of the individual. Theory thus becomes not a body of knowledge formulated outside of day to day experiences, but these experiences of the individual become central to the process of theory building which stands up to the rigour of caring, emotion and personal accountability which have been central to their formulation.

Implications and Recommendations

The method used in this study, together with the data and analysis which informed the preliminary thoughts on a Caribbean feminist theory, has shown the complexities in the lives of women which need to be accounted for. Some implications for further exploration in the use of the methodology of life histories which serves to build up a data base on the varying experiences of women's lives are:

1. Theory can, does and should originate from the everyday lives of ordinary people.
2. Given that women are underrepresented in positions of power within society, research which seeks to understand lives, and hopefully, empower them, must address itself to the lived experiences of 'ordinary' women.
3. Notwithstanding the above mentioned consideration, and given that women occupy a wide range of social positions based on class and skin colour, research which seeks to document women's lives must address women who are privileged as well as those who are not-so-privileged.
4. Those agencies which gather and analyse statistical data on the situation of women should seek to utilize the case study and life histories method to a greater degree largely because these approaches yield information of a different, yet necessary quality from the quantitative approach.
5. There is need to think, perhaps to a greater degree than we do now, of people responding to unfavourable situations in ways which may not be adequately conceptualized under the traditional discourses of 'revolution' and 'resistance'.
6. Despite a widespread recognition that race, colour, class and gender all structure Caribbean societies in complex ways, state agencies continue to develop understandings of the population, especially women, by means of narrow categories. Social policy which impacts on women needs to be more sensitized to the interplay of these structural factors.

3

Life Satisfaction among the Elderly in Urban Jamaica

Donneth Crooks

Introduction

For many years, policymakers have wrestled with the problem of development and, as the conceptualization of development has changed, so have the strategies for its achievement. During the 1960s development was considered to be synonymous with economic growth, measured in terms of an economy's ability to generate and sustain an annual increase of 5 to 10 percent or more of its GNP. The overall economic and social benefits of growth, it was thought, would then 'trickle down' to the masses in the form of jobs and other economic opportunities (Todaro 1985: 87).

By the end of the first development decade, it had become clear that growth alone was insufficient to improve the quality of people's lives. Many 'Third World' countries had achieved the required growth in GNP, but widespread unemployment and growing inequality indicated that the overall levels of living of the masses had not improved. Calls for the 'dethronement of GNP' and 'redistribution from growth' resulted in the 'basic needs' approach which aimed to achieve a specific minimum standard of living for the majority of the world's population. In 1977, the International Labour Organization (ILO) severely criticized this approach, arguing that development must be seen as more than providing the minimum necessary for subsistence. Development thus came to be seen as the improvement of the quality of people's lives through change.

The 1980s saw the rise of neoclassicalism and the emphasis on economic growth. The cornerstone of this view is that the state should reduce or withdraw the level of its intervention in the economy and allow the free market to reign. It was argued that this would result in economic efficiency and growth. During this decade, many developing countries adopted structural adjustment programmes which imposed severe hardships on their populations. The result was that, with the exception of the 'Asian Tigers', many countries experienced a significant decline in living standards. This period has been described as the 'Lost Decade for Development'.

Concern over the continuing poverty and accompanying anxiety led the UN Committee on development planning to propose human development as the international development strategy for the 1990s. At the core of the human development concept is the view that the main objective of development is to benefit people. As used by the United Nations Development Programme (UNDP), human development denotes both the process of widening people's choices and the level of their achieved well-being.

The idea of human development is not an entirely new concept. Between 1985 and 1986 a transdisciplinary team of researchers from Chile, Uruguay, Bolivia, Colombia, Mexico, Brazil, Canada and Sweden presented the concept of human scale development (HSD) which has three main postulates:
1.   Development is about people and not about objects.
2.   Fundamental human needs are finite, few and classifiable.
3.   Fundamental human needs are the same in all cultures and in all historical periods. What changes over both time and through cultures is the way or the means by which the needs are satisfied.

The proponents of this approach to development make it clear that:

HSD does not exclude conventional goals such as economic growth . . . the difference with respect to the prevailing development styles lies in considering the aims of development not only as points of arrivals but as components of the process itself. (Max-Neef, et al. 1989:45)

The main objective of 'human development' as proposed by the UNDP is "enlarging people's choices", the most critical of these being to "live a long and healthy life, to be educated and to have access to the resources needed for a decent standard of living" (*Human Development Report* 1990).

While this approach does not deny the importance of income and wealth for development, it contends that these do not, in total, constitute development. Therefore it measures human development by an index called the human development index (HDI) which reflects the three choices considered to be essential to development at all levels: life expectancy, literacy and command over the resources to enjoy a decent standard of living.

Based on these indicators, the UNDP has concluded that developing countries have made great strides towards the human development ideal in the last three decades. Between 1960 and 1987, for instance, life expectancy in developing countries increased from 46 years to 62 years which is about 80 percent of that of the developed countries. But as Kane, et al, (1990) have pointed out, living a longer life does not necessarily imply an improvement in the quality of life nor that people are more satisfied with their lives. The Human Development Report (HDR) has itself acknowledged the enormous challenge of "making the lives of the old and infirm happy and worthwhile" (*United Nations* 1994:11).

The research problem

Against this backdrop, this study has three main objectives. Firstly, to develop a profile of the elderly who live in private homes and institutions in Jamaica. Is there evidence, for instance, to support the commonly held view that there is a relationship between reproductive failure and the likelihood that an individual will enter a residential home for the elderly in old age? Secondly, to find out how satisfied these elderly persons were with their lives. The third objective is to determine the importance of children for the life satisfaction of the elderly. One important area which the study seeks to shed light on was the extent to which children and the support which they give to their parents affect the way the elderly feel about their lives.

The Elderly in Jamaica and Globally

At present there are about 400 million elderly people in the world (*WHO Report* 1989), 52 percent of whom live in developing countries. By the year 2000, the world elderly population is expected to reach 600 million, with two-thirds of them living in developing countries. As pointed out by

Kinsella (1988), within the developing world, the Caribbean has the highest proportion (12 percent) of population aged 55 years and over, ahead of Asia (10 percent) and Latin America (9 percent).

With an elderly population of 246,910 (10 percent of the total population) in 1992, Jamaica is one of the Caribbean countries with the largest aged population. Over the past decade alone, the proportion of the aged in the population increased by 18.25 percent (Kinsella 1988). And with a percentage growth rate of 3.1 percent annually, Jamaica will experience rapid aging well into the next century (*Demographic Statistics* 1992).

Of the total population of elderly persons in Jamaica, 48 percent are males and 52 percent are females, with Kingston having almost twice as many females as males. Despite the rapid urbanization taking place, Jamaica is still largely rural with approximately 52 percent of its population living in the rural areas. Of the aged population, 62 percent live in the rural areas. Overall, only 7.6 percent of the urban population is aged, compared with 11.3 percent of the rural population. In fact, the proportion of aged persons to the total parish population is lowest in the four main urban areas, namely Kingston, St Andrew, St James and St Catherine.

But not only is the aged population growing; it is getting older as well. The 'old elderly' (75 years and over) now represent 39.4 percent of the elderly population while in 1960 they represented only 21.6 percent (Eldemire 1993).

Two major factors have accounted for this increase in the aged population: increased life expectancy at birth and decline in mortality rates. In the decades between 1950 and 1990, life expectancy at birth increased by 15.9 years for women and 14.7 for men. Currently, life expectancy is 74, the highest among the developing countries (*Demographic Statistics* 1992).

Additionally, improvements in medical science and technology have resulted in life expectancy at older ages increasing at a faster rate than life expectancy at birth. An individual now attaining the age of 60 can expect to live an average of 15 additional years. Relatedly, death rates have also declined moving from 25.8 percent in 1920 to 7.5 percent in 1970. In terms of gender, the figure moved from 27.9 percent to 15 percent for males, while for females it moved from 26.2 percent to 14.2 percent for the same period (*Demographic Statistics* 1992).

Issues affecting the aged

It is traditionally accepted that each family will look after its own elderly and this has been the pattern for the most part. Most of the responsibility falls on children and society holds in disdain those who do not fulfil their filial responsibilities. But as the country experiences the demographic transition, changes are occurring which place increased strain on the family and brings into question the norm of family-based care for the elderly.

While the extended family still functions in the rural areas, there is concern that the trend toward urbanization is changing the structure of the society, leading to a decline in family support for the elderly. The small size of urban housing units which are not conducive to caring for the elderly, and the increasing participation of women in the labour force have been cited as contributing factors. In addition, the extended family tends to give way to the nuclear or conjugal family in the urban areas (*United Nations* 1991a).

Unlike in developed countries where the main source of income for the elderly is social-security,[1] a majority (65 percent) of the elderly in Jamaica cite the family as their main source of income. Very few are covered under old-age pension schemes which started only in 1947. Even the introduction of a formal government pension system in 1962 did not significantly improve the situation as it excluded certain occupational categories and those with earnings below a specified level.

One of the main features of old age is economic inactivity. Irrespective of the statutory retirement age in a country, the fact is that the percentage of persons over 60 years old who are still working is often only a small fraction of the total labour force between 18 and 59 years. This has serious implications for the support of the elderly by the labour force. Labour force participation rates for the 65 and over age group was 37.9 percent in 1991 (*United Nations* 1991a).

The issue of gender is also a matter of concern. Women tend to marry earlier and live longer than men, so they are more likely to spend the remaining years of their lives without a spouse. It is also true that unemployment rates are higher among women than among men, that most women work in low-status, low-paying jobs and that whenever government introduces cuts in its budget, it is usually the jobs that women do and their support services that go first. The result is that older women are generally even more dependent on their children.

It is this combination of social and demographic factors which has figured greatly in the gradual increase of residential care homes as an accepted method of providing maintenance for the elderly. Although these homes go by different names (golden age homes, rest homes, homes for the aged, nursing homes and retirement homes), they all provide room, board, and protection for aged persons.

According to the Homes Registration Act passed in 1934, three types of residential care homes operate in Jamaica:

1. Private nursing homes where residential nursing care is available hourly;

2. Homes for the aged which offer board and lodging and general care for the aged, not including medical care beyond such as is expected in a normal household;

3. Residential homes for functionally independent elderly persons who do not require any special physical protection beyond the public health and fire department regulations applicable to boarding houses and hotels. (Conference on the Elderly 1980)

In addition, there are 12 government infirmaries and two Golden Age Homes which provide institutional care for the elderly.

It is difficult to state with precision exactly how many elderly persons are housed in residential care facilities at any one time. Based on very liberal estimates, no more than 1.5 percent of the elderly population fall into this category. Based on information provided by the Board of Supervision, there are currently 759 elderly persons living in parish infirmaries, 57 percent of whom are males. These 759 represent 62.7 percent of the total population in infirmaries. The two golden age homes have a combined population of 507, of which males constitute 48.1 percent (*Economic and Social Survey* 1992).

So far, there is no policy statement on the aged, but the government has acknowledged the need for a systematic and coordinated approach to deal with the needs of the elderly. The National Council for the Aged was inaugurated in May 1976 with its primary functions being to make recommendations for policies and programmes designed to meet the needs of the elderly, and to advise the relevant minister on all matters concerning the welfare of senior citizens. The achievements of this body include:

1. The establishment of golden age homes to provide opportunities for social interaction, recreation and involvement in income earning opportunities.

2. Feeding programmes which provide a hot meal each working day and a food package on public holidays for the elderly, including shut-ins.
3. Activity centres which offer care and leisure activities to the elderly.
4. Seminars designed to train staff and volunteers as well as the elderly themselves in areas of geriatric care and income-earning skills.
5. Senior Citizens' Month which is observed in September each year and is designed to honour and pay tribute to the elderly.

There are also a number of programmes which provide economic and social assistance to the elderly. These include: old age pensions for those elderly covered under the National Insurance Scheme; old age assistance for those without a regular income or pension; food stamps for those persons at risk of becoming malnourished; and poor relief which provides monthly assistance for the destitute, both in and out of institutions. Elderly persons with bus passes may also travel at concessionary rates on public transportation in the corporate area.

Methodology

Each method of collecting data has its limitations and so a combination of methods is often appropriate to capitalize on their different strengths. In order to get as complete a picture of the social situation under investigation as possible, four main methods were used in the data collection process. These included elite interviews with the matrons and operators of homes for the elderly, personal observation, and a survey based on questionnaires administered to the elderly and secondary sources.

Sampling

The sample comprised 105 males and females out of a total population of 452 residents drawn from 24 residential care homes in the Kingston-Metropolitan Area as Table 3.1 shows.

The respondents ranged in ages from 62 to 97 years and the proportion of females to males in both the sample and the population was 4.5 to 1. In this study, the 'elderly' or the 'aged' refers to persons who are 60 years of age and above.

Table 3.1 Summary of Sampling Frame

Type of Home	Total Number	Sex M	Sex F	Number Sampled	Sex M	Sex F
Nursing Home	174 (38%)	49	125	35 (33%)	13	22
Homes For The Aged	278 (62%)	32	246	70 (67%)	6	64
Total	452	81	371	105	19	86

Homes and institutions

Of the homes sampled 66.6 percent (n= 24) fell in the home for the aged category, while 33.3 percent were nursing homes. Half of the homes sampled are operated by the church, 42 percent of them at monthly rates of between $3,000 and $5,000 per person (Table 3.2).

One of the main criteria for admission into a home for the aged is that the individual be ambulant and not suffering from any kind of illness which requires constant attention, as these homes do not offer nursing services. However, a doctor is on call in all of them and relatives are expected to take their residents for monthly medical checks. Should a resident of a home for the aged become seriously ill or incapacitated, he/she has to be moved to a nursing home. Within this category there were two homes which operated slightly differently. Individuals were allowed to move in with their own furniture and were allowed much more freedom. More individual space was also allotted as there were no shared rooms. One was like a dormitory and the other took the form of clusters of self-contained flats shared by flatmates.

Two of the homes sampled served the members of their sect exclusively. One specified that residents must belong to a church to be admitted; another admitted only persons who had a specific type of illness and one served only the destitute. The others were open to the public as long as they could afford the rates and at least one of the persons responsible for their maintenance is resident in Jamaica.

Nursing homes, on the other hand, accounted for 33 percent of the homes sampled and, as indicated by their names, provide full 24-hour nursing care. Residents of nursing homes were generally more infirm than their counterparts in homes for the aged and the rates were therefore significantly higher, ranging from $2,000 monthly at the lower end to

Table 3.2 Summary of Characteristics of Institutions

Characteristic	Number	Percentage
Type		
Nursing home	8	33.3
Home for the aged	14	58.3
Residential care home for		
functionally independent	2	8.3
Size		
10 – 20 beds	14	63.0
21 – 30 beds	6	21.0
31 – 40 beds	3	12.0
Over 40 beds	1	4.0
Ownership		
Church	12	50.0
Private person	10	42.0
Other	2	8.0
Years Home in Operation		
5 years or less	3	12.5
6 – 10 years	4	16.6
11 – 20 years	2	8.3
21 – 30 years	6	25.0
Over 30 years	7	29.1
Date not ascertained	2	8.3
Monthly Rates		
No fees at all	2	8.0
Less than $3,000	6	25.0
$3,000 – $5,000	10	42.0
$6,000 – $10,000	2	8.0
$10,000 or more	1	4.0

$18,000 at the upper. Three of the homes sampled started off as nursing homes but are now operating somewhere between the two categories.

Measurement

Life satisfaction was measured by interviewees' responses to a series of 14 statements, both positive and negative, about their present and past lives. The statements, which were all taken from standardized life-satisfaction tests, used a Likert type of scale to which respondents were expected to agree or disagree. Positive answers scored two points and negative answers 1 point each, so the maximum life satisfaction score possible was 28. The higher the score, the higher the degree of well-being. The scores were then grouped: 0–13 denoted low life satisfaction, 14–18 moderate life satisfaction and 19–28 high life satisfaction. Some of the items in this section were also looked at separately.

Findings and Analysis

General physical and social environment

All of the homes in the sample were situated in quiet, residential areas, more than three-quarters of them having been dwelling houses. All but three occupied one floor only and most had sizeable verandahs which served as reception and recreation areas for the residents. Where there were no verandahs, there were large reception areas, sometimes also used as dining areas, or residents were taken out into the yard on mornings. The general environment of the homes was clean and tidy except in two cases where the physical environment and furniture left much to be desired.

Most of the residents were observed sleeping, meditating, or having something done to them (eg, hair being combed or nails being done), supporting the finding of many researchers that the majority of a resident's time is spent in 'passive' activity, that is, doing nothing. Watching television and talking to each other were the two most common 'active' activities in which residents engaged. Although the television set was on in three homes, a significant number of the residents just stared blankly at the screen. Lively discussions among residents were seen in just about four homes. Some residents were also seen helping others to manipulate the environment. Only one resident was observed reading and one sewing. In one home, residents who were able were seen in groups playing dominoes and cards. There was also friendly interaction between residents and staff, and between residents and visitors in about four cases. Negative interaction was also observed between residents and staff, and members of staff were heard making negative remarks about some residents and ignoring their calls for attention.

Based on the information gleaned from operators and matrons, most of the homes had very little, if any, planned activities. The fact that a significant proportion of the homes are run by churches is reflected in the heavy religious tone of most of the homes in the sample. In fact, the most common activity in which residents participated on a regular basis was some kind of devotion carried out either by staff members or by various church groups. Some residents did their own washing and domestic chores; others helped to set the table at mealtimes and with the washing up. In the two homes for the functionally independent adults, residents did their own cooking and could hire their own helpers if they wished.

Three homes had well-developed programmes which included: a games evening, art therapy, remotivation sessions where residents listened and danced to the music of their time, or regular outings for shopping or to recreational areas such as the movies or Devon House. In a few others, the residents were involved in physical exercise. In some others, however, it was reported that the staff had tried to get residents involved in craft and other activities but with little success. Almost all operators said, however, that their residents were feted by the Kiwanis and Rotary Clubs at least once per year.

Sociodemographic profile of the elderly

The sociodemographic profile of the elderly examined the following characteristics: age, gender, number of children, previous residence, marital status, education, occupation, income, and church/club membership (see Appendix I).

Age and gender. Only 2 percent of the sample were in the 60–64 age group while 81 percent were in the category classified as the 'old elderly' that is, 75 years and over. In fact, there were four times more elderly, persons in this group than there were in the age groups under 74. This finding supports the view that elderly persons live at home until it is no longer possible for them to do so. Females outnumbered males by four to one. Eighty-two percent of the sample were female and 18 percent were male, which was exactly proportionate to the total number of elderly persons in the homes and institutions sampled. These figures contrast with those for the government infirmaries where the ratio was 1:3 in favour of males. As pointed out by the UN (*Ageing and the Family* 1994a), more old women are institutionalized because old men are usually cared for by their wives while a great majority of old women are widows. However, the fact that there are significantly more in private homes compared to government institutions could indicate a greater willingness of children to provide for their mothers above their fathers. In fact, most of the residents of government infirmaries were destitute. Not only were there more females than males in the sample overall, but women were also more highly represented in the age group 75 and over. Eighty-two percent of the females in the sample were over 75 years old compared with 63 percent of the males. The males in the sample ranged in age from 60 to 95 years while the females ranged in age from 64 to 98 years.

Children. Nearly one third of the sample or 29 percent were childless, while 43 percent had either one, two, or three children. Of the childless population, only 10 percent were males, compared with 33 percent who were females. The median number of children for males was three, while for females it was one. This is not surprising in light of the tendency of Jamaican males to have several informal relationships, often simultaneously. The data also showed that, of the twelve respondents from charity homes, only two had children who were both males.

Previous residence. More than half at 65 percent of the sample had not lived in a home for more than three years while at the other end, only the small number of 5 percent had been institutionalized for over 12 years. This could suggest either that more homes and institutions have come into operation within the last three years or that there have been significant changes in the society which have forced the elderly to seek refuge in residential care homes. The survey data show, however, that only 12.5 percent of the homes sampled started operating within the last five years, so explanations must be sought elsewhere. Two factors can be looked at in relation to this: migration and changes in the status and role of women. Migration is a very selective process. This means that certain elements of the population are more migratory than others. The profile of the typical migrant can be described as a single, fairly well educated female, very likely a professional, between the ages of 15 and 35 years old. One possible explanation for this is that the large-scale out-migration from Jamaica which took place during the latter half of the 1970s and the early 1980s is now having its consequences. The present elderly who were too old to join the migration stream then, have now reached the age where they can no longer live alone and with no children in Jamaica, the next best option is to seek residence in a home or institution. Funding is thus provided by the children who have built up lives for themselves in their adopted countries and therefore cannot do otherwise. The survey data show that 23 percent of the elderly in the sample had no children living in Jamaica, the most common place of residence being the USA. A further 17 percent had more of their children abroad, and 15 percent exactly half.

When the cost of care in these homes and the previous occupation of the respondents are taken into consideration, it becomes easier to understand the role that migration could have played in this process. Equally interesting is the view that more women are challenging the role stereotypes and are passing their role as caregivers to others. The percentages for male and female as regards length of time in the institution were roughly the same except that three times as many women as men had lived in a home for more than 8 years. This is not unexpected considering the greater longevity of women in general.

A significant proportion of the sample 42 percent had lived alone prior to entering a residential care home compared with 15 percent who had lived with a child, more of them being females than males. Further analysis of the data shows that only 25 percent of those who had children had lived with them prior to institutionalization. This situation could also have been created by migration although data from other studies (eg, Townsend and Wedderburn 1969) tend to indicate that many aged persons prefer to live alone.

The data also showed that women were three times as likely as men to have lived with a child. Interestingly though, twice the number of respondents had lived with a son as opposed to a daughter. In fact, none of the males in the sample had lived with a daughter. This finding contradicts previous research findings (Townsend and Wedderburn 1969) which indicate that persons with daughters are less likely to become institutionalized in later life, even given the greater numbers of male children in the sample. Another common place of residence was with relatives, not including siblings. Twenty percent of the sample fell into this category. This represents 64 percent of those respondents who had no children. Most often these relatives were nieces and grandchildren. The greater longevity of females again comes into play. While 21.1 percent of the males had been living with a spouse prior to their move to a home, only 3.5 percent of the females were in that category.

Siblings and friends also provided residence for respondents before they were institutionalized. Roughly one half of the sample had sought admission to a residential care home based on the advice of their children, and there were no gender differences in this respect. Interestingly though, daughters were twice as likely as sons to suggest that their parents enter a home. This could be due to the increasing participation of women in the labour force.

Marital status. Only 10 percent of the sample were still married, 31 percent had never married while 54 percent were widowed. A significant 32 percent had never been married, which represented 30 percent of both males and females. However, while 58.8 percent of the females had been widowed, only 31.6 percent of the males fell into this category, supporting, to some extent, the commonly held view of Jamaican males as being irresponsible and philanderers.

Education and occupation. Fifty two percent of those interviewed had received only elementary education,[2] while only 9.6 percent had received tertiary or university education, none of whom were males. It should be noted that the two persons who had university education were not trained in Jamaica. As should be expected, a larger percentage of males than females had received elementary, secondary and postsecondary education. Thus while more males were exposed to education generally, females were more inclined to pursue higher education. The greater number of males receiving general education represents a cohort effect, as educational opportunities were sparse then and education was generally not encouraged for females. The wider availability of education in more recent times would mean that the future aged would be better educated. Education therefore would be more likely to be significant for their life satisfaction. Quite a number of the respondents also indicated that their mothers had died when they were young and so they had to leave school to work.

Considering the link between education and occupation, it is not surprising that a significant proportion of the sample, 59 percent, had been engaged in semiskilled and unskilled occupations.[3] In fact, there were roughly equal proportions of persons in the three lower categories of skilled (30 percent), semiskilled (30 percent) and unskilled (29 percent) labour. Although the percentage of males and females working in semi-skilled occupations was basically equal, startling differences were seen in the unskilled category where 95 percent of the people who worked in these occupations were females. Conversely, there was a higher proportion of skilled men (52.6 percent) to women (36.6 percent). None of the occupations represented were classifiable as higher professional and managerial; one was in the lower professional and managerial category while five were highly skilled.

Source of income. Thirty-nine percent of the sample reported that their main source of income was remittances from children, and in this regard there were differences based on gender. Although there were only slightly more women than men who received pensions (government and private), the number of women receiving private pensions was almost three times that of men, implying perhaps that more men had been self-employed. Over ten percent of the men (10.5 percent) were more likely, however, to cite property rents as a source of income than the women (7.16 percent).

Church or club membership. In light of the fact that Jamaica is reputed to have the highest number of churches per square mile, it is not surprising that 94 percent of the persons interviewed said that they were members of a church. In addition, it is also not surprising that women are more likely than men to belong to a church. For instance, while 2 pecent of the females did not belong to a church, the corresponding figure for males was 25 per cent.

Life Satisfaction

Life Satisfaction scores for the sample ranged between 1 and 28 with a mean of 16.8 and a median of 16. When examined by gender, several differences were observed. For instance the mean score for females was 18.3, almost 5 points higher than that for males. Median scores also differed – 16 for males, 18 for females – as well as the mode, which was 14 for males and 20 for females. Twenty-nine percent of the females got a score of 21 and over, while no male fell into this category. When the scores were further classified as low, moderate or high, it was shown that nearly one-half of the sample got moderate scores while only about one-sixth of the total sample fell into the low satisfaction group (Table 3.3).

Table 3.3   Life Satisfaction Scores

Score	Frequency	Percentage
Low Satisfaction		
(0–13)	16	15.4
Moderate Satisfaction		
(14–18)	50	48.1
High Satisfaction		
(19–28)	38	36.5

There were twice as many persons receiving high as low scores. Table 4 shows that whereas the bulk of the males 57.9 percent fell in the moderate life satisfaction group, the bulk of the females 47.8 percent fell in the high satisfaction group. Overall, females had higher life satisfaction scores than males, the opposite to what Harris et al. (1975) found among the American population.

Generally, the data show that a significant proportion (65 percent) of those interviewed expressed satisfaction with the sum total of their lives. Although 61 percent of the sample said that they would not change their past lives even if they could, 46.3 percent felt that they had made many mistakes and of these, 62 percent indicated they would do many things differently if they had the chance to live all over again. The mistakes mentioned varied but a number of them made mention of bad marriages, while several others were sorry that they had not married.

Of the respondents, 60.2 percent did not think that old age was the worst time of their lives, but neither did 57.9 percent think it was the best. Many cited the fact that they have lived long, that they have three meals per day, clean clothes and a place to sleep as important reasons for so thinking. Among those who felt that it was the worst time of their lives, bad health, loneliness and difficulty in getting around were the major factors. These findings compare well to those of Harris et al. (1975) for the United States of America.

Some respondents were also worried about how they would be "put away" when their "time" came. More than half of them felt that life could be happier than it is now. Several mentioned terrible tasting food, rough nurses and attendants, dishonest workers and staff members as reasons for this. Among the things that respondents felt made for happiness in old age were: being in good health (93 percent); having social contacts (91 percent); having children around (81 percent); being able to make decisions (73 percent); being able to work (72.3 percent) and having

Table 3.4   Life Satisfaction Scores, by Sex

Life Satisfaction	Males	Females
Low	26.3	17.6
Moderate	57.9	57.6
High	15.8	45.8

enough money (64.6 percent). A number of respondents expressed the view that money cannot buy happiness and further, that with their reduced activity money was not all that important.

In relation to the effect of children, although it was generally felt that children are an important source of happiness in old age, one third (37.1 percent) felt that older people should not reside with their children as that only creates friction. Also frequently mentioned as a source of happiness in old age was knowing God and having a relationship with Him.

As in the Harris study (1975), less than half of all persons interviewed felt that their life expectations had been met. A little less (43.2 percent) felt that things had turned out better than they had expected. Although only a small proportion – about 1 in 4 – felt that they had got the most important things that they wanted out of life, 78 percent agreed that they had been quite fortunate.

Some expressed regret at not having children and one respondent was of the view that if she had a daughter, she would not have been put in a home. Others regretted that they had not been able to follow their career choices or that they had not secured homes. A few even regretted that they had not become Christians earlier. When asked how they felt about not having control over their lives, 42.4 percent said that they felt badly while 44.6 percent did not, a marginal difference of 2.2 percentage points.

Disaggregation of the data by sex showed interesting differences for some items. Only about 1 in 9 men felt that they got the most important things that they had wanted out of life, compared with 1 in 3 women. Men were also more likely than women (62.5 percent to 43 percent) to feel that they had made a lot of mistakes, but because men were not as communicative, it was difficult to find out what some of these mistakes were. Generally, men seemed to be more dissatisfied with their present lives than women. Whereas 59 percent of the men felt that this was the worst time of their lives, only 27 percent of the women did. Lack of control over their lives also seemed to be a big problem for men. Even though roughly the same proportion admitted that they felt badly without control over their lives as those who said they did not, closer analysis revealed that only 34.2 percent of females felt this way compared with 81.3 percent of males. Work was also important for men as almost half of them felt that their worth as an individual depended on it, as opposed to one-third of the women. This can be explained by the system of patriarchy which socializes males to be the 'breadwinner' of the family and to be in control.

Men who become incapacitated are therefore more likely to have feelings of worthlessness.

Associations with life satisfaction

Using statistics appropriate for the data collected, no meaningful associations were found between life satisfaction and any of the independent variables. Environment did not seem to make much of a difference for among the top scorers were respondents from a charity home as well as from the most expensive home. However, two observations with respect to the environment were made. More of the top scorers lived in homes for the aged as opposed to nursing homes and only one respondent from a home where conditions were not satisfactory received a high score.

No differences were found in the scores of those who had children and those who did not. However, a different pattern emerged when further disaggregation was done. Of the sixteen persons who received low scores, eight had no children and five had only one child. None of the respondents with five children or more received a low life satisfaction score. Those persons with only male children scored significantly higher than those who had female children only. In the latter category, no respondent got a score above 19, whereas 60 percent of the former category received scores of 20 and over. Two factors could be considered. First, when girls get married their first loyalties tend to be towards their husbands and their families. Secondly, men assume more dominant positions and command more resources, giving them more flexibility with regard to the amount and type of support that they can give to their parents. But this finding could also suggest that there is some truth in the popular belief that sons care more for their mothers than daughters do.

Additionally, all those who had only one child and who scored greater than 20 were females. This finding confounds the general view that girls are to be preferred as they are more likely than boys to provide care for their parents. It could also lend some support to the popular view of the Jamaican male as one who stoutly defends his mother.

As it pertains to the residential location of siblings, whether children lived abroad or in Jamaica did not seem to affect life satisfaction scores, even where the respondent had only one child. However, none of those persons who reported no contacts with their children scored high on life satisfaction. The converse was also true: those who had very frequent contact with a child (at least once per week) tended to score higher on life satisfaction.

Summary and Conclusion

Several major findings emerged from the study. Most of the sample were in the 'old elderly' category, that is 75 years and older. Females outnumbered males by four to one and the females were also comparatively older than the males. More than half of the respondents were widowed and had lived alone before entering a home. Only a very small percentage of the sample, excluding males, had received tertiary or university education. Consequently, the skilled, semiskilled and unskilled occupational categories were overrepresented in the sample.

A significantly large proportion of the sample had been institutionalized because of illness, but loss of residence was another important factor. Almost all of those interviewed reported affiliation with some religious organization and many expressed hope and confidence in God.

Most of the elderly had children although a significant number did not, of which females comprised the majority. Although the children of many respondents lived abroad, there was frequent contact with them, and for many residents, their main source of income was remittances from their children.

Most of the interviewees received moderate or high satisfaction scores, with females gaining top scores. Persons with children did not necessarily get higher scores but those with male children did. Additionally, no person with more than five children received a low score.

Based on the above findings, the following conclusions can be drawn. First, the aged in private residential care homes have been neither abandoned nor rejected by their children. To the contrary, a significant proportion of those with children are actually being supported by their children and report frequent contact with them. The evidence also suggests that there is no relationship between life satisfaction and any of the variables examined. However, more females received higher overall scores and most of the low scorers had low fertility rates. There also seemed to be some advantage in having male children, as those persons who had only male children received higher life satisfaction scores.

Old age was not the worst time of life for those studied but neither was it the best. Although most expressed satisfaction with their lives and had no desire to change them, the majority said that they would do many things differently, if they got the chance to do so.

The general profile of the elderly in private residential care homes is that of a very old widow who did not receive any education beyond the elementary level and is likely to have worked in a skilled, unskilled or semiskilled occupation for most of her life. Her main source of income is remittances from her children living abroad and she is very likely to have sought residence in a home because of illness.

Life satisfaction is a composite index which reflects the effects of a myriad of variables. The fact that no direct relationships were observed does not mean that no relationships exist. It could suggest, however, that the level of interaction among the variables is very high, making it difficult to isolate their individual effects. Life satisfaction is thus more than the sum of its parts. It seems also that the concept 'life satisfaction' is based on expectations which are culturally determined, suggesting that standardized, universal life satisfaction tests might not yield valid and reliable data in all cases.

The results of the study suggest that the UNDP is justified in its use of life expectancy as an indicator of development. Arguably, the quality of life is more important than the fact of life itself, but the data show that longevity does have an intrinsic value. Even when they were well into the ninth decade, respondents expressed satisfaction with their lives, despite low educational levels and limited income. Income and education are undoubtedly important because they enhance an individual's capabilities of leading a fulfiling life. But, of themselves they are inadequate to produce life satisfaction.

There is no doubt that more information is needed on the elderly in Jamaica in general, and specifically on feelings of well-being among them. Future research should firstly undertake a comparative study among the noninstitutionalized elderly to ascertain if there are differences attributable to institutionalization. Secondly, a longitudinal study would be useful for tracing life satisfaction from middle age through old age.

In the past, little attention has been given to the elderly as a social group. But the rapid increase in the size of this group, coupled with their increasing longevity sends a strong, clear signal to policymakers that issues related to this stage of life must be accorded greater priority. In addition to the government's plans, as outlined in the five year development plan, the following suggestions might be useful in responding to the situation of an ageing population.

1. A complete census of the elderly must be undertaken before any comprehensive plans can be made. All types of data are desperately needed on the health and living conditions of the ageing and the aged.

2. There has to be a national policy on ageing and the aged to provide the necessary guidelines. This policy must address issues relating to pensions; tax benefits for persons providing care for the elderly, especially in cases of chronic illness or incapacity; housing for the elderly; and elimination of discrimination against the elderly.

3. The National Council for the Aged must be strengthened so that it becomes an effective force, providing leadership and direction for this section of the population. The council should be able to perform monitoring functions, to mobilize and/or influence the allocation of resources, and to conduct research and operate a data bank on issues relating to ageing and the aged.

4. Legislation and means of monitoring their implementation must be established to ensure a minimum acceptable level of care for those elderly persons in institutions.

5. The community must be encouraged to play a greater role in the lives of the aged, especially those in institutions. At the moment, church groups, who are the persons most involved with the elderly, are mostly concerned about gaining converts among this population. But there is a great need among the elderly, especially shut-ins, for contact with the world outside their own. Many, for instance, would appreciate having someone to read for them and youngsters could be rallied to that call. It is possible to develop a programme which allows adolescents to perform voluntary service to the aged during weekends and holidays, for which they would be awarded certificates. These hours of service could also count as work experience.

6. Attempts must be made to change the negative stereotypes of the elderly. In this regard, the mass media can be a very effective medium of change. Radio stations especially have a responsibility to the aged. Many elderly persons have lost their sight or find it strenuous on their eyes to watch television and others do not find it entertaining, having not grown up with it. Even one hour per week could be programmed for the elderly in which the music of their time is played and time is

given to their concerns and interests. It would not be unreasonable to suggest that commercial enterprises directly involved in the health care sector should provide sponsorship, considering that the elderly are the largest consumers of these products and services.

7. Public educational programmes should be developed to prepare people for old age and retirement. There should also be programmes which will enable informal caregivers to provide better care for the elderly. The elderly themselves would fare better if they had the knowledge to deal with certain aspects of their condition.

8. Future plans should include giving consideration to locating custodial care institutions for the aged and those for children on the same compound so that children can benefit from the general knowledge and wisdom of the elderly. It is an accepted fact that children need nurturing if they to are become well-adjusted social beings. Since, for obvious reasons, this one-on-one interaction is not always possible, children in care often become emotionally starved. An intervention of this kind could go a far way in alleviating this problem.

9. More social services are needed to reduce the probability of institutionalization of the aged. Many more elderly persons could continue to function independently with a little help.

10. More opportunities should be provided for the elderly to participate in the economy so that they will be able to meet most of their needs themselves.

Notes

1. Townsend and Wedderburn (1969) found that the most important single income source for the aged in Britain was income from the state.
2. Prior to independence, elementary education was provided for all students up to age 15. Only a select few (2 per parish) received scholarships to secondary schools, but those who could afford to pay were able to do so.
3. This categorization is borrowed from Miller (1990).

APPENDIX I Demographic Characteristics of Total Sample

Characteristic	Percentage
1. Age	
60–69	8
70–79	25
80–89	45
90 and over	22
2. Sex	
Male	18
Female	82
3. Marital Status	
Married	10
Never married	31
Divorced	–
Separated	5
Widowed	54
4. Number of Children	
None	29
One only	21
2–3	22
4–5	9
6–9	9
More than 10	4
5. Length of Stay in Institution	
Less than one year	31
1–3 years	34
4–7 years	21
8–11 years	6
12–15 years	3
More than 15 years	2
Missing	4
6. Main Reason for Seeking Admission	
Illness	32
Loss of home	18
Loneliness	10
Lack of home help	11
Loss of spouse or supporting relative	10
Friction in household	10
Other	9

(Table continues)

95

APPENDIX I (cont'd)   Demographic Characteristics of Total Sample

Characteristic	Percentage
7. PLACE OF PREVIOUS RESIDENCE	
Alone	42
With spouse	7
With children	15
With a sibling	7
With other relatives	20
With a friend	5
In another home	6
8. Educational Level	
No formal education	12
Elementary	52
Secondary	17
Post secondary	6
Tertiary	8
University	2
Missing	3
9. Occupational Level	
Higher professional and managerial	–
Lower professional and managerial	1
Highly skilled	5
Skilled	30
Semi skilled	30
Unskilled	29
Missing	6
10. Main Source of Income	
Children	39
Self (savings, property etc.)	15
Pension	21
Relatives	7
Church	6
Public assistance	7
Missing	5
11. Church Membership	
Member	94
Non-member	6

4

Human Development, Economic Competitiveness and Secondary Education in Jamaica

Sharon Kelly-Stair

Introduction

The problematic

The issues involved in an examination of the contribution of any educational system to national development are multifaceted and complex. They are even more so when the educational system under examination represents a kind of hydra. The existing institutional forms, curricula practices and organizational ethos reflect external impulses grafted upon a colonial core. Where, additionally, the development imperatives are more often than not externally derived and fashioned, this produces a situation of dependent economic and social relations within the society in question. The fact that the society is characterized by great social and economic inequities and by the existence of a strong counter-culture, expressed in language, music, dress and other aspects is also significant.

In this context, the central issues concerning the contribution of the educational system to national development centre on concerns of instrumentality but must also have a humanistic and empowering content.

While this study focuses on the economic function of education in respect of the development of human resources as a critical factor in the enhancement of international competitiveness, it does so fully recognizing the continued important role of educational systems in the social, political, and other domains. The study therefore seeks to examine the extent to which certain skills, which are identified as critical to enhancing national competitiveness, are present among school leavers in Jamaican secondary schools.

To this end, the study seeks to measure existing levels of achievement in literacy, numeracy, creativity and critical thinking at the secondary level. Additionally, it will attempt to suggest some of the factors which may contribute to these skills and to propose policy interventions which could be employed to address the situation. English language and mathematics will be used as proxy measures for achievement in literacy and numeracy, respectively.

Hypotheses to be tested

Consistent with the objectives of this study, the following seven hypotheses are examined:

1. There is no relationship between levels of literacy, creativity, critical thinking and numeracy and the type of school which a student attends.
2. There is no relationship between students' levels of literacy and/or numeracy and the levels of creativity and/or critical thinking which they display.
3. Students' levels of literacy, numeracy, critical thinking and creativity are not related to their gender and/or age.
4. Students' socioeconomic status is not related to their levels of numeracy, literacy, critical thinking and creativity.
5. The urban/rural location of the school which a student attends does not relate to levels of performance in literacy, numeracy, critical thinking and creativity.
6. The gender composition of the students' school makes no difference to their levels of achievement in literacy, numeracy, creativity and critical thinking.
7. There is no relationship between students' achievement levels and the methods used by teachers in classes.

Historical Background

The public secondary system in the colonial period

The public system of secondary education in Jamaica had its genesis in the postslavery period with the establishment of the 1879 Schools Commission (Gordon 1974: 31). Earlier efforts by the churches and individuals, through endowments, to establish a secondary system, had resulted in failure for the most part.

A more propitious environment for the promotion of a secondary school system in Jamaica arose as a result of declining sugar fortunes after 1846, which meant that the resources to send the children of the planters to England for education were not available. At the same time, the popular notion was that the upper and middle classes ought to receive an education which was superior to the elementary type education, then available to the majority of the black masses.

The colonial government did little to provide the necessary infrastructure for the secondary system, and it was the churches which had taken a leading role in the provision of elementary education which continued to provide the dynamism for secondary education. This situation obtained until well into the twentieth century.

The system has been variously described as elitist and middle class in ethos, catering to the needs of a fairly small and select proportion of the population (King 1987: 90). The fact that secondary education was largely financed by user charges meant that it became "the educational preserve of those who could afford it" (Gordon 1974: 33). Up to 1911, less than 1 percent of the 10–19 age group was enrolled in secondary school (Miller 1990: 69).

The period 1879–1911 has been described as the formative years for secondary schooling in Jamaica (Miller 1987: 109). It was during this time that a secondary educational system began to be institutionalized in Jamaica, and by 1890 a definite structure could be discerned. The Jamaica Schools Commission was responsible for the general supervision and certification of the secondary schools. These included endowed schools, which were reorganized, as well as secondary schools which were operated by the churches or by private individuals. The secondary system underwent further modifications in its structure up to 1943. There was some expansion in the institutions offering secondary education by the amalgamation of the church schools into the public system through a grant-in-aid scheme as well as the provision of scholarships for capable students from parishes where there were no secondary schools. While in 1911 there were twelve secondary schools, by 1943 there were some twenty-three schools. Enrolment in public secondary level institutions also more than doubled between 1912 and 1943, increasing from 1,012 to 3,637 (Miller 1987: 131). Changes also occurred in the management structure of schools. As a condition for the receipt of government grants, the government could now appoint two members to sit on the boards of these schools.

Between 1947 and 1957, little was done in practical terms to reform the Jamaican secondary education system. A series of studies of the system were however conducted. Reforms of the secondary system were included in the National Plan 1957–1967. The proposed reforms included: the conversion of practical training centres at Holmwood, Vere and Dinthill as well as the Kingston Technical School into technical high schools; the extension of the curricula of existing schools through the provision of facilities for technical subjects in the existing plant of several high schools; the increased offering of awards through the Common Entrance Examination whereby greater numbers of students, from public primary as well as private preparatory schools, were afforded access to the public secondary system; the expansion of some primary schools to offer three years of postprimary education in what were then termed 'senior' schools for those children who were unsuccessful either by virtue of achievement or income in their bid to enter existing secondary institutions. This was the structure of the secondary school system in Jamaica on the eve of Independence in August 1962.

The postindependence period

In the immediate postindependence period, the Independence Plan 1963–1968 was developed. One of the principal policy changes which resulted from this plan was the allocation of places to secondary schools based on the Common Entrance Examination. In the new system, 70 percent of the places were to go to children from primary schools, while 30 percent were to go to children from preparatory (privately owned and operated) schools. The system was further expanded by the establishment of two comprehensive high schools.[1]

As a result of a request for multilateral assistance in the field of education by the first postindependence government, a set of reforms, which became known as the New Deal for Education, were promulgated. The main policy initiative which derived from this plan was the development of junior secondary schools which were to cater to students in the 12-15 age group on a nonselective basis. Some 50 new schools were built with assistance from the World Bank, and two new and 14 pre-existing senior schools were converted into junior secondary schools.

This policy initiative was intended to address the weaknesses and class biases inherent in the system. It was argued that expansion of secondary offerings would afford increased opportunities for secondary education regardless of class position. In this way, more than the ten percent of the age cohort which was then receiving secondary level education would have been able to access education at that level. Quantitative rather than qualitative considerations appear to have been uppermost in the minds of the policy formulators. The populace, however, was concerned with both issues. It was the secondary education which was offered in the high schools that people wanted their children to have access to and not this new, seemingly inferior curriculum which was being grafted onto the existing primary system.

The year 1972 witnessed a change in government in Jamaica and new policy initiatives in education followed shortly thereafter. The education thrust of the seventies heralded the introduction of free secondary and tertiary education in 1973. In 1974, the programme in the existing junior secondary schools was extended for a further two years and the institutions were now termed new secondary schools. To allow for increased access, a shift system was introduced fully in 35 new secondary schools and partially in the 29 others. This allowed two school communities to use a single school plant over a ten hour period: from 7 a.m. to 5 p.m. In September 1975 all 64 schools went on a full shift system. Several secondary level institutions were expanded and better equipped to meet the demands of increasing student intake, and as a result, there was a 25 percent increase in the number of students accessing high school education.

The 1980s saw another change in government and a subsequent downgrading of education in the range of priorities as structural adjustment programmes were implemented. There were two principal policy changes in the sphere of secondary education. These included the introduction of the Secondary Schools Textbook Project. Under this scheme, which was funded by the Governments of Jamaica and the United Kingdom, there was the provision of basic textbooks on a rental basis in all secondary level institutions. Initially, books were provided only for core subjects including English language and mathematics up to the Grade 9 level. The programme was later extended to Grade 11 and included several other subject texts. Incorporated into the project were training workshops for teachers to facilitate effective use of the books. An interim evaluation revealed problems in the administration of the programme as well as the inappropriateness of some of the texts for students of low reading ability, many of whom constituted a significant proportion of the student population of the new secondary schools.

Another policy initiative was the upgrading of 14 new secondary schools and 1 comprehensive high school. Four were converted into technical high schools while the others became high schools. Facilities were also expanded and improved to meet the new requirements, and there was a programme for the upgrading of existing members of the teaching cadre (Planning Institute of Jamaica 1990: 18). Since the 1990s, the newly elected government has promoted a philosophy of continuity: six new secondary schools have been upgraded to comprehensive high schools.

There are plans for the reform of the secondary education system designed to, among other things, rationalize or standardize the curriculum for the first three years (Grades 7 to 9) across all secondary level institutions. Besides a pilot project, little has been done to date, thus comment may be somewhat premature.

Some argue that the average standard of performance in secondary education is declining globally (De Landsheere 1987: 40). In Jamaica, while issues of funding and equity do engage the minds of many, concerns about quality also abound (Hamilton 1991: 3). Notwithstanding the attempted reforms, however, evidence of the unsatisfactory performance of the educational system in promoting the kind of literate and numerate populace capable of the creative thinking and the reasoning which are so critical to technological progress can be seen in the annual performance of Jamaican students in the examinations of the Caribbean Examinations Council (CXC) (Table 4.1).

Table 4.1 shows that of the total number of candidates sitting the CXC General Proficiency Examinations in English language from Jamaica in

Table 4.1 Performance of Jamaican Students in CXC English and Mathematics Examinations, 1992

Subjects	Entries	1	2	3	4	5
English General	13,725	386	2,983	6,593	3,355	408
Maths General	12,388	47	2,599	3,286	4,408	1,248
English Basic	1,250	173	576	324	153	24
Maths Basic	2,887	154	724	718	1,048	243

Source: CXC Western Region Office, Jamaica

1992, 25 percent achieved scores in Grades 1 and 2. Grades 1 and 2 have been recommended as the levels which indicate a candidate's suitability for further study. For mathematics, 28 percent of total candidates gained scores in Grades 1 and 2. Forty-eight percent of total English candidates and 27 percent of total candidates in mathematics obtained scores in Grade 3. For CXC, the General Proficiency Examination had been designed to measure competencies for further study up to Grade 2, with Grade 3 being considered suitable for the labour market. The Basic Proficiency Examination had been conceived as measuring competencies for the world of work at Grades 1 and 2. The elitist assumptions inherent in such categorization has resulted in most students aspiring to sit the General Proficiency Examinations regardless of future plans.

The problem of performance at the secondary level is of particular importance when considered against the background of the purposes of secondary education. Secondary education is supposed to give students a systematic introduction to knowledge, techniques and 'know-how' relevant to functioning in today's society (UNESCO 1987: iv). What is also widely accepted is that secondary education represents terminal education for many students and that the secondary system ought therefore to aim at developing persons capable not only of doing useful work, but also of benefitting from continuing education and training. This is especially important in light of the challenges currently posed by the new technologies.

The foregoing gives some understanding of the historical evolution of the secondary education system in Jamaica but some fundamental questions remain to be answered. What have been some of the underlying assumptions which have served to shape and condition the system which has developed? What are the principal features of the secondary education system today? To what extent has the system been achieving its stated objectives? It is only from some appreciation of these issues that one can attempt to examine aspects of the delivery and output of the system.

The basic underlying assumption which informed the formation of the public secondary system in Jamaica was that secondary education was essentially education for a select few. This was later garnished with the belief that secondary education involved the pursuit of certain predetermined subjects and was therefore curricula oriented. Gradually the perception has developed that secondary education involves the education of a certain age cohort and presupposes the exposure to or the mastery of earlier educational experiences.

The fact that the secondary educational system in Jamaica has been quite segmented or stratified and has not yet been fully articulated with either the primary or tertiary sectors has meant that the secondary system has continued to reproduce rather than transform existing social cleavages. The public secondary school system in Jamaica is characterized by the plethora of institutional types involved in the delivery of educational offerings at that level. This phenomenon developed based on the fact that policy prescriptions have been governed less by the requirements of the society and more by external institutions and formations.

There are differences between the existing institutional types. These centre on the methods by which student intake is determined, curricula offerings, teacher supply and qualifications, resource allocation and the examinations which are sat in the terminal grades. Of no less significance is the existing perception among the populace of a sort of hierarchy among secondary level institutions with secondary high school education being the most valued and all-age and new secondary programmes being the least prized.

In 1990/1991, there were some 31,762 students registered at the Grade 11 level in the secondary level institutions identified above. It is noteworthy that some 33 percent of secondary students registered in the terminal grades were in all-age schools. A small proportion of these would gain access to secondary high, comprehensive high and technical schools through the Grade Nine Achievement Test, but most would have entered the labour market. While Grade 11 is not necessarily terminal for some students who may proceed to pursue programmes of further education, the vast majority enter the labour market at this stage. It is these students who constitute the principal focus of this study.

Education and Development

Various studies have been conducted to establish the relationship between secondary education and the skill and attitude requirements of the new technological age. A dynamic technological environment such as exists today places a greater responsibility and value on education. It has been argued that in such an environment education is likely to have a positive effect on productivity (Cotlear 1989: 76). Cotlear, in examining the relationship between schooling and agricultural productivity, posits that schooling facilitates the process of integrating the new technologies in several ways. Increased numerical skills, in particular a greater capacity for abstraction can help to uncover the causal relationships between technology and output which may remain somewhat obscure to the less educated. Literacy can facilitate the acquisition, storage, interpretation, transformation and retrieval of large amounts of information and ease its transmission.

The need for increased investment in education and training in developing countries in order to develop the capacity to exploit technological change as a stimulus to development has been highlighted. Here, the concern is with the need to transform the education curriculum to make it more technologically oriented thus increasing the supply of scientists and technologists (Commonwealth Secretariat 1991: 62).

Whenever a country begins to lag economically, some attention is often directed at the education system in order to explain or otherwise justify the decline. This would seem to suggest a virtually linear relationship between levels of education investment and national competitiveness. But this is not necessarily so. What is more apparent is that the output of the education system can contribute to the realization of the development potential of a country but, the influence of other factors cannot be discounted.

Some core issues identified by entrepreneurs as relevant to the competitiveness of their countries include the level of human resource development as well as levels of trade and investment flows, the performance of capital markets and the political climate. In the case of South Korea, the quality of the labour force has been cited as a critical factor in the country's gaining a competitive edge in international trade. There, by the 1980s, some 94 percent of students were enrolled in middle school and 85 percent in high school (Lau 1990: 68). Lau attributes the upgrading of the literacy and numeracy skills of the workers to the tremendous expansion of the secondary education system in Taiwan between 1952 and 1981. Similar conclusions are arrived at by Pavri (1990: 85) in his analysis of the technological development of Singapore. The National Committee on Excellence in Education in the United States of America has also stressed that the ability of the USA to compete globally in trade and industry is dependent on the level of educational standards (De Britto 1986: 13). Global competitiveness therefore has an inescapable educational dimension.

Locally, Danny Williams, former president of the largest insurance company in Jamaica, is reported to have bemoaned the quality of education in the island, specifically in relation to the dearth of competent and qualified mathematicians. Pointing to the advantage of an educated work force, he stated that "[T]here is absolutely no substitute for a trained work force if a country is going to increase its productivity" (*Jamaica Herald, 20 May 1993*).

The relationship between education and national economic development has been the subject of many and varied studies (Psacharapoulous 1988). Central to these have been concerns about the relative returns to production and productivity arising from education to different grade levels and from differing expenditure levels. It has been suggested that there has been a high correlation between productivity and percentage expenditure on education (Nettleford 1991: 17).

The characteristics of the new technological age and the prospects which it offers for enhanced development especially to developing societies has been the subject of several bodies of research (Perez 1985). Some of the characteristic features which have been identified include the rapidity and extensiveness of change. No longer will individuals be able to insulate themselves easily from the impact of the widespread application of technological innovations in everyday life. The blurring of lines and functions between occupational categories indicate a need for a more flexible workforce.

The rapid economic development and enhanced competitiveness which have been enjoyed by the newly industrializing countries compared to the industrial economies of Europe and the United States as a result of the widespread application of the new technologies of microelectronics have led to a general assessment of some of the factors which have contributed to this advance. Some have pointed to differing patterns of work organization, to cultural and other factors as well as to the quality of their human resources. Studies have suggested that a principal contributing factor to the lag in western industrial economies is weakness in the training and development of human resources (Economic Commission for Latin America and the Caribbean [ECLAC] 1992). It is the quality of the human resource which facilitates the best use and application of technology in the production process thus facilitating competitiveness.

In examining changes produced by the application of new technologies at the microlevel, studies have concluded that the impact of the new technologies on individual organizations is shaped by various factors. These include the history of the organization, the type of market in which it functions, its culture and, importantly, the quality of the human resource available to it and how it is organised.

There is compelling evidence to suggest a positive correlation between the quality of the human resource available to a nation and its ability to achieve international competitiveness. Some writers posit a nexus between technological advance and the quality of basic education. As Papadopoulus (1988) states:

It should provide the core of basic knowledge, skills and attitudes as the foundation on which subsequent educational and professional careers can be built and the capacity of individuals to cope with change developed.

Others contend, however, that while there can be some justification for suggesting some relationship between the educational system and economic advancement, the ways in which secondary education may contribute to economic development are by no means clear. For instance, the link between education and economic development is not as linear as some might suggest. History has proven that education is neither a necessary nor sufficient condition for economic development to occur. The Industrial Revolution occurred without the trained and educated work force which is considered so vital for development today. The nature of the revolution required a human resource which was uneducated, and whose qualifications were the ability to obey orders and to perform repetitive and tedious tasks. Had they been educated, they would have rebelled as they eventually did. Economic development in that context, was the responsibility of the aristocracy and the human development did not necessarily accompany the economic. The revolution in informatics, however, demands an educated human resource if development is to occur. This is not to suggest that an educated populace can be automatically equated to economic development. The relationship between the two, that is, education and economic development, is very complex and requires the intervention of other factors.

To the extent that there is some kind of relationship between the two, however, the extent to which changes in one contribute to changes in the other is of some import. The implications of this for the formal system is more at issue. For some, increased access to the fruits of technology, such as computers in the classroom is the principal concern. For others, while this may be of some importance, what is even more vital are the efforts to prepare the necessary specialized human resources to design, operate, transform and maintain the new technologies (ILO 1987: 27).

In this regard, the fundamentals of mathematics, science and language have been identified as essential for absorbing the new technologies (ILO 1987: 37). These, together with the development of greater flexibility, creativity, independence and decision-making skills are deemed to be of critical importance. As Rumberger and Levin (1989: 213) posit:

... evidence suggests that the level of skills required in the job market are unlikely to change appreciably in the near future. What is more likely to change are the types of skills required, as new technologies and new forms of work organisation demand different kinds of skills, such as communication and reasoning skills.

The level of skills required for effective functioning in the technological age may not be as clear as at first appears to be the case. On the one hand, the issue of what level of skills are necessary for effective functioning is subject to dispute; while on the other hand, it has been noted that even where certain competencies are identified as critical to the production process, these are seldom promoted within elementary and secondary education (Rush 1987).

Lankshear (1986) and Freire and Macedo (1987) are critical of the concept of "functional literacy" which perceives literacy purely in terms of "a set of skills or as the ability to use skills" within a certain context. It is essential to understand literacy and numeracy within existing social realities. It is difficult in this context to arrive at a standardized approach to literacy or numeracy since the knowledge needed to function in different social situations must of necessity be varied.

Some theorists posit that some reasons for underachievement or the existence of illiteracy in schools may be the dominant middle class culture which pervades the education system, resulting in the marginalization of those whose origins and perspectives do not accord with the assumed norm. In this circumstance, "children who are streamed into lower level school programs are less likely to gain proficiency in reading and writing . . . " (Jules 1987: 79).

But what are the skills and values and the particular knowledge base which are of particular necessity in promoting competitiveness and at what level should they be developed? The issue of the relative importance of the differing levels of the formal education system is a largely spurious debate. The proper articulation of all levels and the nature of the content developed is of more importance if education is to continue to be valued in some societies.

The issue of what is most vital for formal learning is of greater significance in the context of identifying the ways in which the formal education system can contribute to enhancing global competitiveness. This centres on issues of what should be the directions in curricula development in order to promote enhanced competitiveness. The current debate centres on two main issues: first, the promotion of a more "technologically oriented curriculum" (Commonwealth Secretariat 1991: 63), in which science, technology and computer literacy would hold pride of place; and secondly, that precisely because an important feature of the current technological wave is its knowledge intensity, the ability to use information effectively to address production needs is going to be largely dependent on the development of basic skills such as literacy and numeracy (Rumberger and Levin 1989: 210). Pavri (1990), in his examination of the impact of technological advance on the education system of Singapore, cites evidence of a "strong push in both primary and secondary schools to develop computer literacy in students" and a subsequent decline in interest in the more humanistic aspects of the curriculum. Moreover, some argue for a more vocational focus in educational institutions in order to develop lower level skills for industry. The changing skill requirements for technologically driven industries frequently means that the skills acquired in school could be obsolete by the time the student enters the world of work. This could be minimized by increasing articulation between the education system and the industrial sphere, but unless the schools have the resources to change rapidly to meet the new skill requirements arising from technical change, a closer relationship between school and industry may be of little consequence.

Perhaps the issue could be the fostering of a creative and critical thinking ethos to enable students to be more flexible and adaptable in the world of work. It is only by preparing students to have an openness and receptivity to change that they can be adaptable to changing requirements, and be willing to re-tool themselves when new skills are demanded. But some theorists have turned their attention to examining whether or not these skills can be effectively taught. For some, creativity cannot be separated from specific disciplines. Creativity here is perceived as difference within an accepted framework and it is argued that conditions for the flourishing of creativity can be created within a classroom setting (Best 1982: 294). Recent research seems to suggest that critical thought is a necessary although insufficient precondition for creativity.

The institutional level which may be best able to equip students to be able to respond effectively and to initiate technical change is of some concern. Some argue that it is tertiary level education which best lends itself to the promotion of the technical knowledge and the problem-solving skills which are essential for technological innovation (Rumberger and Levin 1989). Others suggest that training for production is best conducted within the particular enterprises which need the skills for development. Still others suggest that a combination of both approaches in the context of a realistic national development plan, best affords prospects for technological advance. As an ILO study succinctly states, it is "now generally agreed that schools should concentrate on where their comparative advantage lies, that is, those activities of skill and knowledge development which firms are relatively speaking ill-equipped to undertake" (ILO 1987).

The secondary system is advanced as being best able to provide the foundation on which higher level skills can be developed as well as providing the critical core necessary for the world of work. Secondary education is supposed to give students a systematic introduction to the techniques of knowledge as well as produce students able to enter and function in the world of work. Changes have occurred in the institutional form and purposes of the secondary system historically. Previously the students were more homogeneous and the purposes of the system were less economic and more social and political. Today, the gap between the secondary school and social reality is widening as obsolete content and methods of teaching hold sway. The challenge of the new technologies makes a revision of the system virtually inescapable. Indeed, it has been argued that one of the principal reasons for the poor performance of students in secondary schools today is the fact that, in most cases, outdated educational methods "have not been systematically modified in the light of changes in the composition of the school-going population" (De Landsheere 1987: 40).

Certain cognitive and affective skills have been identified as being of particular significance in facilitating effective functioning in the new technological environment. These include the "fundamentals of mathematics, science and language". The development of creativity, independence and decision making skills have also been identified as being of critical importance. A survey among workers in the USA concerning the skills which they felt were of importance in the production process today, confirms the primacy of mathematics and reading as important attributes. They identified mathematics as being of critical importance in the programming of computer controlled machinery (Heitner, et al. 1990: 28). The workers felt that the need for basic literacy and mathematics skills will increase in the coming years.

Several studies have identified the sociocultural dimensions of language learning and mathematics education in Jamaica (Isaacs 1984; Craig 1986). These point to social class, ethnic origin and other variables as directly impinging on the ways in which language and mathematics are learned. While these are important, they do not constitute the primary focus of the study. Suffice it to say that the main concern here is in the context of the new technological age where the capacity to analyse, summarize and evaluate will be paramount – what level of literacy and numeracy exists among Jamaican secondary school students and what constraints exist to their improvement.

This study seeks to contribute to filling the gap concerning two of the potentially important educational ingredients in indigenous technological capability. It limits itself to literacy and numeracy because several studies have already pinpointed the relationship between scientific learning and technological capability (eg, McIntyre 1987: 5).

Methodology

Measurement and testing

Operationalizing what can be considered an appropriate level of functioning in the identified skills is fraught with pitfalls. Can there be a precisely defined level of functioning which is desirable for all? Does the concept of minimum levels of competency not contain implicit normative judgements based on assumptions of common values and shared beliefs (De Landsheere 1987: 42)? In a pluralistic society such as Jamaica, does such a concept help to define the parameters of the problem being studied, or does it simply serve to conceal some of the issues in a mire of vagueness and imprecision?

It is undeniable that in the sphere of work there are certain competencies which are vital to the performance of production tasks (Rush 1987). These include performance related to writing, reading and computation skills. What levels of these skills are required for optimum performance? Are they the same for all occupations? There is some debate as to what levels of competency in literacy and related skills are vital for job success. Rush argues that whereas the levels of these skills required in skilled and semiskilled occupations are perhaps more complex than is implied in the term 'functional literacy', only minimal literacy competencies may be necessary for success on the job.

The concepts of literacy and numeracy are themselves multifaceted. Indeed there are some interpretations of literacy which not only incorporate a certain facility with language but also the ability to treat with numbers. Literacy in this study is taken to mean the ability to use language in such a manner as to allow the user to be able to accomplish requisite tasks in the society. Implicit in this definition is an appreciation of not only the instrumental applications of language but also its empowering possibilities within the social context in which it is expressed.

The competencies are defined in terms of operational literacy and numeracy, that is to say, that level of literacy which contributes not only to the ability to read and comprehend the newspaper or a textbook, but also to organize and present ideas logically and clearly. For numeracy, it implies that facility with computation, reasoning and problem solving which would enable the student to engage in the resolution of simple tasks.

Implicit in all attempts to define literacy is the question of adequate levels of literacy. That issue is only meaningful, however, in terms of the needs and values of a particular society (Jules 1988: 375). Jamaican society, as it prepares for the challenges of the twenty-first century, requires persons who have attained a level of competence in literacy and numeracy. Certainly a similar level may not be necessary for all tasks but it is the researcher's view that a certain minimum level is an essential precondition for development.

For the purposes of this investigation, that minimum level is taken to be the qualities which individuals would need in the different spheres in which they function and develop interests. In the area of literacy, the ability to acquire and interpret information; to evaluate opinions; to communicate and express thought as well as to derive enjoyment through a facility with language are considered significant. For numeracy the significant qualities are: the ability to use basic computational skills effectively; to use these in the solution of problems which arise in daily life whether as consumer or producer and to think logically and critically through the application of these skills. Throughout the study, literacy and numeracy are used synonymously with English language and mathematics, respectively. This is done partly in order to give meaning to the secondary school programmes which are principally concerned with the development of these skills and partly to facilitate their measurement. To identify the parameters which delineate the essence of creativity and critical thinking may not be as simple.

Some authors argue that to present a dichotomy between the processes involved in critical thinking and those involved in creativity is inadequate, that "creative thought cannot be uncritical" (Nickerson, et al. 1985: 89). While it is undeniable that there is some interconnection between critical thinking and creativity, some attempt has to be made to specify the essential characteristics of each for the purposes of this investigation. Creativity is a multidimensional trait which can be expressed in diverse ways. In this study creativity is taken to mean not only originality of thought, inventiveness and imagination, but also ideational fluency. Critical thinking is construed to represent that ability to evaluate arguments based on their logical coherence. It measures the qualities of arguments based on the patterns of reasoning displayed. It involves processes of deductive reasoning. The term critical thinking skills will be used interchangeably with reasoning ability.

Neither creativity nor critical thinking are skills which are often explicitly taught in Jamaican classrooms. The assumption frequently made is that they will be acquired in the process of students developing their cognitive abilities in other fields of study. For example, it has been often advanced that creativity is not independent of language and art forms (Best 1982: 287). Neither is critical thinking divorced from the reasoning skills often employed in the solution of mathematical problems. Despite this, however, it can be argued that in the current period both are areas which require direct attention.

In order to measure students' levels of literacy, numeracy, creativity and critical thinking five tests were administered: one each in mathematics and English, two in creativity and one in critical thinking.

The English Language and Mathematics tests

The sixty multiple choice items which were contained in each test represented items based on the Caribbean Examination Council's Basic Proficiency Level for English language and mathematics. Although many students in the sample and a majority of students from new secondary schools were not pursuing CXC type programmes, it was felt that they represented a level of proficiency which had already been assessed as being suited to the world of work. Besides, there are no other official tests which are tailored to measure the curricula of the variety of secondary level institutions which exist in Jamaica. The CXC type items utilized therefore would reflect some, but not all, aspects of the curricula which would be pursued by all students in secondary level institutions which exist in Jamaica.

In the case of mathematics, the items sought to measure performance levels within the following areas: sets, relations, functions and graphs, computation, number theory, measurement, consumer arithmetic, statistics, algebra and geometry. The paper was weighted most heavily in terms of items on consumer arithmetic, algebra and geometry and least in terms of sets. The items were also designed to measure problem-solving skills as well as the ability to think logically and critically.

The English language items were concerned with measuring the ability of the students to understand meaning conveyed through vocabulary, sentence patterns and paragraph construction. The extent to which information was interpreted, relationships perceived, conclusions and inferences drawn, the effectiveness of language devices evaluated, and information communicated were also measured.

The reliability and validity of the items had already been established through regional testing among Grade 11 students. This, together with the measurement objectives of the items, rendered them most suited to the researcher's purposes.

The creativity tests

Creativity was tested using the Minnesota Test of Creative Thinking and an adaptation of the Southern California Test of Divergent Thinking.

The circles test is a nonverbal creativity test which requires subjects to draw as many objects as they possibly can from twenty circles, by adding lines either inside and outside the circles, or both inside and outside. The word association test, on the other hand, is a verbal test of creativity. The subject is in this situation presented with a list of forty-five words, five of which were repetitions so that, effectively, the students were faced with forty. They were required to write as many related words as they could beside each of the words.

Some success has been reported in establishing both reliability and validity for creativity tests. Both measures, according to research findings, provide a reasonably accurate gauge of creativity in adolescents. Getzels and Jackson (1962) obtained a reliability coefficient of 0.87 for the word association test. The reliability coefficients for the battery of tests of which the circles test is one ranged from 0.75 to 0.85 (Torrance and Gowan 1963). Richardson (1984) obtained a reliability of 0.81 for the circles test using Jamaican adolescents.

The critical thinking test

The Ennis-Weir Critical Thinking Test was used. Although specific reliability coefficients could not be located, the test and variations thereof have been used by Nolan and Brandon (1984) and Brandon (1990) in measuring critical thinking abilities among Jamaican secondary school students and teachers in training. Ennis himself argues that the very concept of reliability may be difficult to apply to a critical thinking test because of the heterogenous nature of critical thinking ability. He also pithily states that "those who develop critical thinking tests will find it difficult to make a convincing case for their validity" (Ennis 1984: 7).

The test required that students read a letter concerning problems of street congestion due to overnight parking. They then had to evaluate the arguments presented in each paragraph of the letter for relevance of arguments, ambiguities and other weaknesses. A final paragraph was to be presented containing an overall assessment of the total arguments made. The test contains some culturally specific formulations, which may not readily be considered a part of the experiences of Jamaican students.

Scoring procedures

A key for correct answers to the mathematics and English language tests was developed using Grade 11 teachers of the respective subjects. They were moderated by university lecturers who are specialists in the relevant areas. Each correct answer received one mark and the total marks were then converted to percentages for ease of analysis.

The circles test was scored for originality with weights being attached to the uniqueness of the drawings presented. Where more than 20 percent of the students had a particular drawing, for example a clock, they received 0 for their effort. Designs which were done by 5 percent or less obtained 2, and those done by 6 percent to 20 percent received 1. The word association test was scored for fluency with one mark being awarded for each related word listed by the students.

The Ennis-Weir Critical Thinking Test was scored based on weights being attached to the level of analysis and the number of reasoned arguments presented by the student. Students were not penalized for incorrect grammar, spelling or other flawed application of the techniques of language.

Hypotheses testing

The lambda measure of association was used to measure the extent of the relationship between all dependent variables and independent variables of interest, except in the case of the critical thinking test. This was done because all of the test scores except those of the critical thinking test were grouped prior to analysis, thus reducing them to the level of ordinal data. The lambda coefficient is said to be the most reliable measure of association between a dependent ordinal variable and independent nominal variables. The eta coefficient of association was employed to measure the extent of the association between the scores on the critical thinking test and all of the variables of interest.

The distribution of scores on all tests on the basis of the gender of the respondent was of particular interest. T-tests were used to measure the differences, if any, in levels of achievement based on gender.

Having conducted these tests, it was necessary for the study to have some predictive value and, to do so, some information about the nature of the relationship between the criterion or dependent variables and the variables of interest or independent variables was critical. This was vital in order to inform decisions concerning educational policy. As a result of this, regression analysis was conducted using the test scores as criterion variables and the variables of interest as predictor variables.

Data collection and sampling

Elite interviews and the administration of a questionnaire were the principal instruments employed to gather data.

Elite interviews were conducted among sixteen teachers: eight each from mathematics and English language representing the range of school types included in the survey. Eight principals were also interviewed. These interviews were intended to collect data on the perceptions of teachers and principals about factors affecting the current performance of students in English language and mathematics in schools. This, it was felt, would aid in reconstructing the dimensions of the problem as well as in advancing possible solutions. It also aided in evaluation of the validity of some responses of students to curricula questions, and provided an important qualitative dimension to the research project. The questionnaire was administered to students and was used to ascertain (a) important biographical information about themselves and their parents; (b) their attitudes towards learning the subjects in question; (c) the self-evaluation of their achievement in same; and (d) their assessment of teachers.

The study was based on a stratified, random sample of schools and students of Grade 11. Of the 138 public secondary schools in Jamaica, and at a 95 percent confidence level, 70 were selected, while 397 students were selected at the same confidence level. However, 67 schools and 403 students were actually obtained. The sample was stratified by school type, region, gender and age which are illustrated in Table 4.2.

As Table 4.2 shows, the sample consisted of forty-six (68 percent) urban schools and twenty-one (32 percent) rural schools. The national figures were 69 percent and 31 percent respectively. The gender composition of

Table 4.2   School Location, by Gender Composition of School

School Location	Single-sex Girls	Single-sex Boys	Co-educational	Total
Urban	6	4	36	46
Rural	1	0	20	21
Total	7	4	56	67

the schools reflected all types distributed between both locations. Ten percent of the sample were single-sex girls' schools while single-sex boys' schools accounted for six percent; the national figures were also ten percent and six percent. Coeducational schools comprised 84 percent of the sample, which was the same figure nationally. The sample thus compared quite favourably with the national picture (Ministry of Education 1991).

The gender distribution of respondents across school types is depicted in Table 4.3.

It is shown that 44 percent of the respondents were males, while 56 percent were females. Females thus represented the larger proportion of respondents across all school types. In comprehensive high schools some 60 percent of respondents were female but these schools accounted for only seven per cent of total respondents. In respect of school type, secondary high schools produced some 48 percent of the total respondents, while new secondary schools accounted for 36 percent. Despite changes which have occurred in the status of some new secondary schools as a result of the secondary schools upgrading programme, the number of respondents from secondary high schools seems disproportionately high.[2] The situation in Grade 11 may be some what different since, it could

Table 4.3   Respondents, by Gender and School Type

School Type	Male	Female	Total
New Secondary	62	81	143
Secondary High	89	105	194
Technical High	16	22	38
Comprehensive	11	17	28
Total	178	225	403

Table 4.4   Grade 11 Students, by Gender and School Type

School Type	Male	Female	Total
New Secondary	7,197	7,037	14,237
Secondary High	5,305	7,262	12,567
Technical High	1,619	1,606	3,225
Comprehensive	830	906	1,736
Total	14,951	16,811	31,762

Source: Ministry of Education statistics 1991

be argued that, there is likely to be a higher rate of drop-out for students of new secondary schools.[3]

In 1991, females accounted for 53 percent of the total school population in Grade 11 while males accounted for 47 per cent (Table 4.4). Forty-five percent of all students attended new secondary schools, 40 percent attended secondary high schools, while 5 percent attended comprehensive high schools. The fact that six new secondary schools had been upgraded to comprehensive high schools in September 1991 may explain some of the observed difference between the population and the sample.

The ages of respondents ranged from as low as fourteen years, to as high as nineteen years (Table 4.5). While this variation seems large, it is possible given the existing admission practices in Jamaican secondary schools. When combined, 81 percent were either sixteen or seventeen year olds, while fourteen and nineteen year olds accounted for a mere 1 percent. Fifty-two percent of females and 51 percent of males fell in the age group sixteen years and under.

Table 4.5   Age of Respondents, by Gender

Age	Male	Female	Total
14	0	1	1
15	20	20	40
16	72	95	167
17	69	89	158
18	15	19	34
19	2	1	3
Total	178	225	403

Table 4.6   Students Sitting CXC, by Students Sitting Other Examinations

| | CXC | | |
Other Exam.	Yes	No	Total
Yes	133	148	281
No	108	14	122
Total	241	162	403

Some 60 percent of respondents indicated that they expected to sit subjects in the CXC examinations this year, (Table 4. 6). Forty percent indicated that they would not be doing so. Thirty percent indicated that they were not entered for any other examination during this academic year. Some of the students entered for CXC were also entered for a range of other examinations with 4 percent of total respondents being entered for no examination.

Analysis and Findings

Table 4.7 reveals the opinions of students towards learning English language and mathematics. Thirty-eight percent had less than positive feelings about learning mathematics in school, while for English the figure was 25 percent. However, a varying majority of students expressed a positive attitude towards learning English (75 percent) and mathematics (62 percent).

Table 4.7   Students' Opinions About Learning English Language and Mathematics

| | English | Mathematics |
Students' Opinion	Frequency (%)	Frequency (%)
Strongly dislike	0.7	7.4
Dislike	1.7	10.4
Indifferent	22.8	20.3
Like	30.3	25.3
Like very much	44.4	36.5
Total	100	100

Most students felt that the methodologies employed by both their mathematics and English teachers in class facilitated their learning (Table 4.8).

In the case of English, 89 percent felt that the methods employed by their teachers aided student learning, while the corresponding figure for mathematics was 81 percent. On the negative score, while 19 percent of students felt that their mathematics teachers did not facilitate learning, 11 percent opined similarly for the teachers of English.

When students who assessed their teachers' methods positively were asked to specify the methodologies employed which they believed assisted the learning process, most students identified expository, teacher-centred methods. As one of the respondents succinctly stated: "the teacher goes over and explains until we understand". Some 70 to 71 percent of respondents identified these types of methods as those which particularly facilitated their understanding of English language and mathematics respectively. Little weight was attached by students to more inductive or more creative methodologies.

For those who evaluated their teachers' contribution to learning negatively, several identified various professional limitations in the teacher. Attending classes late or not at all; assigning tasks from the textbook and without adequate explanation; leaving the students unsupervised to conduct conversations with other teachers, and verbally abusing students were just some of the weaknesses cited. In 57 percent of the cases where students evaluated their English language teachers' contribution to learning negatively, they suggested that some personal attribute of the teacher needed improvement. For mathematics, 56 percent who expressed the view that their teacher did not aid their learning responded similarly.

Table 4.9 shows students' evaluation of their current levels of achievement in mathematics.

Table 4.8   Students' Assessment of Teachers' Input in the Learning Process

Assessment	Mathematics Frequency (%)	English Frequency (%)
Positive	80.6	88.8
Negative	19.4	11.3
Total	100 (N=396)	100 (N=400)

Table 4.9   Student Self-Evaluation of Performance In Mathematics

Evaluation	Frequency	Percent
Very poor	16	4
Poor	60	15
Fair	138	34
Good	124	31
Very good	64	16
Total	402	100

Fifty-three percent evaluated their current level of achievement in Mathematics as being either 'fair' or less than 'fair'. However, 31 percent assessed their performance as 'good', while for 16 percent it was 'very good'. Their self-evaluation for English language is revealed in Table 4.10.

In respect of English Language, 44 percent of respondents evaluated their performance as 'fair' or worse. 41 percent assessed their level of achievement to be 'good', while for 15 percent, it was 'very good'.

The possession of textbooks was identified as a variable which could critically affect the learning process for English language (Table 4.11) and mathematics (Table 4.12).

More than three-quarters of respondents at 78.3 percent reported access to an English textbook. This includes those who would have rented their texts through the existing Secondary Schools Textbook Rental Programme, as well as those who might have purchased the book.[4] For mathematics, some 79 percent of respondents, almost the same propor-

Table 4.10   Student Self-Evaluation of Performance in English Language

Evaluation	Frequency	Percent
Very poor	2	1
Poor	19	5
Fair	53	38
Good	168	41
Very good	61	15
Total	403	100

Table 4.11 Student Access to English Textbook

Response	Frequency	Percent
Yes	314	78.3
No	87	21.7
Total	401	100

Table 4.12 Student Access to Mathematics Textbook

Response	Frequency	Percent
Yes	317	79.3
No	83	20.8
Total	400	100

tion as for English, reported possession of a textbook by either of the two means mentioned above.

Almost the same proportion of students did not have access to textbooks for mathematics (21 percent) and English language (22 percent). Actually in many cases the same students had neither English nor mathematics textbooks. The reasons advanced for not having access to a textbook revolved principally around either a lack of financial resources to purchase or rent them or, the fact that the book was not being used in class.

As revealed in Table 4.13, the students identified several factors which, in their view, adversely affected their ability to learn English and mathematics. Of these, one-third (32 percent) identified student related factors while smaller minority proportions identified problems associated with the language of instruction (8 percent), the school/class (7.5 percent), teachers (7 percent), resource gaps (6 percent), and student/teacher relationship (0.3 percent). It is interesting to note that one-third (33 percent) of the students did not identify any factor as affecting their performance in English.

It should be noted that the category 'teacher' refers to the range of variables which students identified as affecting their performance and which could be construed as emanating from the teacher such as teacher competence. 'Student' factors include the student's perception of the

Table 4.13 Perceived Factors Affecting Performance in English Language

Factors	Frequency	Percent
Teacher	26	7.0
Student	121	32.4
Resource gaps	23	6.2
School/Class	28	7.5
Teacher/Student	1	0.3
Socio-linguistic	31	8.3
None	124	33.2
Other	30	5.1
Total	403	100

extent to which their learning was hampered by their own limitations. It is possible that greater probing could have elicited more information about the source of the problem. For example, when a student said: "I need to read more", was this indicative of the student's own distaste for reading or did it signify a lack of appropriate reading material? 'Resource gaps' refer to areas where students identified either financial or material liabilities. 'School/class' refers to aspects of the organization of the school and/or classroom which the student identified as exerting a negative influence on their learning of English language. These included: inadequate time allocated to teaching the subject; the large size of classes and the impact of undue and excessive noise in the learning environment. 'Sociolinguistic' factors were taken to be those which alluded to the influence of the dialect and other environmental factors on their ability to learn standard English. Those who indicated that there was nothing which hampered their ability to learn English were also included for analysis because it was felt that the failure of a student to identify anything as adversely affecting the process of their learning English language was itself of significance. Those who failed to isolate a specific problem performed throughout the entire range of scores.

Student achievement on tests

Table 4.14 presents a summary of the performance on each set of tests. Only scores for English and mathematics are presented in percentage form. For the other tests, the raw scores are presented.

Table 4.14 Summary of Achievement on all Tests

Test	Valid Cases	Mean Score	Range
English	394	46.5%	7%–83%
Mathematics	394	41.1%	5%–87%
Creativity 1	367	2.9	0–19
Creativity 2	366	29.9	0–95
Critical thinking	219	0.9	0–15

In Table 4.15 below, the scores for English are examined by school type.

Table 4.15 English Scores, by School Type

Scores %	New Sec.	High	Tech.	Compr.	Total
80–99	0	2	1	0	3
60–79	2	70	8	5	85
40–59	42	87	18	13	160
20–39	83	31	11	8	133
0–19	8	3	0	2	13
Total	135	193	38	28	394

Less than 1 percent of the sample received English scores in the fifth quintile (80–99) and among these, the largest proportion, two-thirds, represented students from secondary high schools. No student from a comprehensive high school or a new secondary school gained scores in this range. In the next category of scores, the fourth quintile, 82 percent of the cases were from the secondary high schools with new secondary schools registering only 2 percent. In categories 4 and 5, of those receiving scores below 40 percent, new secondary schools registered the highest proportion of cases, with technical high schools recording the least.

Eighty-two percent of all cases from secondary high schools recorded scores of 40 percent and above. Forty percent of the entire sample obtained scores in this range. In new secondary schools, only 32 percent of respondents had scores in that range. Table 4.16 presents the scores for mathematics.

Table 4.16 Mathematics Scores, by School Type

Scores %	New Sec.	High	Tech.	Compr.	Total
80–99	0	9	1	0	10
60–79	2	44	9	4	59
40–59	22	78	12	7	119
20–39	99	55	14	14	182
0–19	14	6	2	2	24
Total	137	192	38	27	394

For mathematics, respondents from secondary high schools accounted for almost all scores above 79 percent. One student from a technical high school was the only exception.

Forty-eight percent of the sample obtained scores above 40 percent. The scores of 68 percent of respondents from secondary high schools were between 40 percent and 90 percent. For respondents from new secondary high schools only 18 percent obtained scores of 40 percent or more. Generally, 52 percent of the respondents obtained scores of 0 to 39 percent on the mathematics test.

The scores on the circles test were grouped so that 4 represented scores of 0 through 5; 3 indicated scores of 6 to 10; 2 represented scores of 11 through 15, while 1 signified scores of 16 and above. The findings are shown in Table 4.17.

Seventy-nine percent of all scores fell in category 4. This category accounted for the largest proportion of respondents from all school types. It accounted for the scores of 93 percent of all new secondary respondents.

Table 4.17 Scores on Circles Test, by School Type

Scores %	New Sec.	High	Tech.	Compr.	Total
1	0	1	1	0	2
2	0	23	3	0	26
3	9	29	7	4	49
4	118	124	26	22	290
Total	127	177	37	26	367

Table 4.18   Scores on Word Association Test, by School Type

Scores %	New Sec.	High	Tech.	Compr.	Total
80–99	0	3	0	0	3
60–79	2	13	1	2	18
40–59	21	63	8	4	96
20–39	39	60	11	12	122
0–19	66	43	10	8	127
Total	128	182	30	26	366

The low scores recorded in this test were primarily due to the fact that the test was scored for originality hence many students who produced shapes which were common, received a score of 0 for their efforts. One secondary high school and a technical high school accounted for the only students who scored either 16 or above. Neither comprehensive high schools nor new secondary schools had any respondents gaining scores above 10.

The scores on the verbal creativity test, the word association test, were grouped using the same categories as those employed for the mathematics and English tests except for the fact that scores on the verbal creativity test are not expressed in percentages. These are shown in Table 4.18.

Sixty-eight percent of all respondents obtained scores of thirty nine or under. New secondary students accounted for the highest single proportion in this category, with 82 percent of all new secondary respondents recording scores between 0 and 39. Less than 1 percent of all respondents accounted for scores between 80 and 99. Only students who attended secondary high schools gained scores in this range.

The critical thinking or reasoning ability test scores were grouped in the following manner: 5, which refers to those who received 0 and which represented the largest number of cases; 4 refers to those who received 1 and 2; 3 those who obtained 3 to 5; 2, those who attained 6 to 8 and 1, those who got 10 and above. Table 4.19 shows the scores on the critical thinking test.

The largest proportion of students of all school types obtained a score of 0 on this test. Some of the possible explanations for this have already been discussed. It should also be noted that this test involved reading skills,

Table 4.19   Scores on Critical Thinking Test, by School Type

Scores %	New Sec.	High	Tech.	Compr.	Total
1	0	7	0	0	7
2	0	3	0	1	4
3	3	14	2	0	19
4	4	10	5	2	21
5	53	91	12	12	168
Total	60	125	19	15	219

in addition to reasoning ability. The instructions were written and many respondents appeared to have totally misunderstood them and proceeded to support the arguments of the writer in equally emotive language rather than weighing and assessing their merits and logical validity.

Students from secondary high schools accounted for virtually all the scores in categories 1 and 2. One respondent from a comprehensive high school constituted the only exception to this.

The examination of the scores on all of the tests according to the type of school which the students attend showed that students of secondary high schools performed at a higher level than did those from any other type of secondary school. Only in the case of the two creativity tests and the critical thinking test did more than a half of the respondents from secondary high schools register scores in the two lowest groups. Students from new secondary schools performed worse than students of all other school types on all the tests. It was expected that this would not have been necessarily so with respect to the nonverbal creativity test. But, many new secondary students apparently misunderstood the instructions which were written on that test and instead of producing drawings in which the circles were an integral part, simply drew figures inside of the circles which did not incorporate the circles into the design.

Perhaps one factor which may have made the greatest contribution to the low performance of new secondary students was the apparent and, in a few cases, stated poor reading skills. In all cases, instructions for the tests were written and the researcher tried not to depart from the terms used in the written format when a verbal explanation was requested.

The extent of relationships

The results of the statistical testing of the postulated relationship between the dependent and independent variables under study are examined in this section. In Table 4.20, the coefficients of association are presented for all the variables of interest.

In all cases the lambda coefficient is close to 0, indicating that the variables of interest do not help significantly in predicting performance on all the tests for which it was applied. In the case of the nonverbal creativity test, the circles test, neither the type of school that a student attends, its location (urban vs rural), its gender composition, nor the sex of the student doing the test seem to be of any value in predicting student performance.

The fact that the respective lambda coefficients are close to 0 in most cases and 0 in one case does not necessarily mean that there is no relationship between the variables. Such a relationship could be observed by examining the distribution of the dependent variable for each independent variable. An example of this kind of association is depicted in Table 4.21.

In Table 4.21, it is shown that the most frequently occurring score, zero, categorized in group 4, occurs most often for both urban and rural schools. This suggests that regardless of the location of the school attended, Jamaican secondary school students will demonstrate a low level of achievement on the nonverbal creativity test. However, higher performance was associated with attendance in an urban school. The extent to which these apparent associations are significant was tested further.

Table 4.20 Coefficients of Association, Lambda/Eta of all Scores, by Variables of Interest

Scores	School Type	School Location	Gender Composition	Student's Sex
English	.17521	.09402	.02991	.02564
Maths	.10849	.00472	.12736	.00000
Circles	.00000	.00000	.00000	.00000
Word association	.10460	.03347	.07950	.08368
Critical thinking	.20030	.10613	.08018	.00438

Table 4.21 Scores on Circles Test, by School Location

Test	Urban	Rural	Total
1	2	0	2
2	21	5	26
3	43	6	49
4	189	101	290
Total	255	112	367

The differences in performance in all the tests which could be attributable to the sex of the student were tested more rigorously using the students' t-test. The null hypotheses were that there would be no statistically significant differences between the means of the male and female population on any of the test scores. That is to say the average score for males and females on all tests would not be different.

Table 4.22 summarizes the results of the t-tests for each set of test scores by the sex of the student. For none of the scores except for both creativity tests, verbal and nonverbal, did the results suggest that it was unlikely that males and females would perform similarly on the tests. To make a type 1 error as small as possible, an observed significance level of below .01 was employed in determining whether or not the sample variances in performance on all tests were similar. For the two tests mentioned before, the observed significance levels were .0005 in the case of the nonverbal test and, .003 in the case of the verbal creativity test. For all other tests the results suggest that it is likely that both males and females perform in the same way on the tests.

Efforts were made to test the hypotheses while controlling for other factors which could influence performance such as school type, school

Table 4.22 T-Values for all Test Scores, by Sex of Student

Test Scores	T-Value	Degrees of Freedom	2-Tail Prob
English	-.76	392	.451
Mathematics	1.71	392	.088
Circles	3.88	365	.000
Word association	-2.94	364	.003
Critical thinking	.06	217	.949

location and the gender composition of the school. Additional t-tests were conducted while isolating particular variables. For example, t-tests were conducted using performance on the tests from students who attended urban schools.

The test involving students from secondary high schools only, had a 2-tail probability of .001. This seems to suggest that for students attending secondary high schools the performance of both males and females on the nonverbal creativity test does not appear likely to be similar. A comparable result was obtained from the test which examined performance in urban schools and in coeducational schools. The observed significance levels were .0005 and .002 respectively. This seems to indicate that the likelihood exists that differences in performance of students who attend coeducational schools and urban schools on the circles test could be linked to the sex of the student. Performance in mathematics for schools in urban areas produced an observed significance level of .011. The sex of a student therefore could be an important factor in explaining levels of achievement in mathematics for students attending schools which are located in urban areas.

For those tests which generated observed significance levels which were too large to reject the null hypothesis (Table 4.22), there remains the possibility that there are small differences in performance on those tests which could be linked to the sex of the student. In the case of English, there is a 45 percent chance that the t-value would be observed in a population in which males and females performed at comparable levels in English language. For mathematics, there is a 9 percent probability that the levels of achievement would be observed in a population in which there was no variation in performance which could be attributed to the sex of the student. The critical thinking test results suggest that there is a 95 percent chance of observing such a difference in achievement if levels of achievement on critical thinking were similar for males and females. This conclusion would have to be very tentative, however, in light of the problems with the test which have been previously outlined.

More rigorous testing of the hypothesis that there is no difference in levels of achievement in mathematics and English language based on the type of secondary school attended was done using the one-way analysis of variance. The data satisfied one of the preconditions for its use, that of randomness and the equal variance assumption held for the mathematics and English language tests. The F-statistic for school type is highly significant (.000), suggesting that the probability of F values of 49.127 is less than .0005 if the null hypothesis is true. Therefore the null hypothesis should be rejected. Students do not have the same average performance in English regardless of the type of secondary school which they attend. School type does influence levels of achievement in English language.

In the case of the mathematics test, the one-way analysis of variance produced results which were similar to those generated by the English tests. The F value was 43.392 and the F-statistic was .000. This suggests that the null hypothesis that the type of secondary school attended makes no difference to levels of achievement in mathematics should be rejected. Hence students' performance in mathematics is influenced by the type of school which the student attends. New secondary school students performed worse in both English language and mathematics with students of secondary high schools performing best.

The nature of the relationship between the scores and selected variables

In order to identify which of the variables were most important in explaining variation in all the test scores, some regression analysis was conducted. A multiple regression model was developed to obtain that combination of variables which would best explain variance in students' levels of achievement in English language, mathematics, creativity and critical thinking.

The variable age was added for analysis to determine the extent to which it helped to explain variation in performance on the tests. Two other variables were added for analysis. These were composites created from the survey data collected. One was an indicator of occupational status (occstat) created by averaging the occupational status of both parents/guardians where both existed or using the occupational level of one where only one was present in the household. The other was an indicator of educational status (edstat) created in the same manner as outlined above. Both were interpreted as indicators of the respondents' social and economic status. To facilitate analysis, several dummy variables were created: newschl = new secondary schools; sechigh = secondary high schools; techhi = technical high schools; singirl = single sex girls' schools; coschool = co-educational schools. The original variables school then became comprehensive high schools and gendcomp became single sex boys' schools. The full models contained the following variables with 'e' as the error term:

English $= a + ß_1$schooltype $+ ß_2$location $+ ß_3$gendcomp $+$
$(Y_1)ß_4$sex $+ ß_5$occstat $+ ß_6$edstat$+ ß_7$age $+ ß_8$
newschl $+ ß_9$techhi $+ ß_{10}$coschool $+ ß_{11}$sechigh $+$
$ß_{12}$singirl $+$ e.

Mathematics $= a + ß_1$schooltype $+ ß_2$location $+ ß_3$gendcomp
$(Y_2) + ß_4$sex $+ ß_5$occstat $+ ß_6$edstat$+ ß_7$age$+ ß_8$
newschl $+ ß_9$techhi $+ ß_{10}$coschool $+ ß_{11}$singirl$+$
$ß_{12}$sechigh $+$ e.

Creativity 1 $= a + ß_1$schooltype $+ ß_2$location $+ ß_3$
(Y_3) gendcomp $+ ß_4$sex $+ ß_5$occstat $+ ß_6$edstat$+ ß_7$
age $+ ß_8$newschl $+ ß_9$techhi $+ ß_{10}$ coschool $+ ß_{11}$ sechigh
$+ ß_{12}$singirl $+$ e.

Creativity 2 $= a + ß_1$schooltype $+ ß_2$ location $+ ß_3$
(Y_4) gendcomp $+ ß_4$ sex $+ ß_5$ occstat $+ ß_6$ edstat$+$
$ß_7$ age $+ ß_8$ newschl $+ ß_9$ techhi $+ ß_{10}$ coschool
$+ ß_{11}$ sechigh $+ ß_{12}$ singirl $+$ e.

Critical thinking $= a + ß_1$schooltype $+ ß_2$location $+ ß_3$
(Y_5) gendcomp $+ ß_4$sex $+ ß_5$occstat $+ ß_6$
edstat$+ ß_7$age $+ ß_8$newschl $+ ß_9$techhi $+$
$ß_{10}$ coschool $+ ß_{11}$ sechigh $+ ß_{12}$singirl $+$ e.

The decision to include the independent variables was made based on existing theoretical perspectives concerning some of the factors which can impinge on educational achievement. Studies in Jamaica have also identified several of the variables mentioned above as being related to academic achievement. The full models produced adjusted r_2 as identified in Table 4.23.

In an effort to try to incorporate those variables which best helped to explain variation in performance on the tests, and thus facilitate prediction, reduced models were calculated. The variables which were retained in the reduced models were based principally on previous observation of the distribution of scores and analysis, which indicated those which were associated with achievement levels in literacy, numeracy, creativity and critical thinking. In addition, examination of the t-values pointed to variables which contributed significantly to the observed variation in

Table 4.23   Regression Coefficients of Multiple Determination for Full and
Reduced Models on all Tests

Y-Values	Adjusted R Square Full Models	Adjusted R Square Reduced Models
English	.35252	.35205
Mathematics	.40592	.39553
Creativity 1	.17922	.16309
Creativity 2	.19231	.20375
Critical Thinking	.10370	.13474

performance. For English, all except new secondary schools (newschl) and single sex girls' schools (singirl) had t-values below a .01 level of significance. In the case of new secondary schools, however, Table 4.15 showed that attendance in new secondary schools was associated with low performance in English language. Also much has been written about the facility which females often display with language, hence the retention of the singirl variable.

For mathematics, the variables with significant t-values were location, technical schools (techhi), secondary high schools (sechigh) and comprehensive schools (school). Although new secondary schools and occupational status did not have significant t-values they were included in the reduced model based on observed contribution as well as theoretical reasons.

A similar approach was adopted for the other three tests resulting in the following reduced models from step wise procedures. The reduced models were:

English $(Y_1) = a + ß_1newschl + ß_2occstat + ß_3location + ß_4singirl + e.$
Mathematics $(Y_2) = a + ß_1newschl + ß_2occstat + ß_3 location + ß_4school + e.$
Creativity 1 $(Y_3) = a + ß_1newschl + ß_2sex + ß_3school + e.$
Creativity 2 $(Y_4) = a + ß_1sechigh + ß_2sex + ß_3singirl + ß_4newschl + e.$
Critical thinking $(Y_5) = a + ß_1occstat + e.$

To test whether or not the full models or the reduced models offered the best explanation of achievement differences in all the tests, the F-test for restrictions was calculated. Prior to this, however, the F-ratios were examined to establish that the variables did assist in explaining the variability of scores. The F-ratios for all scores were significant suggesting

Table 4.24   Results of F-Tests of Existence and Restrictions

Variable	F-Ratio	F-Calculated	F -Critical $a = .01$
English	0.0000	1.10	2.51
Mathematics	0.0000	2.26	2.51
Creativity 1	0.0000	2.12	2.51
Creativity 2	0.0000	0.80	2.51
Critical Thinking	0.0098	0.74	2.18

that all of the independent variables in the full models helped to explain student performance on all tests and appear to be related in a linear fashion to performance levels on the tests. The F-ratios for all tests are shown in Table 4.24.

From Table 4.24 we can see that in none of the instances could the null hypothesis be rejected. That is, the variables which were omitted from the reduced model did not add significantly to explaining performance on any of the tests. Therefore the reduced model was better at explaining score variability than the respective full models.

Consideration of interaction effects was limited to performance in English language and mathematics. This was so because these were the principal variables of interest and time did not allow further analysis.

For this analysis two new variables were computed, for English $ß_{13} = ß_1 * ß_2$, that is, a variable which would combine the effects of occupational level and the school type variable, that is, newschl. Theory suggests that students of lower socioeconomic status tend to be concentrated in the least valued type of secondary level institution, the new secondary school. For mathematics a similar procedure was followed with the sole exception of the inclusion of an additional variable computed from the combining of the effects of occupational status and comprehensive school, $ß_{14} = ß_2 * ß_4$. This produced two new full models including the interaction effects:

English $(Y_1) = a + ß_1 newschl + ß_2\ occstat + ß_3\ location +$
$$ß_4\ singirl + ß_{13} + e.$$
Mathematics $(Y_2) = a + ß_1 newschl + ß_2\ occstat + ß_3$
$$location + ß_4\ school + ß_{13} + ß_{14} + e.$$

Table 4.25   Results of F-Tests for Interaction Effects

Evaluation	F-Calculated	F-Critical a=.01
English	22.79	6.85
Mathematics	3.96	6.64

Partial F-tests were conducted to determine whether or not the impact of school type on levels of achievement in English language and mathematics varied with the level of the parents'/guardians' occupational status. The null hypotheses were: for English Ho β_{13} = 0; for Mathematics, Ho β_{13} = β_{14} = 0. Table 4.25 shows the results of these tests.

For performance in English, the calculated F-value was greater than the critical F-value. The null hypothesis that the new full model including the interaction effects would not add to explaining variation in levels of achievement in English language has to be rejected. The opposite was true for mathematics where the calculated F-value was less than the critical F-value hence the null hypothesis could not be rejected in this instance. For English therefore, occupational status is involved interactively with attendance at new secondary schools in contributing to levels of achievement. Occupational status influences achievement in English language across school types.

The scores were then examined in relation to each other because correlation analysis had revealed a high level of correlation between scores. Theory also suggests that performance in mathematics is associated with levels of achievement in English language (Isaacs 1974).

Table 4.26 shows the correlation coefficients between all scores with the term 'letter' indicating the results pertaining to the critical thinking test. All except the scores in critical thinking and the scores in mathematics and the word association test had 1-tailed significance levels of .001. The strongest linear relationship was evident between mathematics and English language scores, with the weakest being between scores in the critical thinking test and those in the nonverbal creativity test. There was no significant linear relationship between performance in critical thinking and either performance in mathematics or in the verbal creativity test.

Performance of students on all tests, therefore, is related to their performance on others. Except for critical thinking in two instances,

Table 4.26 Correlation Matrix Showing Association Between Scores

	Engscore	Mthscore	Circles	Assoc	Letter
Engscore	1.0000	.6031	.3461	.4292	.2748
Mthscore	.60311	.0000	.4586	.2825	.1632
Circles	.3461	.45861	.0000	.3077	.2567
Assoc.	.4292	.2825	.3077	1.0000	.1030
Letter	.2748	.1632	.2567	.1030	1.0000

higher scores on any test are associated with higher scores on all other tests. Performance in mathematics helped to explain some 40 percent of the variation in levels of achievement in English, $r_2 = .40326$. When performance in the verbal creativity test and performance on the critical thinking test are added to the model a half of the observed variability in achievement levels in English is explained, $r_2 = .50285$, adjusted $r_2 = .49574$.

The critical variables in explaining variation in performance in mathematics were performance in English and performance on the nonverbal creativity test. That model had an $r_2 = .51207$ and an adjusted $r_2 = .50916$. A student who performs well in mathematics therefore is likely to be a high achiever in English language and in nonverbal creativity.

The Other Perspective – Interview Findings

Teachers and school administrators all conceded to awareness of, and concern for, improving levels of achievement in literacy and numeracy. Differences existed as to interpretations of causative factors and consequently, of methods for alleviating or minimizing the problem.

All teachers identified student related factors as principal contributors to low levels of achievement. Demotivation, poor reading skills, lack of parental guidance, low levels of concept formation were a few of the problems mentioned. Only two teachers mentioned inadequate training, competence and retention of teachers as a contributory factor. Yet, a half of the mathematics and English teachers interviewed confessed to not having been trained to teach those particular subjects. English teachers of all school types cited the existence of the dialect and its central position in the speech pattern of students as an important factor affecting the development of facility in Standard English. Shortage of teaching materials and inadequate allocation of time for teaching were other shortcomings mentioned.

Summary of Findings

The levels of achievement of the sample of Jamaican secondary school students in literacy and numeracy fell below the performance recorded for CXC candidates in 1992. For English language, 22 percent of the sample recorded scores of 60 percent and over while 18 percent obtained a similar level in mathematics. This is not surprising since the CXC does not measure as wide a range of abilities as this survey sought to do. Also, for the CXC, final scores are based on performance on two papers for each subject while this was not the case for this survey. Nonetheless as an attempt to measure the range of abilities across the range of public secondary institutions, the survey has assisted in offering insights into the dimensions of the problem and some of the possible contributory factors.

The critical variables influencing performance in English language were: attendance in a new secondary school, parents/ guardians' occupational status, attendance in a school located in an urban area and attendance in a girls' school. Attendance in a new secondary school was negatively associated with improved levels of achievement in English language. A student from this type of school therefore was more likely to perform poorly in English language than a student attending any other type of secondary school. On the other hand, students whose parents had higher occupational levels or who attended girls' schools or secondary schools in urban areas, were more likely to perform better in English. It should be noted that the most important explanatory variables of performance in English language were attendance in a school other than a new secondary school and the occupational status of parents/guardians. These two served to explain 30 percent of the variation in levels of achievement in English, (adjusted $r_2=.30062$).

Eighteen percent of all students obtained scores of 60 percent or more on the mathematics test compared to 28 percent who obtained Grades 1 and 2 in CXC mathematics in 1992. Students who attended new secondary and comprehensive high schools had a greater probability of performing badly than students from any other type of secondary school.

Improved levels of achievement in mathematics were also associated with higher occupational levels of parents/guardians and attendance at schools located in urban areas. Of students who attended schools in urban areas, however, males were likely to perform better at mathematics than females, ($t = 2.56$, $p = .011$). For instance, 32 percent of all males in urban schools obtained scores of 60 percent or over in mathematics. For females, the proportion was 17 percent. More than twice as many males than females obtained scores of 80 percent and above.

Most students displayed a lack of originality on the nonverbal creativity test. This seems to suggest an inadequacy of inventiveness among Jamaican secondary school students. It may, however, be a spurious association as the conditions under which the tasks were performed, although untimed, may not have been conducive to creative expression. Students of new secondary and comprehensive high schools exhibited less nonverbal creative skills than students of all other types of secondary schools. Males exhibited significantly higher levels of nonverbal creative skills than females. The opposite was true of the verbal creativity test where females tended to attain higher levels of performance than males. Attendance at a secondary high school and a single sex girls' school was also associated with greater ideational fluency. Students who attended new secondary schools performed badly on this test also.

There was some association between the sex of the student and performance on the critical thinking test but the most powerful factor explaining levels of attainment on this test was the occupational status of the students' parents/guardians.

Conclusion and Recommendations

The principal concern of this investigation was to identify the current levels of achievement in Jamaican Grade 11 students in literacy (proxy measure English language), numeracy (proxy measure mathematics), creativity and critical thinking, variables identified as being vital in facilitating the kind of human development necessary for national competitiveness.

Allied to this was the attempt to isolate some of those factors which were of importance in explaining poor learning performance. In this respect, although the investigation employed measuring instruments which assessed achievement in terms of rank order, and these are popularly employed throughout the education system in Jamaica, perhaps a plurality of instruments to capture the different ways in which excellence is expressed would have been more effective. Certainly, Jamaicans have been noted for responding to real life crises in a creative way. Perhaps creative responses were not forthcoming to the circles test since it was not deemed to be crucial to survival. In addition, any evaluation of competencies or proficiencies must be informed by current knowledge of the specific conditions which help to shape the particular environment, for the impact which these have in mediating student performance is of significance.

Educational development can either facilitate or stymie social development. The reverse is no less true. Declining or low standards of performance must cause disquiet. This is especially so in the context of the unprecedented pace and scale of change occurring as a result of the new technologies.

The findings indicate a relationship between the type of school, occupational status of parent, school location and literacy and numeracy levels. Of course, the occupational status of parent/guardian is closely related to the type of school which a person is likely to attend, with higher occupational levels being associated with attendance in a secondary high school and lower occupational levels being associated with attendance in a new secondary school. The very conceptualization of the Jamaican secondary education system has rested on an ideology of elitism and reflects and reinforces the social disparities and inequities which are evident in the wider Jamaican society. This is a context which predisposes elite groups to reproduce themselves within the society through access to, and in some instances control of, the principal institutions of influence and power, including the education system.

The mastery of literacy and numeracy skills in the sample was shown to be fairly low especially in new secondary schools. This has implications for the programmatic content of the offerings of secondary schools. To the extent that teachers use principally didactic rather than creative methodologies, the classroom climate is unlikely to promote the kind of creativity and critical thinking which is needed for development.

There is the need to address the segmentation of the secondary system as a matter of urgency. This needs to be done in such a manner as to remove all structural impediments to students developing self-confidence and a sense of self-worth. These include organizational factors such as the methods of selection of students for entry to secondary schools and their placement within the school. This study highlights the weaknesses in the system generally and in new secondary schools in particular.

No improvement can occur in the output of the secondary system without serious attention being paid to teacher quality and remuneration. This also involves improved supervision of schools and classrooms.

Based on the findings of this study, one offers the following recommendations for policy and research:

1. Institutionalize the practice of collecting data regularly pertaining to young people whose entry into the labour is most imminent, and to develop the instruments which will help to reveal the dimensions of the problem as well as to identify causative factors with greater precision. Collaborative efforts between the Statistical Institute, the Planning Institute of Jamaica and the Jamaican Ministry of Education should be able to produce quality data to inform policy.

2. A reassessment of training programmes for teachers of English and mathematics is needed to emphasize the importance of experiential components in the learning situation and to provide the basis for targeted interventions for males in English and for females in mathematics.

3. Greater articulation between the lower grades (7–9) and the upper grades (10–11) of secondary schools and between secondary schools and primary schools, the world of work and the society to ensure that schooling truly offers the enhanced life chances which many expect.

4. The forging of a national consensus about the purposes of education in general and secondary education in particular with regards to preparing persons for the world of work. The responsibilities of the school as well as the responsibilities of enterprises for specialized training must be clearly delineated to avoid an overlap of roles and the inappropriate allocation of scarce resources. Firms and organizations need to be prepared to provide on-the-job training for school leavers as well as to provide upgrading programmes for current employees who may not possess the requisite literacy/numeracy skills.

5. The identification and replication through the school system of the cultural patterns which are essentially Jamaican are of vital importance to developing the national confidence which is vital for development.

6. The full implementation of proposals made by Craig (1971) and others for the use of foreign language methodologies in the teaching of English to Jamaican students.
7. The removal of elitist ideology and structures in education including selection procedures, curricula offerings and evaluative mechanisms, to release the potential of all our children.
8. Attention must be paid to system gaps which aid in perpetuating uneven levels of achievement. These include:
   (a) the lack of competency standards for Grade 11 students;
   (b) the practice of automatic age promotion of students regardless of performance levels;
   (c) the lack of an effective programme to provide teachers who are equipped to assist with remediation in all schools at all grade levels.
9. Ensure that quality secondary schooling is accessible to all students regardless of socioeconomic status. The implications of increased cost recovery programmes for national development needs to be studied carefully before implementation.
10. Parents/guardians need to demonstrate positive valuation of educational achievement to undermine the association between low achievement and low occupational status.
11. Content analysis of the English and mathematics test papers would offer additional insights into where gaps in competencies exist.
12. Further investigation into the obstacles which hamper effective policy implementation in education is vital.

Notes

1. The Trench Town and Frankfield (later renamed Edwin Allen) Comprehensive High Schools in Kingston and Clarendon respectively, were the schools established.
2. In 1991, secondary high schools accounted for 41 percent of the total population of public secondary institutions, excluding all age and vocational agricultural schools. For new secondary schools, the proportion was 43 percent (Planning Institute of Jamaica 1992: 18).
3. This would be due in part to the public perception that the programme of new secondary schools is not as worthwhile as that offered by secondary high schools. Additionally some new secondary students do gain admission to secondary high schools through unofficial channels based on sports and other cultural activities.
4. The Secondary Schools Textbook Rental Programme was inaugurated with funding by the government of the United Kingdom and the government of Jamaica to provide texts on rental to students in all public secondary institutions in Jamaica.

5

Community Protection in Inner-city Kingston, Jamaica

Oral O'Brian Khan

Introduction

The fear of criminal attack held by many Jamaicans of all social strata has been mounting for years, and has become one of the most pressing concerns of the Jamaican public today. Although Jamaica has one of the leading per capita crime rates in the world, rising crime is not unique to the island.

While there is the desire to bring about a reversal of the growing trend and the feeling of insecurity, under the prevailing socioeconomic conditions the police are aiming for "containment" of crimes. According to police statistics 80 percent of all major crimes of violence occur within the six police divisions in the Kingston Metropolitan Region (KMR) and St Catherine. When the locations of major crimes are plotted, a high concentration emerges in the southern and western sections of the city. The areas of concentration have been traditionally called 'crime prone areas'. It is within this crime prone belt that Jamaica's inner-city communities are to be found.

The recent alarm with the crime rate has, to some extent, come about because more crimes have started to be reported outside of the crime prone belt. 'Containment' of the crime rate, if it were to be successful, would mean that some sections of the corporate area would not experience any significant growth in crimes. For the crime prone areas, however, 'containment' could mean no reduction in the level of crime and violence which their residents face. The protection of lives and property in crime prone inner-city areas presents a real challenge to both the residents of these areas and the country's security agencies.

The Research Problem

There are many communities that lie within the crime prone belt of the city. Some of these communities have managed to preserve relative peace and safety within their borders, while others have witnessed wave after wave of outbreak of violence. The primary objective of this paper is to explain this phenomenon.

Life in the inner-city is fashioned by an informal economy (Buchanan 1992). It can be argued that this informality extends to the people's own efforts to see about their safety and the protection of their property, often independent of police input. This paper seeks to identify the popularity and level of dependence on these methods and to determine what implications they bear for security policymakers and persons concerned about the security of their local environment. Another related objective is to show that contrary to popular belief, some inner-city communities are still relatively safe. Thus the benefit of microlevel as opposed to the divisional and national level analyses which are usually undertaken[1] will be highlighted.

It is hoped that security policymakers as well as members of the wider society will benefit from an understanding of the potential of informal protective security measures, and the contexts within which such measures are likely to succeed or to fail. With an appreciation for the potentials and the limitations – the opportunities and the threats – posed by people's efforts to protect themselves, new options may emerge for community protection, which is seen as a basic human need.

Theoretical framework: security as a basic need

Social policymakers have refocused attention on the provision of basic human needs. It is the satisfaction of these basic needs that affect the quality of people's lives which the process of human development seeks to improve. Among the basic needs which must be satisfied is the need for protection. People from all social strata, all cultures and in all historical periods have had this need.

The ways and the means by which the need for protection is satisfied may vary from one culture to another and from one time period to another, for "human needs are discerned differently, according to the ideological and disciplinary lens of viewers" (Max-Neef, et al. 1989: 17). Since the basic needs of subsistence, protection, affection, understanding, participation, idleness, creation, identity and freedom are all interrelated in a dynamic way, then activities to meet one impacts in some way on the achievement of some other need (Max-Neef, et al. 1989: 20).

Care must therefore be taken to ensure that 'satisfiers' applied for the sake of protection, especially those imposed on people, do not cause more harm than good, ending up in one of the following categories:

(a) As violaters, where they block the possibility of meeting the need overtime and impair the satisfaction of other needs.

(b) As pseudosatisfiers, where they generate a false sense of security.

(c) As inhibitors, which oversatisfy one need while curtailing the possibility of satisfying other needs.

(d) As singular satisfiers, which are neutral in respect of other needs.

What is needed is a mix of 'synergic satisfiers' which will satisfy the need for protection and simultaneously stimulate and contribute to the fulfilment of other needs. In this way, human development advances. Needs will be satisfied at varying levels with varying intensities within three contexts: the individual, the social group and the environment.

The state's obligation to afford the protection of the law to the people is binding. Nevertheless, in keeping with the aim of human development, the thinking is that the state has to move from its traditional role as a generator of satisfiers, which are exogenous to civil society, to being a stimulator and creator of processes arising from the bottom upwards (Max-Neef, et al. 1989: 36). In the case of community protection, there has to be an examination of the 'prescriptions' which have been applied from top down, while we seek to learn about the security measures that people at the grassroots level have made work.

Several economic, political, social, cultural and psychological factors, either singularly or in combination, have been advanced to explain the incidence of crime in Jamaica. These pertain to inequalities in the distribution of income, wealth, power and social opportunities (Eyre 1986; Headley 1992; Stone 1988), the absence of strong moral values (Taylor 1992; Headley 1992), and family disorganization and the lack of positive role models (Task Force Report 1992). In addition, the Task Force Report on crime in Jamaica (1992) has directed attention to the ineffectiveness of crime containment strategies which have been pursued in Jamaica over nearly twenty years. The failure was blamed on shortcomings in the areas of quality intelligence, preventive measures, and the deployment of uniformed foot and vehicle patrols, all of which were said to be critical to the success of crime containment.

Apart from improvements in the above mentioned areas, several strategies have been proposed for dealing with the problem of crime at the community level, some of which were also dealt with in the Task Force Report. Some of these strategies relate to community policing, the character of control mechanisms, community leadership and the general approach to security provision (viz. statist/top down vs grass roots/bottom up).

The purpose of community policing is to "develop a team of officers who have an intimate knowledge of local conditions and who develop special skills in dealing with them" (Roach 1987: 84). Commander Lawrence Roach of the London Metropolitan Police advises that there are three themes to be considered by every officer intending to adopt the community policing approach. These were: the nature and extent of consultation between the police and the public; the relationship between policing and the social context; and the proper arrangement for police accountability and control. He emphasizes the importance of understanding the specifics of the social and political environment, for these are crucial in defining the role of the police and accountability. The principal role of the police is:

to afford the protection of the law to the citizen, to be his support and servant in creating the conditions of peace and security which make social life possible and freedom a reality in his daily life (Roach 1986: 78).

The adoption of the community policing approach was seen by Roach as an acknowledgement that traditional methods were not delivering, leaving the only real option that of asking the 'customer' himself to participate in the design of the 'product' that is required. He was careful to point out that the police were not meant to take a passive role in the discussion. The police still had to specify what was or was not an acceptable level of policing. They had to insist on their role as custodians of the people and their right to take action to prevent and to detect offences (Roach 1987: 83). The new approach had far reaching implications for the police service: its structure, the attitude of its officers, its planning and management process, its structure of accountability, and the political structure to which it is related. All these must become open to the influence of the community affected by them if this approach is to be effective. Relatedly, a more extreme approach is suggested by Headley (1992: 78), who does not just advocate greater community involvement in policing but "complete community control" of the police service.

Writing on community treatment and social control, Learman (1975) recognized that there were many informal mechanisms such as praise, blame, shame, ridicule and social isolation which may operate to induce compliance to social standards. These informal methods rely on the acceptance of the customs, folkways and mores of the society (Learman 1975: 8). This passive mode of social control may retain its effectiveness in situations where efforts by formal regulatory agencies fail. The mode of behaviour that will prevail will reflect the values of the community. The more cohesive the community, the greater the effectiveness of the passive forms of social control.

In respect of leadership, Allen (1993) recognizes this as a very significant community variable. He describes two types of local power structure, namely the vertical and the horizontal power systems. In the vertical power system, the community is led by a few powerful individuals who make the majority of decisions within the community. In the horizontal power structure, leaders perform roles based on expertise or personal interest. Decisions are based on consensus and may change over time (Allen 1993: 156). However, Streeten (1984) expressed the concern that local self-determination could conceivably work against the interests of the poor, if power were to be handed to members of the local power elite. He noted that the unrepresentativeness of the leadership of many local groups may impair the ability of such leadership to identify with the local needs and aspirations. He feared that the local power elite could "grind the faces of the poor" (Streeten, 1984: 975).

Another vertical but more dictatorial mode of control relates to what has been termed the "Top Ranking" leader. Buchanan (1992) raised concern over the Top Ranking leader from the ghetto whose legitimacy, power and influence was related to his economic base, which was itself traceable to the political contract system. He portrayed the Top Ranking leader as a very formidable character, whose "utterances and action form the prevailing philosophy and community norm, especially among the youth" (Buchanan 1992: 41). According him, the Top Ranking leader of an area is the prime gunman and the leader of local gunmen. He is the principal in the drug enterprise and the chief contractor on government projects. He is treacherous and will kill to preserve his title. He called the "Ranking" phenomenon a disease, which he said was creating a barrier to the economic development of a community. He saw it as a curable disease, but one for which the healing process may be accompanied by some disorder in the community (Buchanan 1992: 63).

Overview of Policing in Jamaica

The formal approaches to the policing of communities, as announced and practised publicly, may be grouped under three headings: (1) routine policing; (2) community action against crime; and (3) special crime fighting squads.

Routine policing

The Jamaica Constabulary operates some 181 police stations across the island, from which police service is delivered to communities. These stations and supplementary police posts are usually established in response to an increasing threat of criminality and the weight of representation and political clout of the interest groups concerned. The presence of a police station or post is intended to enhance a community's sense of security and allow for a speedy response whenever the service is needed. The high crime rate in the South Western belt of the city is itself an indication that policing from local stations in these areas has many shortcomings.

Community action against crime

Formal endorsement of community action against crime came in 1973, with the establishment of the National Home Guard, which was to complement traditional law enforcement forces (*Daily Gleaner*, 21 November 1973). This conferred official recognition under a formal structure upon residents supporting the police in fighting crimes in their own locality.

Participants in the Home Guard were allowed to bear arms and were granted powers of arrest. The concept was abandoned after the change of government in 1980, because of the perception that the Home Guard was more of a political institution and therefore a threat to national security.

Neighbourhood Watch was introduced in 1987. Like the Home Guard, Neighbourhood Watch sought to unite citizens at the community level to protect themselves and their properties, by reducing the risk of crime. The concept of the Watch calls for less activism than the Home Guard displayed. Householders are asked to lend their support by participating in a system to alert the whole neighbourhood about an intruder. They are asked to participate in mock practices of how a community alarm system should be used. Victim support groups are also encouraged to provide moral or even financial support to crime victims by, for example, accompanying them to court to reduce the possibility of intimidation.

According to the Police Community Relations Department, there were 186 registered Neighbourhood Watch groups in the corporate area by May 1994, distributed across police divisions as follows:

St Andrew North	87
St Andrew Central	49
St Andrew South	23
Kingston Central	3
Kingston East	24

The divisions within which inner-city communities are located recorded only a few Neighbourhood Watch groups. Kingston West Division, which is noted for frequent outbreaks of intercommunal and intracommunal strife, did not have one single Watch registered. The concept of Neighbourhood Watch has not been embraced by inner-city communities. The police identified a number of difficulties which curtail the establishment of 'Watches' in these areas. Among them were the following:

1. Ignorance of the role of the police in communities.
2. Fear on the part of residents of being described as police informers.
3. Fears held by residents concerning the risk of criminal reprisals.
4. Lack of support by some community leaders.
5. Insufficient knowledge of Neighbourhood Watch programmes.
6. Lack of self-esteem and self-worth of some people.

7. The influence of some religious persuasions whose members disasso-
    ciate and disavow themselves from the concept of a Watch.

Since February 1994, the police authorities have taken steps to implement the concept of community policing in accordance with the recommendations of the National Task Force on Crime (1992). Under this
concept the police force aims to become more of a police service, as police
officers seek to get involved in the life of the communities they serve. The
process is still in the experimental stage in some three corporate area
communities, namely Harbour View, Southside and Mona, and also in
Greater Portmore, St Catherine.

Southside is the only pilot area that could be classified as an inner-city
area. In the case of Southside, the police speak of encouraging results.
Residents there, however, had not heard much about what the concept
meant up to the time of the research. Nevertheless they expressed the
view that until the local police changed their attitude towards local
residents, then it would not work. The police expect that community
policing will help to bridge the gulf which had been created between the
people and the police.

Special crime fighting squads

Special crime fighting squads have been established from time to time as
short term responses to crime waves. They usually have wider areas of
responsibility than local police stations with a mission to combat hard
core criminal groups wherever they exist. The police are often supported
by the military in arrangements of this nature. At the time of this study
special squads included the Special Anti-Crime Task Force (SACTF); Joint
Military/Police patrols (Rat Patrols); Operation Shining Armour and
Operation Ferret.

These special squads depend heavily on intelligence for planning and
execution of their duties. They usually record significant successes in the
early stages of implementation. 'Rat Patrols' have become a matter of
routine in many inner-city communities where they have played a significant role in diffusing intercommunal strife. SACTF continues to record a
good measure of success against hard core criminals on whom intelligence
is available. Stone (1988: 40) was of the view that there would always be
the need for such "strong, well trained, mobile, militarized, special squads
able to repel gunmen". From this general overview of policing approaches

and the limited success they have had in the inner-city, questions arise as to the suitability and sustainability of these methods.

The Vulnerability of Corporate Areas

The data in Tables 5.1 and 5.2 show that, at least for the calendar year 1993, some relatively safe corporate area communities were to be found not only in the prime residential areas where private security is beginning to take off, but also in average working class communities such as Mountain View Gardens, Rollington Town and Duhaney Park. The presence of two inner-city communities, namely Craig Town and Rema, among the safe areas suggests that the approach to security employed within them may be considered appropriate for their own contextual reality. These inner-city areas which reflected relatively minimal risk were, however, exceptions, most inner-city areas bore assessments of unsafe to critical levels of risk.

It is significant that all the safe communities had registered Neighbourhood Watch groups except for the two inner-city communities. The existence of a registered Neighbourhood Watch group, however, was not a sufficient condition for safeguarding a community. There were some communities with 'Watches' which were relatively unsafe.

The lack of a registered Neighbourhood Watch group did not necessarily mean an unsafe community, as Craig Town and Rema clearly demonstrate. It may be that these communities take a somewhat different approach to community protection.

Those communities which had critical levels of risk did not have registered Watches. It may not be concluded, however, that those communities had no interest in their own protection. What may be deduced is that the means of satisfying the need for protection as they were applied in these areas were not suitable and should be re-examined. Eyre (1986) suggested that insecurity was a primary factor in the migration from urban zones. From the available data, it is easy to see why people would desire to move from areas like Tel-a-Viv, Matthews Lane and Hannah Town to anywhere else. But migration need not be the only recourse. For many inner-city poor, it is not an option. If people are more interested in their personal safety than in their profile or in their personal image, then the upwardly mobile working class people emerging from the inner-city

Table 5.1   Distribution of Major Crimes in Corporate Area Communities (1993)

Community	Incident Type				Total	Pop. Est	Rate*
	mur	sh	rob	rape			
East Kingston							
Franklyn Town	10	9	41	2	62	5,199	11.9
Newton Square	2	4	8	0	14	3,017	4.5
Passmore Town	1	4	13	0	18	6,826	2.6
Rennock Lodge	3	3	14	4	24	5,567	4.3
Norman Gardens	1	2	13	1	17	2,276	7.4
Rollington Town	1	1	2	0	4	8,969	0.4
Bournemouth Gardens	0	0	8	1	9	4,710	1.9
Central Kingston							
Rae Town	5	5	26	3	39	4,317	9.0
Allman Town	7	13	31	4	55	10,340	5.3
South Side	3	4	25	2	35	3,296	10.6
Tel-A-Viv	0	8	17	1	26	1,052	24.7
Down Town (commercial)	4	20	127	2	153	4,644	32.9
Western Kingston							
Tivoli Gardens	6	5	12	3	26	4,704	5.5
Denham Town	11	27	76	5	119	11,635	10.2
Hannah Town	10	16	38	6	70	1,671	41.8
Mathews Lane	1	5	19	1	26	863	30.1
Fletchers Land	1	2	21	1	25	4,664	05.3
S/East St Andrew							
New Kingston	1	5	11	1	18	1,903	5.7
Swallowfield	6	0	2	0	8	3,465	2.3
Vineyard Town	3	5	11	1	20	13,982	1.4
Mt View Gardens	0	2	5	0	7	13,502	0.51
Cross Roads (commercial)	13	10	55	2	80	8,871	

(Table continues)

Table 5.1 (cont'd) Distribution of Major Crimes in Corporate Area Communities (1993)

Community	Incident Type				Total	Pop. Est	Rate*
	mur	sh	rob	rape			
N/E St Andrew							
Barbican	7	13	58	0	78	10,979	7.1
Grants Pen	4	7	23	1	35	13,818	2.5
Cherry Gardens	1	3	18	0	24	74	2.8
E/C St Andrew							
Richmond Park	0	9	13	1	23	3,086	1.7
Cassia Park	1	0	1	0	2	12,157	0.1
Kencot	3	16	20	1	40	9,866	4.0
Half-Way-Tree (commercial)	4	25	70	2	101	5,984	16.8
W. St. Andrew							
Patrick City	1	4	4	0	9	5,495	1.6
Seaview Gds	18	21	22	2	63	12,502	5.0
Washington Gads	1	4	32	1	38	10,668	3.5
Riverton City	1	7	5	0	13	1,123	11.5
Duhaney Park	0	0	7	4	11	17,445	0.6
Bay Farm	2	3	7	0	12	7,922	1.5
S/W St Andrew							
Delacree Park	6	5	12	3	26	4,704	5.5
Whitfield Town	11	27	76	5	119	11,635	10.2
Greenwich Town	10	16	38	6	70	1,671	41.8
Payne Lands	1	5	19	26	26	863	30.1
N/W St Andrew							
Meadowbrook	0	2	8	1	11	2,076	5.2
Havendale	0	1	14	0	15	7,025	2.1
Arlene Gds	1	3	23	3	30	11,667	2.5
Pembroke Hall	1	4	15	2	22	5,611	3.9

(Table continues)

Table 5.1(cont'd) Distribution of Major Crimes in Corporate Area Communities (1993)

Community	Incident Type				Total	Pop. Est	Rate*
	mur	sh	rob	rape			
South St Andrew							
Jones Town	10	32	35	4	81	12,040	6.7
Trench Town	9	16	20	5	50	10,831	4.6
Craig Town	0	0	1	1	2	59	0.8
Rema	1	2	1	0	4	4,241	0.9
N/C St Andrew							
Whitehall	0	4	21	2	27	12,411	2.1
Constant Spring	0	6	28	2	36	4,927	7.3
Stony Hill	0	0	3	0	3	8,472	0.3
Dunrobin	4	4	11	3	18	1,096	16.0
E. St Andrew							
Hope Tavern	0	4	19	0	23	7,134	3.2
Beverly Hills	1	10	44	2	57	3,830	14.9
Hope Pastures	0	0	4	2	6	6,249	0.9
Mona/ Mona Heights	0	0	9	1	10	7,327	.13

*Incidents per 1,000 residents
Source: JCF daily crime reports and Statistical Institute of Jamaica 1982 census.

should consider if they really want to move to places such as Meadow-brook, Barbican or the environs of New Kingston.

The higher status of middle income communities carry higher costs for rent, insurance,[2] and for commuting. At the same time their greater affluence make them targets for criminal attacks, bearing a resemblance to the "Robin Hood mentality".[3] The data show that some of these affluent communities are not much better off in terms of risk of criminal attack than some of the less aesthetic, lower income communities. The upwardly mobile in search of a better life may yet consider the alternative to migration, the option to remain in their communities and to contribute to the lifting of the image and the status of their area.

Table 5.2 Ranking of KMR Communities in Order of Increasing Vulnerability to Major Crimes per 1,000 Residents Recorded in 1993.

Community	Crime rate	Risk Assessment	N. Watch
Cassia Park/Eastwood Park	0.1		*
Stony Hill	0.3		
Rollington Town	0.4	SAFE	*
Mnt View Gardens	0.5	(minimal risk)	*
Duhaney Park	0.6		*
Molynes Gardens	0.6		*
Craig Town	0.8		
Rema (Wilton Gardens)	0.9		
Hope Pastures	1.0		*
Cherry Gardens	1.0		*
Balmagie	1.0		
Vineyard Town	1.4		*
Mona/Mona Heights	1.4		*
Bay Fm/Seaward Pen	1.5		*
Greenwich Farm	1.5		*
Patrick City	1.6		*
Richmond Park	1.7		*
Cockburn Gardens	1.8		
Bournemouth Gardens	1.9		*
Havendale	2.1	TOLERABLE	*
Whitehall	2.1	(low risk)	
Swallowfield	2.3		*
Tower Hill	2.4		
Grants Pen	2.5		*
Arlene Gardens	2.5		*
Passmore Town	2.6		*
Marverly	2.7		*
Hope Tavern	3.2		*
Washington Gardens	3.5		*
Delacree Park	3.7		*
Pembroke Hall	3.9		
Kencot	4.0		
Rennock Lodge	4.3		
Newton Square	4.5		*
Trench Town	4.7		

(Table continues)

Table 5.2 (cont'd)   Ranking of KMR Communities in Order of Increasing Vulnerability to Major Crimes per 1,000 Residents Recorded in 1993.

Community	Crime rate	Risk Assessment	N. Watch
Seaview Gardens	5.0		*
Meadowbrook	5.2		*
Allman Town	5.3		*
Fletchers Land	5.3		*
Tivoli Gardens	5.5	UNSAFE (significant risk)	
New Kingston	5.7		
Whitfield Town	6.0		
Waltham Gardens	6.6		
Jones Town	6.7		
Barbican	7.1		*
Norman Gardens	7.4		
Rae Town	9.0		
Cross Roads	9.0		
Denham Town	10.2		
Constant Spring	10.3		
South Side	10.6	HIGH RISK	
Riverton City	11.5		
Franklyn Town	11.9		*
Payne Lands	12.7		
Beverly Hills	14.9	VERY UNSAFE (very high risk)	*
Dunrobin	16.0		*
Half-Way-Tree	16.8		
Tel-A-Viv	24.7	CRITICALLY DANGEROUS	
Matthews Lane	30.1		
Down Town (commercial)	32.9		
Hannah Town	41.8		

*Information on Neighbourhood Watch groups came from the Police Community Relations Department

The community of residents will have to decide the sort of environment they wish to foster. They may then begin to work together to reduce the threats to their survival.

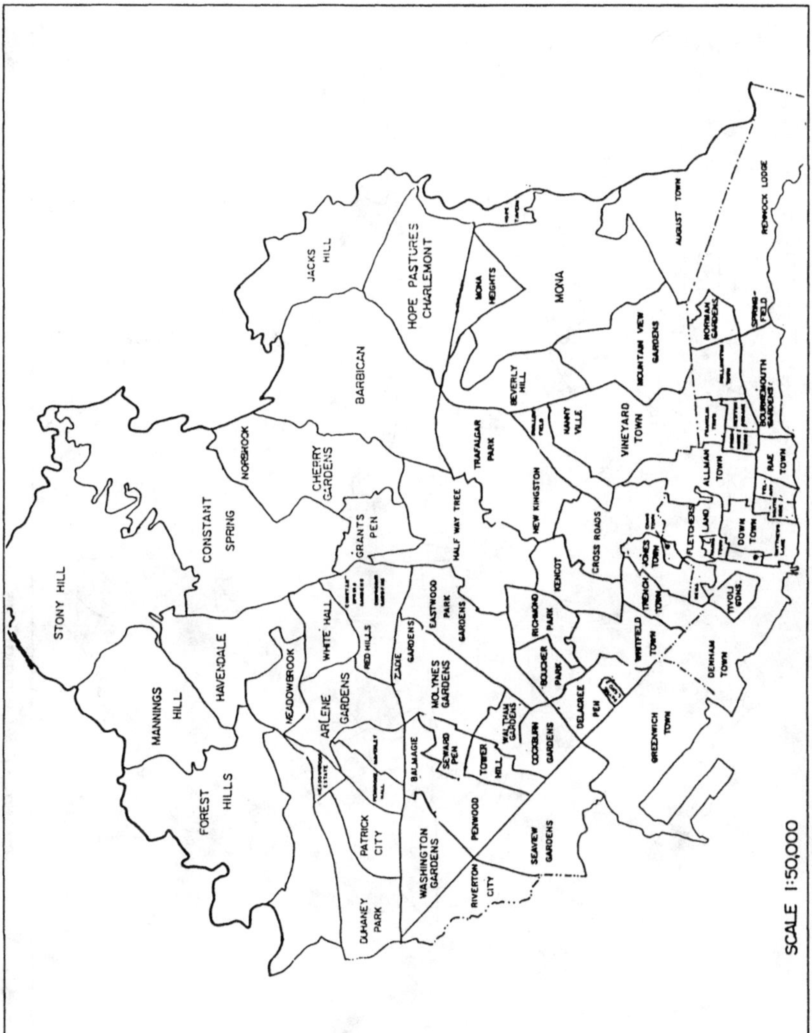

SCALE 1:50,000

Figure 5.1: KMR Communities

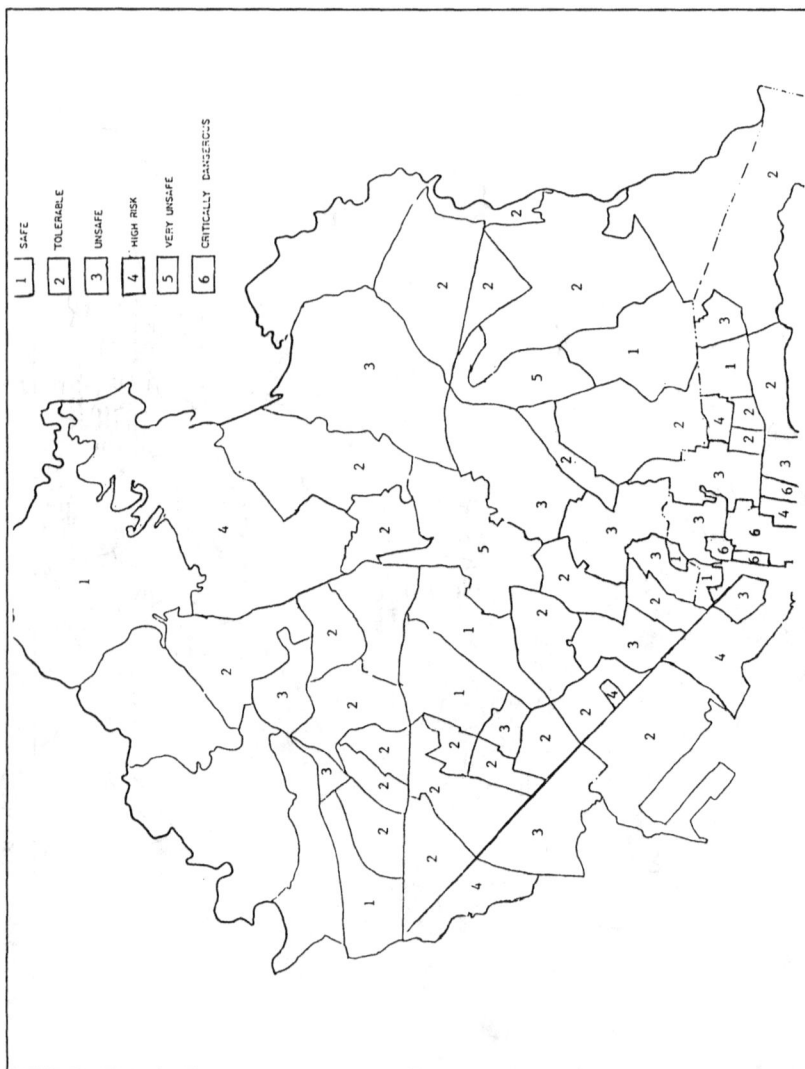

Figure 5.2: Vulnerability of KMR Communities

Methodology

The study was based on two urban communities which were at opposite ends of the continuum of crime: Hannah Town, which registered the highest crime rate of 41.8 (per 1,000 population), and Craig Town whose crime rate was 0.8. Both qualitative and quantitative techniques of collecting data were employed although greater emphasis was placed on the former. The qualitative methods involved principally the use of elite interviews and direct observation, while the quantitative involved a questionnaire administered to the members of the community and the victims of crime. For security reasons, the police were asked to administer the questionnaire, although this was not done effectively. For the elite interviews, respondents were chosen using a snowball technique, while other members of the community were conveniently chosen in groups whose composition ranged from 4 to 14 individuals. Eight group interviews were conducted.

Findings of Victim Survey

During the period of the survey (from 23 May to 30 June 1994) it was found that sixteen crimes (including petty crimes) were reported to the police in Hannah Town, as having occurred *within* Hannah Town. There were no reports of any incidents recorded from the Craig Town community at the Admiral Town police station during this period. The number of victims of shooting surpassed the numbers recorded for every other single category of offence, including robbery. Shootings accounted for 37 percent of total crimes, up from the 22 percent which was recorded for 1993.

In ten (or 58 percent) of the cases, the crime victims were female. In all the cases where the offender's sex could be determined (12 out of 14), the offender was male. Only one offence was reported against persons under age 13, and three against persons aged 13 to 19. The most frequent victim age category was between 19 and 29, in which there were eight offences. Four offences were reported against persons over 30 years.

In 50 percent of the offences, the victims were surprised, not sensing danger at all. Victims responded in several ways, of which the most common were keeping quiet, doing nothing or trying to escape. There was only one recorded instance of a plea for mercy being made. Although incidents were witnessed 56 percent of the times, the victims concerned did not call for help. However, victims received assistance only 18 percent of the times. Only on three occasions did victims report anyone coming to their assistance. On two occasions assistance came from friends. The police reported going to the assistance of just one victim in the case of a shooting.

In five of the cases, primarily the assault cases, attackers were known very well. Women who were the prime victims of assault nearly always offered resistance by fighting back their male aggressors. In most cases where attackers were well known, the victims expected that the police would make arrests. Where the attackers were not known, the victims requested the police to investigate and to recover lost property. In some instances, it appeared unclear what the victims really wanted. In seven cases attackers were total strangers to victims, but we cannot be certain whether attackers who were total strangers came from outside the community. However, total strangers were used to estimate attackers from outside, after excluding the two reports of nonresidents who had been victims of robbery. Outsiders involved in attacks on the community were more likely to be engaged in shootings.

Unfortunately, the victim survey did not provide some of the data expected because of the inconsistency of the local police in soliciting some of the information required. Nevertheless, the data still confirm the high level of vulnerability of Hannah Town vis à vis the relative peace of the neighbouring Craig Town, and also reinforce the need for fresh efforts to provide protection for the residents of Hannah Town.

The residents made it appear that the majority of Hannah Town's problems were being caused by persons from outside the community. This is true for the category of shooting, for which five out of six were committed by persons who could not be identified. The fear and intimidation caused by the relatively high number of shootings is indeed a serious problem if we consider that there were other incidents of shooting which are not reflected in the survey because they had fortunately not caused casualties.

It should be noted that at least half of the victims knew their attackers very well. When we consider that the two nonresidents were among those who stated that their attackers were total strangers, then the cases in which attackers were total strangers to Hannah Town could possibly be reduced to four. This means that a significant portion of the crimes committed within Hannah Town and chiefly against Hannah Town residents are being committed by residents from within the community. This high internal threat is indicative of an enemy within and raises questions about the solidarity of this community.

The higher vulnerability of Hannah Town women compared to the men reflects the attitude of the community towards the use of violence in settling disputes. However, there are opportunities for countering conjugal violence in Hannah Town and similar inner-city areas where there is less privacy, and where some of the confrontations between men and women are played out in the streets. If the community were to change its attitude to these incidents, then the greater publicity may deter potential aggressors, and thereby curtail offences.

Hannah Town

Although the community of Hannah Town has existed for many years, the Statistical Institute was still in the process of delimiting its boundaries for the process of designating the community a special area. The area known traditionally as Hannah Town used to cover a fairly large section of the Western Kingston constituency. With the passage of time, as Hannah Town came to be regarded as the People's National Party (PNP) support base in the area, the boundaries have contracted. Residents generally identify their community as a small enclave bordered to the East by Slipe Road, the South by North Street, West by Drummond Street and the gully, and to the North by Studley Park Road.

The majority of the community's residents have lived there all their lives. There was reportedly an influx of persons to adjacent areas which, up until recently, had been regarded as part of Hannah Town. There has also been outward migration of some families to the nearby community of Torrington Villa to the north where a government housing project was established. Some of these demographic changes were said to have come about as a result of the West Kingston Redevelopment Programme initiated by the Jamaica Labour Party (JLP). This same redevelopment programme has been blamed for the gradual breaking down of the unity and community spirit that used to be characteristic of the community because of the dislocation it caused. There was some evidence of a degree of neighbourliness among the residents of the community, all of whom appeared to be of similar economic means, but this neighbourliness did not spill over into either a strong sense of cohesiveness or solidarity. One resident said the majority of persons just mind their own business while another likened the community to a piece of patchwork, with its many small cliques and corner groups. Residents are suspicious of each other as trust had broken down. This breakdown of trust among residents was making it difficult to build support for any sort of community endeavour requiring wide scale community participation.

In respect of physical and social amenities, Hannah Town could boast of several key institutions: the Kingston Public and Victoria Jubilee Hospitals, the Mel Nathan Institute, and the Social Outreach arm of the United Church which provides community services and training for various interest groups including children and the elderly. In addition, there is The Edith Dalton James Community College which provides technical/vocational training in a range of skills at a reasonable fee, a new Ministry of Health Laboratory and a Blood Bank.

Unfortunately, the youth scarcely made use of the opportunities for skills training offered right there in the community. Several persons interviewed knew generally about the institutions, but they had not taken the time to find out what opportunities were available and how they could benefit. The institutions themselves seemed to have given up hope of reaching a wide cross section of the community.

One might have expected to find residents of Hannah Town gainfully employed in the various institutions but, surprisingly, none of the employees at the Mel Nathan Institute resided in Hannah Town. Unemployment in the community, judging from the number of the work force seen idle in the community, was very significant. The main source of livelihood was described as "higglering and hustling" downtown. Those employed in the community were engaged in bar operations, hairdressing and petty trading from small stalls. It was learnt that the women who conducted trading in the school compound and those operating food stalls were nonresidents which served to confirm the very open nature of the community to outsiders. Residents were allowing outsiders to take advantage of the few opportunities which existed in the community to earn a livelihood, while at the same time they complained that they were being victimized when they sought employment outside the community.

In respect of security, the police station did not have a serviceable vehicle assigned to it. Moreover, the building was very poorly maintained and the accommodation seen was in a dilapidated condition. From observation the primary school was also in dire need of repairs. The principal stated that the gravest need at the school was the erection of a perimeter wall for security. There was said to be good support from parents in the area for the school, but that the community did not have the resources to support the school financially. It was also stated that services obtained from the community had to be paid for. Residents said the government had already provided funds to the area leader for the construction of the wall, but the area leader has not been made to account for the funds.

The incidence of crime within Hannah Town has had serious implications for its reputation, its leaders, its sense of values, intra- and intercommunity relations, and its relations with the police.

In relation to its reputation, Hannah Town has been portrayed in recent years as a very unsafe place to live, which has had several related negative consequences. For instance, it has diminished community solidarity, resulted in outward migration and the refusal of persons outside the community to send their children to school there, which have had the further effect of reducing the school population.

Unfortunately, most residents were not willing to or could not readily identify the most influential person in the community. Those who held positions of responsibility in institutions which served the community did not reside there. Most residents said that the community had no don,[4] declaring that the days of donmanship in the community were over. An area leader who acted as the official link between the community and the political party, who had been chosen by majority decision of the local party group was identified. The local police recognized the area leader, who made frequent visits to the police station. Among the functions of the area leader were the securing of bail for persons who ran afoul of the law, and the allocation of work which flowed through the political system. In addition, the residents had also expected that the leader would have helped to control 'wrongdoers' and bring peace to the community. Some respondents expressed disappointment with the area leader, stating that he had taken the side of the wrongdoers. Those who were dissatisfied with the area leader's performance did not feel that they could voice their concerns openly out of fear of reprisals. Moreover, those who have an intimate knowledge of the community, particularly those who launch frequent attacks, consider the community weak in its internal defence capabilities which is locally called having a 'weak fence'.

Despite the negative image and its associated problems, some basic values were still held dear by some members of the community, particularly in relation to children and their physical security. For instance, it was observed that when guardians/parents sensed danger in the community, they showed up at the school early to collect their children. In relation to the youths, however, they were generally described by the police as violent, and minor disputes would frequently end in confrontation. In addition, they were said to be not as caring or respectful towards the elderly. As regards religion, this did not figure prominently either in the lives of the youths or in the community as a whole. The majority of residents did not attend the services of the Christian churches in the area.

Intercommunity relations

Except for a gully which forms part of the dividing line, a mere street and a low wall in some places separate Hannah Town from its neighbours. The relationship between Hannah Town and its neighbours to the west and the north was found to be very antagonistic and fragile. Everyone in the community, from children to senior citizens, is aware of the threat which the community faces from its neighbours in Denham Town to the west, who may be regarded as common enemies. Most blame for the acrimony was attributed to the neighbours who were said to attack without much provocation from Hannah Town. Ironically, while residents of Hannah Town considered their community to be less safe than their neighbours', they saw the latter as posing a greater threat to their safety than they posed to that of the neighbours. There were some residents who admitted that the youths on some of the corners in Hannah Town helped to provoke attacks on the community because of confrontations they have with residents from outside. This has helped to make the corner groups in the area unpopular. It was generally felt that the reputation of their community was not within the power of individuals to change.

Police and community relations

The relations between the police and the community were very poor. Community members did not cooperate with the police in identifying and apprehending criminals because they distrusted them. This distrust was linked to the belief that some of the persons whom they considered criminal had associations with the police. The general opinion was that the local police could not be relied upon to come to the defence of the community when they faced violent attacks from their rivals. In fact, there was unanimous agreement that it was a waste of time to wait on the police to protect them, for they were considered to be more interested in protecting themselves. There was an extreme minority view that the community would be better off in withstanding the frequent attacks from outside if there were no local police in the community. In addition, the local police were sometimes regarded as the enemy of the residents. This attitude towards the police was more common among the young men who concurred that they considered themselves more at risk because of the presence of the local police in the community.

There was reference to former years when police officers were well known and very responsive, but only the administrators of some institutions in the area spoke favourably of the local police. During the period of the study, no foot patrols by the local police were observed in the community, although the 'Rat Patrol' was seen on several occasions. The residents in general appreciated the presence of the 'Rat Patrols' which they felt helped to keep out the aggressors as well as local 'bad men', thereby making the streets safer. But residents were very displeased with the reaction of police and military units whenever incidents of violence occurred in Hannah Town. They complain that although the aggressors generally come from outside, the response units would come into Hannah Town and harass the youths there, while the attackers are unmolested. Everybody in the groups surveyed were of the view that the residents of the community were living in constant fear and were therefore in dire need of protection.

Despite poor community-police relations, there was still no general commitment among residents to cooperate in order to apprehend criminals resident in the community. Some said it depended on the identity of the 'criminal', meaning that some 'deviants' would be disciplined while others would go free. There was general agreement that the community leader was involved in organizing the youths to help protect the community, but residents generally maintained that there was no one don in the community any longer. The majority were of the view that security was an individual responsibility. Those who objected to that view maintained that the youths helping to withstand attacks were acting beyond individual responsibility.

From the police viewpoint, a hopeless picture was painted of the community. It was said that the community did not assist the police in any way. It was remarked that they "see nothing and hear nothing . . . they do not display a caring spirit towards each other . . . their attitude is as if they hate themselves". The sergeant in charge of the local station related his own efforts to start a police youth club in the area. The response from some of the youths, according to him, was that "youth club can't eat" and that what they needed was "guns to look food". It was alleged by some youth that the last attempt to get a police youth club off the ground failed because of the inconsistency of the police in showing up for meetings.

When asked about the activity of the local police in the community very little information was provided. The policemen do not really try to become a part of the community. The subofficer related the difficulty he had in keeping his staff motivated to come out to work. During visits to the community and the police station, only once was a uniformed officer observed. One interviewee related that when a new officer came to the station he would be given a familiarization walk around the community and that would be about the only time that he would be seen moving about in the community. In light of this, residents have had recourse to both conventional and unconventional measures to protect themselves from criminal attack.

Conventional and unconventional protective measures in Hannah Town

The conventional methods of protection employed by the community included: perimeter walls, burglar bars and security lights. There were several premises with perimeter walls around them, but this was more common in the newer buildings. The premises housing the older structures had zinc (galvanize) fences. A number of the newer properties, however, were still without any form of fencing. The majority of the structures were of very strong concrete construction although some bore the original doors which appeared weak.

The majority of the houses were fitted with burglar bars. Nobody in the community had guard dogs although there were many 'mongrels' in the community. Most of the houses would have several locks and bolts installed on their doors to enhance security.

The use of electric alarm systems and security guards was unheard of, and no one knew of any household which attempted to set any sort of contraption in their yards. Although a telephone service was not common, hardly anyone would think of calling the police if any suspicious activities were seen in the community. The use of two way radios as a means of calling for help was also unheard of in the community.

Several persons were said to keep on security lights, but it was held that the majority of residents did not do this. Any valuables or large sums of money would normally be safely secured either informally (at home or with a friend in a nearby community) or placed in a bank.

Unconventional measures included knives, icepicks, machetes, acid, firearms, establishing ties with government security forces or 'bad men' and keeping vigils. Nearly everyone in the community travelled with a knife or ice pick for their own protection. In relation to acid, however, a significant number of respondents felt that this was an uncommon practice, although it was carried on by several persons. There was a majority view that nearly all households would always have someone at home to keep an eye. There were some young women, however, who did not consider keeping an eye the purpose for being at home. Nearly everyone was believed to sleep with some implement nearby for protection, the commonest being a knife or machete. There was great reluctance by residents to comment on the prevalence of firearms. In this regard, two groups offered no answer while one group did not know, and those who ventured to comment were divided in their views. For instance, while children believed that nearly everyone possessed a fireman, some believed that hardly anyone did.

The idea of befriending a member of the police force or the Jamaica Defence Force as a means of additional protection was hardly practised by anyone. It was more likely for associations with security personnel to be with soldiers than with policemen. On the other hand, it was felt that the majority of residents would seek to be friendly with persons regarded as 'bad men' because of the protection this afforded.

Residents were generally not comfortable with regarding the political area leader as a don, and there was also some vacillation in expressing how the community regarded him. The dominant perception was that only a few persons would try to keep a good rapport with the area leader.

There are times when the threat against the community increases, and on these occasions the area is considered to be 'running hot'. Whether or not persons leave the community depends on why the area is considered 'hot'. Women would tend to sleep out when opposing factions threaten the area, while the young men would remain to fight. On the other hand, if the area 'runs hot' because of raids by the police, the women would remain in the area while the young males would tend to leave the community to sleep out. Children were more frequently sent out than women. The residents were of the view that the majority of the young men especially took turns to stay awake at night to maintain vigilance.

While persons passing through the community were not paid any particular attention, strangers would neither be avoided nor isolated. One key informant disclosed that a system of lookouts was maintained from various corners, manned by both men and women. They use hand signals to warn of the approach of police patrols which give armed youths early notice to conceal weapons or avoid detection. If attackers are spotted then an alarm is shouted and the defenceless women and children would leave the streets.

Craig Town

This is a small community within the larger boundaries of the more well known Jones Town. The community is a part of the political constituency of Southern St Andrew and falls within the highly volatile Kingston Western Police Division. The community has managed to escape the scrutiny of the media and so very little information about the community has come to public attention. The Statistical Institute did not regard Craig Town as a special area, but the residents of Craig Town were certain about their identity. The boundaries of the community were said to be Baker Street unto Madden Street, Bryne Street taking in Clarence Road and down to Asquith Street.

The community was said to have more in common with a rural community than a city community in terms of the relations between the residents. It is believed that the majority of its residents were born in the community and most of the families were related in some way. There were few newcomers in the community, and these were the ones said to be causing trouble.

Craig Town falls within a 'political garrison' constituency of the PNP. The community was neglected by the PNP when it formed the government in the 1970s and again, following the party's return to power in 1989.

The community has not benefited from improvements in the housing stock and other social amenities that the other loyal communities have received. Social services were nearly all obtained from other communities. As a result, the community has lost confidence in its political representatives and interest in politics. As a further consequence, the community has developed a sense of autonomy and has been removing itself from the level of political subordination of other areas and leaders in the 'garrison'.

In relation to social activities, there is a community centre which was rebuilt by the community youth club after the original centre constructed in the 1970s had been vandalized and destroyed. The youth club is the chief institution in the community providing limited family life education, organized sport, summer camp projects for the children and a meeting place for the community. In addition, the youth in Craig Town came together in 1989 to form the Craig Town Youth Organization, which survives to this day. One of its major annual projects is a musical promotion staged in the community called a 'Ghetto Splash', which has assumed international proportions and has drawn very large attendances. This event has been staged successfully for six years in succession and has always been incident free. Unfortunately, the youth knew very little of the opportunities for skills training offered by the Mel Nathan Institute in neighbouring Hannah Town. Moreover, they were not very enthusiastic about going into Hannah Town as they feared for their safety.

There are several churches on the borders of the community but, except for the Salvation Army which runs a lunch programme for needy children, the churches do not have much of an impact or influence on the community.

In respect of the cohesiveness of the community, no real social divisions were described and none were observed. Everyone knew each other and there was no segregation based on status or economic position. Apart from the youth club, the sense of communal solidarity was evidenced in the informal assistance provided to the unemployed and the provision of gifts to the needy. Some of the youths, however, were said to be disrespectful of their seniors who attempted to teach them. Ironically, the youth club also served as an agency to transmit values to youths themselves.

As regards its leadership, one person was unhesitatingly identified as the leader of the community. This was a young working woman who grew up in the community. The police responsible for the area could not say if there was a local leader for the community at the time, although it was the norm that there should be one. The person whom the police expected to emerge as leader was more of the 'Top Ranking' stereotype. At the time of the study, the closest person to a 'Top Ranking' leader had been in police custody for some time. The leadership attributes deemed important by residents included the ability to get things done, to show empathy and problem-solving skills whether that person resided in the community or not.

Intercommunity relations

Craig Town has been having conflicts with some of its neighbours, especially since 1989, notwithstanding the fact that they have a common political allegiance. It is said that residents from Craig Town would feel threatened by residents of Hannah Town, Jones Town and Torrington Villa who were said to be untamable. Peace initiatives did not last for long. The standoff with Hannah Town was attributed to the fact that a leading bad man from Hannah Town had been killed within the borders of Craig Town at the start of 1994. However, the community was not considered to be at constant odds with their neighbours.

Police and community relations

Both the police and the community generally held dim views of each other with respect to the issue of crime. The police were constrained in performing their function by certain infrastructural deficiencies, their own fears and attitudes.

Interestingly, there is no police post in the immediate community. The nearby Admiral Town Police Station services the area. The police said they did not have any officer specially assigned to service the community, although the police force was said to be moving in this direction. They described Craig Town as a dangerous place and were of the view that officers walking through could become easy targets for gunmen. No police officer from the station was resident in the community although policemen who were not assigned to the Admiral Town station would visit. The community was said to have a number of resident soldiers.

The police indicated that they tried to be responsive to the needs of the community but were hampered by the lack of transportation, and the fact that policemen were apprehensive about going to certain areas at night.

The residents viewed the police as ineffective and stated that they chose to respond more readily in cases of domestic disputes than for more serious offences. Residents would like to see a more responsive police service but not necessarily more police.

The police have been invited to functions and private affairs in the community but they admit a reluctance to going into the community alone. They were of the view that a strong criminal element in the community resented their presence. They felt that the majority of the law abiding residents are afraid to be associated with the police lest they be branded as informers. This contradicted the view of the residents who held that they cooperated with the police in identifying and prosecuting criminals. They also believed that community policing would take a long time to reach Craig Town because of the attitude of the police, who lacked any attachment to the community.

Notwithstanding their claimed cooperation with the police, both residents and the police concurred that locals were afraid to report major crimes to the police. Victims of lesser offences such as robberies did make complaints.

As regards the incidence of police brutality, while there was no recent occurrence of such, there were complaints of threats made by a 'rat patrol' in their attempt to get people off the streets by nightfall. In addition, it was felt that the approach of some security personnel may cause them to be regarded as oppressors.

The majority of residents strongly agreed that there was a heavy dependence on joint patrols by the military and the police in the area to keep crimes down. Some dissenters were of the view that the presence of these patrols posed a threat to the residents.

While it was generally felt that residents were not interested in cooperating with each other to apprehend and deal with criminals themselves, there were both individualistic and collective tendencies within the community towards dealing with crime, although the former was more dominant. The nature of the approach was a function of both the nature of the crime and the identity of the individual or the victim. For instance, a more community oriented response would occur in the case of murder or when someone prominent was attacked, which could prove fatal to the offender. In such instances, it was the youth on the 'block' who played the major role in organizing retaliatory action. In addition, the police felt that the community members protected themselves from outsiders, and that strangers to the community would be harassed, robbed or even killed in most instances. However, persons closer to the community made a distinction between those visitors who had a legitimate, positive purpose and those who could not state their purpose. The treatment of visitors was also said to depend on who the visitor knew in the community. The consensus was that total strangers with no legitimate purpose or connections were in danger. Generally speaking, when all was calm individuals took responsibility for their own security.

There was strong disagreement over the idea of a don and his associates providing security for the community. The claim was that the days of donmanship over the community were over and would not return. Residents expressed fear because of what they said was occurring around them in neighbouring areas which could spill over into Craig Town. The feelings of fear with residing in the community, however, were not unanimous.

Conventional and unconventional protective measures in Craig Town

Some of the conventional measures employed in varying degrees in Craig Town were: walls, burglar bars, locks and bolts and common dogs. Very few households had their premises secured with high walls and padlocked gates. Although a few premises did have low perimeter walls, the main sort of perimeter used was zinc fencing. There were only a few firm concrete structures. From what was described and observed, the housing stock was in dire need of upgrading. The use of burglar bars was very uncommon, although residents expressed the feeling that the absence of burglar bars was due more to cost than to any desire not to have them. Hardly any of the households had installed multiple locks and bolts on their doors. Again, some expressed the view that it was a matter of cost. One popular resident stated that no locks were used on her door at all; the door was just drawn up at nights and furniture used to reinforce it.

No one knew of any household that kept guard dogs, although there were said to be many common dogs which helped to keep watch. Several security measures which were becoming popular in communities outside inner-city areas were unheard of in Craig Town. There was no employment of security guards, no electronic alarm systems, no use of security lights, and no contraptions to entrap or deter prowlers. There was no telephone service to the community, thus this means of alerting the police or neighbours of suspicious activities was not available to residents. Nearly everyone was believed to put away valuables. This was considered to be more a case of hiding valuables since there were no real physical means of locking things away. There was varied opinion on the question of securing large sums of money; while some held that it was taken to the bank, others held that it was kept at home.

In relation to unconventional measures, these included knives, ice picks, acid and firearms. Residents were of the view that nearly everyone in the community travelled with some implement to protect themselves, the chief one being a knife or ice pick. Acid was said to be carried by several women but this was not a very common practice. Firearms were also kept by several persons although it was illegal to do so. In nearly all households, persons slept with a knife or a machete nearby.

Nearly all residents in the community were said to have someone keeping an eye either at home or nearby. The majority of residents were hostile to informers since these were associated with the passage of information to the police. Consequently, they were discouraged from the community.

The idea of befriending a member of the police force or of the military as a means of enhancing one's personal security was not considered to be very popular. Several persons were said to be friendly with police personnel who were not assigned to the local station. There was believed to be a greater tendency to befriend soldiers than policemen. There were differing views about friendship with so called bad men. Some of the young men held the view that those regarded as 'bad men' were 'good men' to have around because they were more helpful than the police. However, there were significant numbers who felt that no one would befriend 'bad men'.

Scarcely anyone would seek to avoid strangers although strangers were not very common in the community. Most persons in the community were said to stay up and on the streets late at nights even when the area was 'running hot'. When the area is said 'to run hot', several persons, mainly women, would leave the community. The young men, however, would remain in the area.

The community was not hostile to the idea of mob beatings of criminals who were caught but this method was not unanimously supported.

Hannah Town and Craig Town Compared

Both communities displayed several similarities and differences with respect to certain contextual factors, and in their attitude towards protection and the practical measures they employed. These differences and similarities will be examined to determine if they may help to explain the variation in levels of vulnerability to major crimes experienced.

There were marked differences in the level of cohesiveness, spirit of unity and sense of community between the two areas. The existence of a common enemy to Hannah Town was not sufficient to unite the community. There was a great deal of mistrust and suspicion among Hannah Town residents. There was a much deeper sense of community and demonstration of solidarity in evidence in Craig Town, a community which had begun to chart a course to find solutions and to advance the interests of its own members after years of neglect.

The issue of the communities' relationship with neighbouring communities stood out as important. In the case of Hannah Town the community had no strong friendly relations with any of its neighbours. Those to the west were political rivals and long standing enemies. Craig Town, on the other hand, had neighbours of the same political persuasion. Although their relations were not very harmonious, it was considered more as having a 'standoff' than as having enemies.

The communities varied in their image and reputation. Hannah Town houses some facilities that were very promising which could make it the envy of a poorer community. However it had a public image of being a very unsafe place to live. Its chief enemy had the reputation of being a 'garrison', while Hannah Town was regarded as an easy target.

Craig Town, on the other hand, had no special features that would make it a desirable place to live, except for its low crime rate which was not well known. Its residents were evidently poorer in traditional resources. But Craig Town was part of a defended 'garrison', one which was hostile to its enemies and aimless strangers. Its neighbours were more vulnerable than it was.

There were significant differences in the character of the local leadership in each community. In the case of Hannah Town the leader came through the political process and was still seen as an instrument of the political party. Hannah Town was divided over support for its leader, a businessman, whose reputation has been tarnished and whose integrity has been brought into question. On the contrary, the community leader in Craig Town was a woman who still enjoyed the support of the majority. She emerged from among the people and was officially recognized because of her enthusiasm and interest in the development of the community. She was not regarded as a 'henchman' of the political directorate and she was able to influence a wide cross section of the community.

Control of access to the communities also showed significant differences. Hannah Town, being more open to outsiders because of the facilities which were housed there, allowed visitors to pass much more freely than Craig Town, where strangers were more likely to be questioned and faced a greater risk of harassment.

In respect of the similarities, many were evident in the protective/security methods adopted by both communities, yet the results were vastly different. Both communities had indigenous, active, informal systems for local defence against external threats. This involved alerting the community to the presence of persons (civil or police) who could pose a threat, and actually engaging armed intruders in gun fights. The traditional physical measures such as burglar bars, locks and bolts, security lights and secure buildings were more common in Hannah Town than in Craig Town.

Their defences against the internal threat were in both cases far less active, tending to resort to the passive forms of social control. This laxity towards the internal threat worked to the detriment of Hannah Town because of the lack of solidarity and cohesion which are necessary to give strength to the passive means of control. Both communities had gone beyond the provisions of the Neighbourhood Watch programme in participating in their own protection, except that they withheld information from the police.

Both communities were very dissatisfied with the attitude of the local police, their provision of security for the residents and with the quality of the service they were receiving. Hannah Town claimed to be in a worse position because of the presence of the local police. Craig Town did not have a local station in its environs and did not have any special officers specifically to service their needs. Police-community relations were poor in both cases, but in the case of Craig Town the police expressed fears about working in the community because of some of the residents. In the case of Hannah Town, the residents spoke of the fear of the police because of the threat from Hannah Town's enemies.

In the case of Hannah Town, intervention by the local police was a 'violater' rather than a 'satisfier' as it curtailed the ability of the locals to protect themselves. The intervention by special police squads could be regarded as a 'pseudosatisfier', giving a false sense of security, because the external threat would only be reduced temporarily while special squads were present, but then increased as soon as they left. For these reasons the greater presence of the police in Hannah Town did not satisfice for community protection. Local police interventions were rare in Craig Town. Interventions by special police were also frequent and were beginning to violate the people for idleness and recreation which was often to be found on the streets.

Both Hannah Town and Craig Town had grown hostile to the idea of a 'one don rule'. In this regard, both communities are undergoing a transition, with Craig Town at a more advanced stage. In Hannah Town, the political area leader still maintained some of the characteristics of a don, but his influence is diminishing. The absence of an alternative indigenous community group in Hannah Town, allowing for community expression and participation (as there is in the Craig Town Youth Organization) may retard the transitional process. It was important in both communities to have someone who could organize a community defence, but neither community desired a 'ruler'.

The ethical code bore some similarities in both communities. Persons who would normally be regarded as deviants by the police were sometimes viewed in a positive light in the community. Some groups of residents made a distinction between the common criminals or 'wicked men' and those who made positive contributions to the well-being of the community. The communities were not united in their support for these elements, however, and seemed to accept the 'bad men' out of expediency.

Implications of Findings

The informal means of community protection being applied in the areas of study were sometimes found to be 'violaters' or 'inhibitors' to the satisfaction of other basic needs, which were just as important to human development, as the need for protection. This renders such practices unsustainable. Protection is provided but at a high social cost, that of the retardation of human development.

The indications are that residents of the communities under study have begun to recognize the limitations of their protective strategies and that a process of reform was underway from within. The diminishing role of the Top Ranking and the don man system of control should be interpreted in this light. Faced with real threats to their survival and a dire need for protection which was not being met by the police, the people had taken the next best option. They appeared to be moving towards a new reality, a new form of social organization, but one in which they retain their stake in providing their own defence. They insist that a distinction be made between those persons who have helped to keep the communities safe from intruders, from those really 'bad men' who are themselves a threat to the safety of residents.

They wish for some legitimacy (perhaps similar to that granted under the Home Guard) to be accorded to the former category, so they may be removed from the police target list. If the residents were to be convinced that the police were truly concerned about protecting them and would afford them the backing or 'backitive' of the law, then the residents would move swiftly to expose the rogues residing among them.

If the state and nongovernmental bodies are to reap positive results from their interventions to bring peace, stability and human development to the inner-city, then they must take account of this trend detected in Hannah Town and Craig Town. Furthermore, they should understand the importance of the factors identified here as being crucial for the success of protective security measures, namely:

1. The reputation of the community and that of its immediate neighbours.
2. The quality of the local leadership coupled with the level of cohesiveness and solidarity amongst members of the community.
3. Control of access to the community.

These factors were more important than the physical protective measures and the established law of the land in providing a secure environment for the residents in the areas of study. Policymakers would be well advised to seek out credible means of influencing these factors, beginning with an identification of the barriers which prevent or curtail the ability of a community to act.

The reputation of being a defended area which comes with being part of a 'garrison' was a useful deterrent to external threats. In dismantling a 'garrison' a void or a weakness in a community's passive defence will be created. It is a void that the current concept of Neighbourhood Watch is unlikely to fill, for as our study has shown, inner-city communities have already gone past the concept of a watch. However, the police, in cooperation with a legitimate civil defence group, could cause a retention of the reputation of a defended area.

Whatever the grouping that emerges, it should have a broader focus than just protection. It was found that in both communities, protective measures tended to be individualistic during periods of calm. What is needed is more along the concept of a community council, in which civil defence is just one of the tasks. The desirable arrangement would be for a democratic form of organization based on solidarity and collective effort, since it is this aspect of community that best counters the internal threat.

The cohesiveness and solidarity within the community is closely linked with the quality of the local leadership. More important than physical security (fences, walls, locks etc.), social amenities, a stock of firearms, or financial resources, is a strong community spirit. The absence of a strong community spirit was an obvious barrier to the mobilization of community resources.

Residents are seeking an alternative to the local political party group as the organ through which they participate in the decisions that affect their lives. Whether the party group will reform itself before the transitional process that is underway in both Craig Town and Hannah Town dismisses it as irrelevant, will depend on the state of reform in the political parties. The people are clear, however, about the type of leadership they want. As was found in the case of Craig Town, this quality of leadership is emerging. The potential may also be found in Hannah Town if only the people could get 'backitive'.

External intervention in communities should aim to contribute to the strengthening of the forces of cohesion and avert any further splintering of the community. Interventions are necessary especially to strengthen linkages between 'corner groups' that are now a feature of many inner-city communities. The other critical factor is the control of access to communities. The idea should not be to lock out outsiders, but to select those who enter and those who are turned away. The reputation of a community contributes in this regard, but it falls short in that persons who would bring trade to these areas are also inadvertently barred because of their own fears.

In considering how access should be controlled it must be recognized that the presence of a smartly attired officer of the law does much to reduce fears and uncertainty about the safety of the average citizen. At the same time, a warning signal is sent to the rogue element of society to stay away. It is essential that foot patrols of uniformed law officers return to the inner-city.

This may be attempted under the concept of community policing. For the concept to work, however, there has to be a great change in the attitude of the police towards the residents of the inner-city. This is unlikely with the policemen currently servicing local stations. The relationship between these local policemen and residents cannot be remedied because the animosity and mutual distrust goes deep. A new corps of community policemen will be required for inner-city areas, but it must be a corps of policemen who will seek to meet the priority needs of protection of the community.

Notes

1. Police crime data are not aggregated below the level of parish, except for Kingston and St Andrew, where data are aggregated at divisional level. It is also to be noted that boundaries of police divisions do not correspond with electoral boundaries.
2. Most inner-city areas fall within a belt of the Kingston Metropolitan Region that general insurance companies consider as unsuitable for insurance risk.
3. Stone argued that the socialist ideology of the 1970s legitimized the Robin Hood philosophy leading to an increase in violent crimes against the middle class and the rich. See *Daily Gleaner*, 2 November 1987.
4. The word don is used in the Jamaican vernacular to denote a 'big man' or someone who, in the eyes of the community, is somehow more 'powerful' than the others. This power might derive from unmatched wealth, contacts, or firepower.

6

Urban Bias and Livelihood Strategies in Grenada

David M. Franklyn

Introduction

This study examines the extent to which rural to urban migration and the livelihood strategies which rural migrants to the capital adopt are consequences of spatial polarization in the structure of the Grenadian economy and 'urban bias' in the development process. Rather than scrutinize any existing hypotheses, it analyses aggregate data and the findings of field research and identifies trends that might inform policy interventions.

A spatially polarized economic structure refers to the concentration of market economic activities in the capital, usually the only truly urban centre of small island states like Grenada. This is contrasted with production of predominantly primary agricultural raw material for export and subsistence-oriented economic activity in the rural areas (Newels, et al. 1990). O'Conner (1989) refers to it as "uneven development", which he defines in political and sociological terms as the historically produced, uneven, spatial distribution of, inter alia, industry, banking, commerce, wealth, consumption, labour relations, and political configurations. Most of these are concentrated in urban areas with a corresponding neglect of the rural areas.

'Urban bias' is defined as a bias in the development process against the rural areas, resulting in a situation in which power, decision making and industry are concentrated in the urban centre while the rural areas remain relatively powerless, poor and underdeveloped (Lipton 1977, 1993; Bates 1981, 1993). In other words, the rural economy remains relatively backward while the urban economy is advanced and 'modern'.

In the context of this study, the urban area is defined as the locus or main centre of integration of the local economy with the world economy. Through the urban centre the forces of international integration are transmitted to the rural areas. The dominant functions of the urban area are (a) the processing and marketing of agricultural products from the rural area; (b) the provision of tourism (not necessarily in all cases but certainly in Grenada) and other services; (c) capital formation and finance; and (d) central government administration (Newels, et al. 1990; Lipton 1977, 1993). The rural area is defined in terms of its functional relationship to the urban area. It is peripheral to the urban centre. Its economy is based predominantly on the production of primary agricultural commodities for export, cash crop, and subsistence-oriented economic activity. Its economy functions to (a) supply primary, particularly agricultural products to urban distributors; (b) purchase manufactured goods produced or imported by the urban area; (c) feed the urban centre; and (d) produce an 'invisible surplus' of savings and taxes (Newels, et al. 1990; Lipton, 1977; Bates 1981).

Issues of space and people's ability to make choices are important to human development and development planning. As Porter (1984) has pointed out, in developing countries national economic planning units tend to focus attention on the macroeconomic rather than the spatial, social and equity aspects of development planning. Nevertheless, the research which informs this paper is predicated on the view that the issue of space in relation to economic development and livelihood strategies is crucial to national development. The spatial structure of the economy and 'urban bias' in the development process may affect people's choices (Lipton 1977, 1981; Bates 1981, 1993). Indeed, the first UNDP *Human Development Report* (HDR) put choice at the centre of development objectives and defined development as "a process of enlarging people's choices". The Haq Committee (1990:1) argued that:

[The] most critical of these wide-ranging choices are to live a long and healthy life, to be educated and to have access to resources needed for a decent standard of living.

Additional choices include political freedom, guaranteed human rights and personal self respect.

Ability to make choices influences to a great extent people's decision to migrate and squat, as well as the livelihood strategies they adopt. Chambers and Conway (1992) defined a livelihood, in its simplest sense, as a means of gaining a living. A livelihood, they argue, provides the support for the enhancement and exercise of capabilities. Capabilities are an end, but they are also a means to the extent that it enables a livelihood to be gained (Chambers and Conray 1992). Livelihood activities are determined by the social, economic and ecological environment in which individuals find themselves. Those who are better off usually have a wider choice than those who are worse off (Chambers and Conway 1992; Chambers 1989.

Against this backdrop, this study hopes to make a contribution to the literature on rural/urban development and the formulation of policies to address the problems examined.

Background to the Study

Grenada is located in the southern Caribbean. Together with its dependencies of Carriacou and Petit Martinique, it has a population of approximately 95,950 (1991 Census Report) and a land area of 345 sq. km (1991 Census Report). The population is largely rural. It is distributed among the six parishes and the dependency of Carriacou as follows: St Patrick's, 10.7 percent; St Andrew's, 24.6 percent; St John's, 9.2 percent; St Mark's, 4.1 percent; St David's, 11.6 percent; Carriacou, 6 percent; the capital, St George's, 4.9 percent and the rest of the parish of St George, 28.9 percent. The rural parishes and Carriacou account for over 66 percent of the total population (1991 Census Report). Up to 1990 only 8 percent of Grenada's population was considered urban (Armstrong 1990).

Economic structure

The Grenadian economy exhibits features which suggest a spatially polarized structure: the concentration of major industries and market economic activity in the capital, the predominance of primary agricultural commodities for export, and cash crop and subsistence oriented activity in the rural areas (Newels, et al. 1990). This polarization is historically produced.

The colonial economy concentrated largely on the export of primary agricultural production, namely cocoa, nutmeg and bananas (Persaud 1985). This has remained the nature of the rural economy, complemented by some cash crops and subsistence oriented economic activities.

Traditionally, most of these export crops were – and to a certain extent are – still grown on large estates (Brierley 1992). Nevertheless, a substantial contribution to the volume exported was and is made by Grenada's small farmers. Small farmers did not only provide employment for themselves; they created employment for their families and others as well. But land reform policies in Grenada failed to make more land accessible to the rural masses and diversify the rural economy (Pool 1989; Brierley 1992). During the 1940s approximately 52 percent of Grenada's farmlands were devoted to large estates, ranging in size from 40 to 486 hectares (*Grenada Handbook* 1946).

Colonial Governments attempted to correct the situation with the peasant land settlement schemes of 1903, 1946, 1949 and the period 1956 to 1963. As Brierley (1992) has noted, these schemes played only a minimal role in reducing the size or number of estates between 1946 and 1968, and most of the lands distributed were marginal and inaccessible. Under Eric Gairy's Land for the Landless programmes granted by the Land Settlement Development Act (1969), many large estates were appropriated but only 20.2 percent or 430 hectares of the 45 acquisitions totalling 2128 hectares were actually divested to the landless. The remaining acquisitions remained either idle or fragmented into sizes which could not develop production patterns that could make use of economies of scale (Brierley 1992). The People's Revolutionary Government's (1979–83) attempts to restructure the rural economy through agrarian reform and the creation of state farms failed, nevertheless, to put private ownership into the hands of the rural peasantry, reform the existing marketing structures for nutmeg, cocoa and bananas, and diversify the rural economy (Pool 1989; Brierley 1992).

The colonial economy, as Frank (1969) and others have pointed out, was structured to meet the market demands of the metropolis, thus encouraging production formation in a dynamic relationship of underdevelopment. In this way, agricultural commodities were produced for export to the metropolis through the chief port, while its manufactures and most of its food were imported from the metropolis. This kind of structure has meant that conditions on the international market adversely affected the economy in general and the rural economy in particular, whose economic base is the production of primary agricultural commodities for export to metropolitan markets. Thus, between 1979 and 1981 the rural economy finally collapsed due to a fall in commodity prices on the world market. The fall in world cocoa prices of 45 percent was accompanied by a glut of nutmeg on the world market. This was compounded by the destruction of 40 percent of the banana crop, 27 percent of nutmeg, and 19 percent of cocoa production by hurricane in 1979, and a storm which destroyed 40 percent of the island's banana stems in 1981 (Brierley 1992). Grenada's agriculture has not recovered since. Indeed, *The Grenada Annual Economic Report* (1993) noted that in real terms agriculture declined and contributed only 13 percent to GDP for that year, continuing a trend which began since 1988.

In the colonial era the urban economy was based largely on commerce. The urban area was also the chief port and administrative centre. Most importantly, it served as a centre for collecting and storing export commodities and distributing imported manufactures. It did not attract large populations (Clarke 1983). Whereas the economy of the rural areas was dominated by a plantocracy and agricultural commodities for export, that of the chief port was dominated by a merchant class, commerce and the import/export trade (Clarke 1983). Traditionally, the rural area was dependent on the urban area and its infrastructure for its imports and the export of its agricultural goods, but the rural economy formed the basis of the national economy and supported the urban economy. With the collapse of the rural economic base, however, and the increasing importance of tourism and manufacturing – both concentrated in and around the capital – a rural-urban shift occurred. It is through this shift that an 'urban bias' in the development process became apparent.

Urban Bias

'Urban bias' in Grenada is largely historically produced. In large measure, it is a result of the polarized nature of the colonial economy and the increasing dependence on imports, tourism and manufacturing all concentrated around the capital, which also contains the chief port and the best infrastructure. It is also related to power and class interests.

The urban based local bourgeoisie which replaced the expatriate planter and merchant class following the collapse of the estate system and the decolonization process that started in the 1950s, established links with international finance capital to become junior partners in relations of trade with the latter (Persaud 1985). The result of this partnership has been the perpetuation of economic structures and functions similar to those that had been established in the colonial era. The local urban based commercial class continued to represent, as agents, the interests of overseas manufacturers, and to engage in import/export trade rather than manufacturing and agricultural diversification. In many respects economic activity is structurally linked to the metropolitan economies to facilitate their interests and demands rather than those of the local economy.

It was, however, with the development of tourism that the 'urban bias' became more evident. Tourism is controlled by an urban entrepreneurial class with little or no interests, vested or otherwise, in rural development. Tourism was introduced in Grenada in the 1950s and by the 1970s its impact on class differentiation and the spatially polarized structure of the economy became increasingly apparent. By 1971, a local urban based capitalist class owned 67 percent or ten of the 15 hotels on the island and was playing an important role in services associated with tourism (Persaud 1985). The *Grenada Annual Economic Report* (1993) suggests that tourism and the hotel industry and manufacturing are increasingly becoming the main employers, due to the steady decline in the fortunes of agriculture. It is estimated that 98 percent of tourism and manufacturing and other job-creating economic activities are concentrated in the south in and around St George's. An official at the Grenada Industrial Development Corporation explained this development as follows:

The best infrastructure is within the parish of St George's, in and around the capital – the main port, the international airport, the industrial park, the best roads, the most developed beaches. *Most of these industries, including the hotel industry, do not use local raw materials.* They must therefore locate close to air and sea ports, both in the south, through which the imports upon which they so heavily depend come.

Table 6.1 on page 186 illustrates the spatial distribution of manufacturing and guest houses among the parishes – St George's (S/G), St Patrick's (S/P), St Andrew's (S/A), St David's (S/D), St John's (S/J), St Mark's (S/M) and Carriacou (C).

These data are a graphic illustration of the uneven distribution of industries and tourism in Grenada. More than 50 percent of all industries are concentrated in the parish of St George, which strongly suggests the existence of bias toward the capital in the current development process.

Table 6.1 Percentage Manufacturing Industries and Guest Houses Operating under Concession by Parish

	Parishes (%)						
Industries	S/G	S/P	S/A	S/D	S/J	S/M	C
Garments	75	8	8	-	-	-	8
Handicraft	40	20	-	-	20	-	-
Construction	50	17	17	-	8	8	-
Furniture	64	27	9	-	-	-	-
Food/Beverages	47	5	15	11	11	-	11
Ag-processing	67	-	-	17	8	-	8
Light industries	78	27	-	4	4	7	-
Boat building	50	-	-	-	-	-	50
Guest houses	84	-	2	-	5	-	9

Source: Computed from a listing of manufacturing companies and guest houses operating under government concession made available by the Industrial Development Corporation, St George's.

Rural to Urban Migration and Urban Squatting

The focus of rural to urban migration is the capital, St George's. This is precisely because of the historically produced polarized structure of the economy and the consequential 'urban bias' discussed above. The collapse of the rural economy combined with the failure to diversify the rural economic base and implement sustainable and effective land reform policies by successive regimes left rural people with little choice but to migrate overseas and to the capital in search of jobs and other opportunities. This situation is illustrated by the significant unemployment differences that exist between rural parishes and the capital. All rural parishes except St Johns, perhaps because of fishing, recorded unemployment rates above the official national level of 16.7 percent in 1993 up from 14.4 percent in 1991. This is illustrated in Table 6.2 on page 187. The figures for the previous years were not available, but an official at the Central Statistical Department noted that it is the continuation of a trend which began with the collapse of the rural economy.

Table 6.2   Unemployment Rates, by Sex and Parish in the Week before
the Census, 1991

Parish	Total	Male	Female
		Unemployment Rate	
St George's (Town)	8.4	9.1	7.6
St George's (Rest)	10.6	11.5	9.7
St John's	9.7	11.1	8.3
St Mark's	27.4	26.3	28.5
St Patrick's	19.9	18.1	21.7
St Andrew's	17.3	17.7	16.9
St David's	14.7	16.2	13.2
Carriacou	8.0	8.6	7.3

Source: 1991 *Census Report*

The relatively recent phenomenon of the incidence of suburban squatting is evident in Table 6.3 below, which compares types of tenure between 1981 and 1991. The 1991 *Census Report* suggests that the incidence of squatting moved from zero percent in 1970 to 0.1 percent in 1981 to 0.3 percent in 1991. Table 6.3 shows that by comparison, squatting was, up to the last census, very unpopular as a form of tenure.

Possibly because of rural to urban migration, the parish of St George's registered a substantial increase of 8.9 percent while that of the rural parishes of St Patrick's and St Mark's fell by 0.1 percent and 2.7 percent,

Table 6.3   Households, by Type of Ownership

Type of Ownership	1981	1991
Owned	74.1	78.7
Squatted	0.1	0.3
Priv-Rented	13.4	12.9
Gov't-Rented	0.2	0.5
Leased	1.0	0.4
Free-Rent	9.1	5.2
Other	1.2	1.4
Not stated	0.9	0.6

Source: 1991 Census Report

respectively (1991 Census Summary Report). St George's parish itself, together with the town, contains 34 percent of the national population (the town, 5 percent; the parish, 29 percent and growing). A picture emerges in which the distribution of the population has taken a fairly polarized pattern. It represents what Rojas (1989) identified as two types of historically produced settlements – the capital and the small farming communities. Grenada has one settlement, the capital St George's, with over 40,000 inhabitants and most of the others with populations less than 2,500 (Armstrong 1990). *The Overview Report on Human Settlement in the OECS*, (Armstrong 1990), noted that although this may not be high by international standards, the potential and perhaps rapid growth must be considered against the physical limitations of the capital. Expansion of the town of St George's itself is restricted by its hilly topography, which raises further infrastructural development costs. As a result, expansion is toward the south in the direction of the international airport, the main export processing industrial areas and the hotel zone.

Review of Literature and Theoretical Framework

Space and development

Few studies have been done on the relationship between space and development. This is presumably because the geography of development has not yet begun to preoccupy economists. Porter (1984) looked at spatial perceptions and public involvement in Third World urban planning, using the example of Barbados. His argument centred around the assumption that individual and group perceptions of and people's relative preferences for different regions of the national space is valuable to development planning.

In the same vein Mabogunje (1989) points out that development is a creator and organizer of space and argues that the motive forces of development projects are political and economic. Moreover, space represents within itself relationships that arise out of the economic, political, social, cultural and other values that people associate with particular locations. In a localized Grenada situation, the capital is the space in which the most powerful political and socioeconomic decision makers reside and meet. It is the commercial and manufacturing as well as tourism centre; it contains the central government bureaucracy, is the seat of government and contains the symbols of power and everything else that expresses and affirms national identity. It is the chief entreport; it is the space in which opportunities for higher education are concentrated and it contains the arena for national cultural and recreational events (Mabogunje 1989). The capital is also the contact point between the nation state and the world economic market, international communications and international financial networks.

The market value and social importance of physical and economic space in the capital is, therefore, very much higher than space in the rural areas. Its power is limited and it must depend on the centre for political decisions pertaining to its economic development, resource allocation, management of its environment, and distribution of the benefits of economic growth to its inhabitants. Thus, the perception and social and economic evaluation of differential space (centre/periphery or rural/urban), as Mabogunje (1989) has noted, can have a powerful influence on the pattern of behavior of members of a particular society.

The rural area and the urban area are spatial forms or elements. The ordered relations that exist between them constitute the spatial structure. Some studies have sought to explain this relationship between rural and urban areas in terms of an 'urban bias' in the development process.

Urban bias thesis

The urban bias thesis, associated primarily with the works of Michael Lipton (1977; 1993) and Robert Bates (1981; 1993), is centered on the notion of the existence of an economically poor and politically powerless rural area at one end of the pole and an economically and politically powerful urban area at the other end. Urban bias theory, as advanced by Lipton and Bates, is an ahistorical, society-centred theory which suggests that public policies are biased against rural areas and this bias is rooted in relations of power between urban classes and rural classes. This may not necessarily be the case, at least not in all situations but it is essentially the sense in which urban bias is used in this study. This study argues, however, that urban bias is historically produced and agrees with Colburn's (1993: 61) criticism of Lipton's and Bates' thesis which held that:

Focusing on the state, on its autonomy, on its capacity, on its perniciousness, has obscured the question of how rural folk have survived, and under what conditions – if any – they have prospered.

'Urban bias' and the spatially polarized structure of the economy are manifested most dramatically in a historically produced urban/rural contradiction, rooted in dependency. Thomas (1974: 192) identified the urban/rural contradiction as a contradiction "immanent to the present anarchic pattern of growth in most underdeveloped countries" (Thomas, 1974: 192). He argues further that the historical concentration of activities in the urban centre and the immiserization of the rural area only serve the interest of international capitalism:

With the economy functioning to ensure that local production is geared to servicing and satisfying metropolitan needs, the spatial differentiation of these activities must inevitably be a response to these influences. The conflict between agriculture and industry, urban and rural economy, are deeply entwined with these basic social forces (Thomas, 1974).

This holds true in the Grenadian context. The same historical forces that structured the economy and organized space created Caribbean capitals – the focus of rural migrants. Clarke (1983) contends that Caribbean urban systems, as well as societies, have been moulded by colonialism and slavery. Caribbean cities are not indigenous creations as such but transplants from Europe. Many have population growth well above the island's annual average of about 2 percent but lack the commensurate economic expansion since they lack the mercantile and manufacturing base necessary to support such growth. This is so because of the continuing relationship of dependency that structurally integrates Caribbean economies into the world economy. Nevertheless, development is concentrated in the urban area and as a result the imbalances between population and resources have only been rectified by rural to urban migration.

Rural to urban migration

Theories of rural to urban migration often describe migration as economically motivated. These theories focus on economic considerations, including labour forces, income and employment opportunities. Most of these economic models of migration are based on the human investment approach. Since the early exploratory studies of 1960 and 1962, such persons as Todaro (1969), for example, have done empirical research which confirms the importance of economic factors. Essentially, the model proposes that man is economically rational and therefore his decision to migrate is based on rational choice (Shaw 1975).

The strength of this model is that it allows insights into the relationship between individual decision making and structural considerations. It assumes that an individual will migrate if the value of the expected income at the destination of migration in this case the urban area exceeds the sum of the value of the expected income at the migrants place of origin – the rural area. The mathematical rigour of the model and its ability to predict fairly accurately the direction and magnitude of migration, as well as its possible outcomes, are its other strengths.

This approach is helpful in this study, since the impact of the polarized spatial structure of the economy on individual choice and livelihood strategies are its core concerns. It does not, however, explain the behavior of the individual and some of its assumptions are flawed. For example, there is no empirical evidence that all or most human beings are rational economic beings and make decisions based on calculations of potential costs and benefits. Secondly, this kind of decision-making must be based on information often beyond the knowledge of the individual migrant, as Savasdisara (1984) has observed in his study of rural to urban migration in Thailand. Additionally, others have argued that the model cannot adequately identify the impact of migration on the migrants themselves.

The impact of migration on the migrants themselves is central to the functionalist model of migration (Mangalam and Schwarzweller 1970). This model places emphasis on the social collective aspects of migration and combines structural elements with the behavioral and decisional aspects of migration. Du Toit's (1975) "Decision-making or Voluntaristic model" of African rural-urban migration is useful here. It postulates an effective and continuous link between rural and urban communities that takes the form of frequent communication links and the flow of both personnel and goods in both directions. Pool (1989) observed, for example, that in the case of Grenada, it is sometimes cheaper for rural people with urban jobs in St George's where many of the service and government jobs are concentrated, to remain in their home community because of the communication linkages between the rural and urban areas.

The decision making or voluntaristic model deals with the individual migrant. Each migrant has a rural and urban microfield which connects the rural and urban structures in a migration continuum. The decision to migrate within such a microfield will be determined by a multicausal nexus of stimuli – economic, personal, familial, social and so on. What is interesting here as far as our study is concerned is the argument that the network of loyalties, obligations, pressures, and cost-benefit considerations within which potential migrants decide to move or stay is essentially open, and can change at any time as new stimuli are taken into account. It makes it necessary to gather information from individual migrants in order to establish the real reasons for migration and the basis of choice.

Studies on migration which have focused on Grenada have tended to be exclusively based on out-migration. Pool (1989) examined shifts in Grenadian migration from a historical perspective. After reviewing the patterns of Grenadian migration over an eighty-year period up to 1983, she concluded that a culture of migration pervaded the society. Herbert Blaize, a former Prime Minister of Grenada, seems to have supported Pool's (1989) reference to a culture of migration among Grenadians when he remarked that: "The question is not whether to migrate, but when. It is the normal pattern of behavior; you don't have to teach it" (*Miami Herald*, 16 December 1984). Nevertheless, Pool's population sample made it clear that although many plan to migrate they would rather live in the country if the reasons for migration did not exist. Migration was viewed as a necessary evil. The main reasons for migrating were invariably a desire to own land, low wages, particularly in the rural agricultural economy, and the search for higher education and skills training. Migrant shifts over the years were related to the economic and social conditions as well as the degree of welcome in the destination of the migrant. The main destinations were Trinidad, Britain, the United States and Canada. The existence of relatives and friends in those countries was crucial to the migrant's invitation, reception, accommodation and ability to obtain a job.

Tobias (1976, 1980) studied out-migration from Grenada as culturally determined. This paper agrees with his argument that the migrant's own explanation of the reasons for his/her migration has great explanatory power as those of other models, including those of anthropologists and models of economic determinism. Tobias concluded that the ambition to accomplish the cultural goals of the society – owning one's own piece of land, one's own house, and so on – are powerful noneconomic reasons for migration. This, however, is in reference to emigration, rather than rural to urban migration.

Governments in Grenada have not sought to make out-migration an issue, except in the case of the former People's Revolutionary Government (PRG) which saw it as a loss of human resources and skills to the process of national development (Pool 1989). Out- migration has otherwise been perceived as a good thing. It kept the unemployment rate down, helped stave off absolute and relative poverty and deprivation through the benefits of remittances sent to dependents at home, and served to control population growth. In fact, a study by Harewood (1966) showed high rates of population growth up to the 1960s and quoted estimates that predicted an increase in population to 150,000 by the 1980s. On the contrary, migration doubled by the 1970s and a 1982 census showed a decline in natural increase by approximately 30 percent, thus prompting the PRG to question the validity and reliability of the census data.

Squatting and urban poverty

In his work on urban poverty in the French Caribbean, Laguerre (1990) suggests that when one observes squatter settlements in the Caribbean one realizes that there is a correlation between poverty and space. The rural poor who migrate to the city tend to settle in lower class neighbor- hoods. Since there is much speculation in urban land, the urban elite buy up what is perceived as the best location, leaving the marginal lands to the poor. In this argument, space is not a totally neutral concept. It contributes to the reproduction of poverty. This is so because those who control the productive forces can use the power vested in that control not only to control space but also to reproduce it. Space is hierarchicalized in relation to the centre, the place where the reproduction of the relations of production is located. For Laguerre, the phenomenon of urban poverty is part of the larger process of the reproduction of the state, and the reproduction of urban poverty is partly due to the 'urban bias' of devel- opment policies. He argues that "This bias gives a tremendous importance to the city as the political, administrative, and economic centre of the nation (Laguerre 1990: 161). As a result the country is totally dominated by the urban establishment. In the context of this study, therefore, the extent to which the occupation by rural migrants of urban space creates a challenge to the urban elites and how this challenge is met, may impact upon the choices and livelihood strategies of the rural migrants who occupy those spaces in their squatter settlements.

Other studies on squatting in Caribbean towns, for example Montego Bay (Eyre 1984) and Port of Spain (Conway 1981) describe the urban squatter settlements (shanty town in Jamaica) as "the poor man's suburbia''. That 'captured' space provides a locale and milieu relatively free from the restraints of title and mortgage. Here spatial and social mobility is relatively more rapidly achieved than in the formal institutional structure where title and mortgages may pose restrictions. Others (eg, Laguerre, 1990) describe these settlements as marginalized communities in marginalized space, evidence of the consequences of the exploitative nature of capitalism in the Third World. They see in them poverty and alienation. On the other hand, studies done by Clarke (1983) and Eyre (1984) have found marginality which produces poverty, alienation, frustration and discouragement and at the same time in those same communities there is visible social mobility, self-improvement, investment and community involvement. Eyre reviewed selected data from a comprehensive survey of twenty peri-urban shanty towns in Jamaica, carried out by a multidisciplinary team between 1978 and 1982. Among his findings were much evidence of both marginality and self-improvement; a population structure biased somewhat towards persons of the younger reproductive age groups, with high fertility rates and characterized by the less educated, lower income sector of society. The basic problem in those settlements was not so much lack of money as the irregularity and casual nature of employment. Inhabitants survived by engaging in a variety of jobs – domestic service, street vending, higglering and so on. Locher's (1980) case study of rural to urban migration and living conditions of rural migrants in three neighbourhoods of Port-au-Prince, Haiti, reached similar conclusions. Locher found in those neighbourhoods a multiplicity of occupational roles played by the lower economic circuits: maintenance of rural ties; the existence of migration networks; the transfer of privileges from one generation to another; successful survival strategies and an enormous amount of resourcefulness. Although there was much deprivation, the deprived were not helplessly allowing themselves to be marginalized.

Methodology

A combination of quantitative and qualitative techniques were utilized to gather data. These methods or sources of data collection included archival research, aggregate data, elite interviews, and an open-ended questionnaire administered to sixty heads of households in the two communities selected – Mon Tout and Darbeau. Case studies, which these two communities represent, can provide a richly detailed portrait of a particular social phenomenon, as Hakim (1987) has shown. They provide a real life context within which it is possible to answer the specific research questions (Hakim 1987).

In relation to the sample, sixty respondents, with an equal proportion each drawn from thirty communities, were randomly selected from a list of households in Darbeau and Mon Tout compiled by the Land and Survey Department of the Ministry of Agriculture. The list was compiled for the purpose of surveying the areas and offering the squatters entitlement to the house spots which they currently occupied. In terms of gender, the sample comprised 27 male heads of households and 33 female heads.

In relation to the elite interviews, these were conducted with several government and non-government officials. The latter included the vice-president of the Industrial Development Corporation (IDC), two officials from the Land and Survey Department of the Ministry of Agriculture directly responsible for surveying and distributing lots to squatters in the Darbeau and Mon Tout areas, community leaders and an official of the Criminal Investigation Department of the Grenada Police Force.

Findings and Analysis

Basic social characteristics of respondents

Sixty-eight percent of the respondents were migrants from the rural parishes with 3 percent from the dependency of Carriacou but 32 percent were from the parish of St George. This strongly indicates rural to urban migration and, in the case of St George's, intraparish migration. Eighty-four percent of the respondents were largely of African descent, 10 percent were mixed – dougla,[1] mulatto, half Carib, while 3 percent were East Indian. This compares with the findings of the 1990 national census which recorded an ethnic breakdown of 85 percent African, 11 percent mixed and 3 percent East Indians.

Fifty-eight percent of the respondents were Roman Catholic, followed by the Full Gospel with 15 percent, Spiritual Baptist 10 percent, Anglicans 6 percent and Seventh Day Adventists 3 percent, in that order. In addition, there was one each of the Jehovah Witness, Rastafarian, and atheist persuasion. Fifty-eight percent of the respondents were of the working age 25 to 45, while 33 percent were in the age group 35 to 44. On the whole, the Grenada population is fairly young, for as the Census Summary Report (1991), revealed 38 percent of the population is under 15 years. As regards gender, more younger women than men were heads of households, and there was a higher proportion of younger heads of households in Mon Tout. Heads of households in Darbeau tended to be older.

Socioeconomic status, social ranking and gender inequality

There are several indicators or determinants of social status, and for this study these include marital status, land tenure, home ownership, education, occupation and income.

Marital status: Marriage is culturally perceived as socially desirable and the most approved form of marital status in which sexual relationships are pursued. This is defended on legal, economic, moral and religious grounds. Consequently, families in which the sexual mates are married are accorded greater social respectability in Grenadian society (Smith 1965). All other forms of marital status are tolerated but not to the same degree. For example common-law marriage enjoys a greater degree of tolerance and respectability than visiting unions.

Most of the respondents shared their household with a mate – 31 percent married, 23 percent common law. The others were single (21 percent), committed to visiting relationships (20 percent) or divorced (3 percent). Those persons categorized as single are those who claimed not to have a mate or sexual partner at the time of the research. The majority or 68 percent of the respondents thus were not legally married. Census data shows that for 1981, 69 percent and for 1991, 67 percent of the adults in Grenada were never married. Fifty-two percent more male than the 15 percent female heads of households were married, and 64 percent of the households with common-law marital status were headed by men than by women. Thirty percent of the women who were heads of households were either single as opposed to 11 percent males or had visiting relationships. All of the 12 households with marital status classified as visiting relationships were headed by females.

This trend is reflective of the patriarchal nature of the society. Where male and female lived together in a steady settled household, legally married or common law, the male was generally regarded as head of the household. Generally, the female was regarded as head in households where a man was absent, either because the woman was single or the relationship was a visiting one.

The trend depicted in the above findings is reflected in other independent studies. For example, a 1991 UNICEF study estimated that around 40 percent of households nationally were headed by women, the majority of whom are involved in visiting unions. In fact, it estimated that 82 percent of births in Grenada are to unmarried women.

Land tenure: Land tenure and home ownership may also influence the decision to migrate and survival and livelihood strategies such as squatting and the struggle to own land. Landlessness is also an indicator of poverty in a society such as Grenada whose economy is largely dependent on agriculture. Ninety percent of the respondents were the landless poor, forced to migrate and squat. Forty-five percent of the respondents gave landlessness and the inability to purchase a house lot as the most important reason for squatting.

As with ownership of land, home ownership is perceived as a cultural goal. Ninety-two percent of the respondents owned the shelter in which they lived. This is not surprising as the ambition to own their own rent-free housing arrangements was one of the most compelling reasons given for squatting in the first place.

Housing type: Three categories of housing were observed: wooden houses generally of the poorest, the wood and concrete of the not so poor, and the concrete houses of those who were better off.

Sixty-five percent of all respondents lived in wooden houses, 38 percent in Mon Tout and 27 percent in Darbeau; 20 percent lived in concrete houses, 7 percent in Mon Tout and 13 percent in Darbeau, while 15 percent lived in concrete/wood houses, 5 percent in Mon Tout and 10 percent in Darbeau.

Closely related to housing type as a socioeconomic indicator is the number of bedrooms, and the number of bedrooms in relation to the

Table 6.4 Settlement by House Type

Community	House Type (%)		
	Wooden	Concrete	Concrete/Wood
Mon Tout	38	7	5
Darbeau	27	13	10
Total	65	20	15

number of children. A majority of 51 percent of the respondents lived in two bedroom houses, 27 percent in three bedroom houses, 12 percent in one bedroom houses, and 10 percent in four bedroom houses. The total number of children in the sample amounted to 274; 70 percent belonged to unmarried heads, 27 percent to single heads, while 24 percent and 19 percent were found in common-law and visiting relationships, respectively. Thirty percent of the children were to married heads and 3 percent to divorcees. There was an average of 5 children per household, 45 percent of them were crowded into two bedroom houses, 34 percent in three bedrooms, 11 percent in four bedrooms and 10 percent in one bedroom houses (Table 6.5).

Educational status: Education influences decisions to migrate, the ability to make choices and make use of opportunities, the livelihood strategies adopted, occupation and income. Ninety percent of the respondents had only a primary education, 8 percent secondary and 2 percent tertiary (vocational). The predominance of individuals at the lowest levels of the education scale in the squatter settlements studied is understandable. Low level of education is also associated with low status occupation and low income. Although the transportation system is fairly adequate and most rural villages are no more than three or four hours from the capital in a small country like Grenada, the cost of commuting would consume most of their already low income. The alternative is to find accommodation in the town, close to the job. For those for whom rent is too expensive, the alternative is to squat.

Employment and occupation status: Employment status and income along with education are three of the most important indicators of socioeconomic status. If low levels of education are associated with low status occupation, low status occupation is associated with low income levels and all three to low socioeconomic status. Hodge (1962) has

Table 6.5   Number of Bedrooms, by Children
(Total Children 274)

No. of Bedrooms	No. of children (%)
1	10
2	45
3	34
4	11

Table 6.6   List of Occupations Engaged in by Respondents
(Past and Present)

	Occupations		
1.	Cabinet maker	17.	Beach vendor
2.	Cook	18.	Bartender
3.	Gardener	19.	Baker
4.	Security guard	20.	Plumber
5.	Waiter	21.	Hairdresser
6.	Domestic helper	22.	Janitor
7.	Drinks vendor	23.	Assistant surveyor
8.	Food vendor	24.	Salesman
9.	Housewife	25.	Dockworker
10.	Cleaner	26.	Landlord
11.	Shopkeeper	27.	Factory worker
12.	Tradesman	28.	Groundsman
13.	Small farmer	29.	Mechanic
14.	Shoemaker	30.	Office attendant
15.	Charcoal burner	31.	Solid waste worker
16.	Bus driver	32.	Civil servant

correctly pointed out that the functional relation between education, occupation and income allows for a more meaningful relationship of other criteria of social rank to occupational groups. Occupation could be considered the intervening variable between education and income, since income may be regarded as a reward and education an ability index that would ensure higher rewards both social and economic. The respondents were well aware of this functional relationship between education, occupation and income (or social mobility).

Occupation and occupational status may influence the individual's evaluation of his/her environment, decision to migrate, choice and livelihood strategy. It is therefore important whether the individual is unemployed, underemployed, an unpaid family worker, self-employed, an employer, working for the government or working in the private sector. The respondents were engaged in a wide range of occupations; some of them engaged in two or three at the same time. Many of them are quite versatile, considering the different types of occupations they held in the past and continue to occupy from time to time. The list of 32 different occupations in the table on page 199, compiled from claims of past and current occupations is illustrative of this range of occupations.

The categorization of these occupations into low status, intermediate status and high status, as outlined below, is based on the perception of the respondents themselves and the status ratings they attached to these occupations. This method was adopted in order to avoid the possible influence of any academic bias.

Low status jobs: housewife, cook, cleaner, gardener, small farmer, domestic helper, shoemaker, drinks vendor, janitor, charcoal burner, food vendor, beach vendor, groundsman, solid waste worker.

Intermediate status: cabinet maker, shopkeeper, security guard, tradesman, waiter, bus driver, dockworker, bartender, landlord, baker, plumber, mechanic, office attendant, salesman, assistant surveyor.

High status: middle level civil servant.

Findings suggest an association between the educational level of the respondents and low status jobs, but more rigorous research may be required to confirm this. Sixty percent of the respondents were restricted to low status occupations, 23 percent to intermediate and only 1 person (the middle level civil servant) was regarded as having a high status occupation. Fifteen percent of the respondents were unemployed. This level of unemployment represents people who at the time were not engaged in any income generating activity at all. Additionally, it indicates hidden unemployment.

Income status: Income levels may be translated into ownership of consumption items, type and quality of housing, ownership of home appliances, ability to purchase land, pay rent, travel, educate children, enter the formal and informal economy as self-employed, and generally improve standards of living, broaden choices, and facilitate whatever livelihood strategy is adopted.

Based on responses, a scheme suggesting levels of household incomes was developed ranging from as low as EC$100–299 to EC$1,000+ per month at a rate of US$1.00 = EC$2.57. The minimum wage in Grenada is estimated at EC$300 per month. Table 6.7 on page 201 gives the levels or ranges of household income and the number and percentage of respondents that fall within each range. The total number of respondents who disclosed their household incomes was 57.

As Table 6.7 illustrates, a majority of 60 percent of the heads of households who disclosed their household incomes run their households

Table 6.7   Households and Income

Household Income (EC$)	Total	Percentage
100–299	15	25.0
300–499	14	23.3
500–699	7	11.7
700–899	9	15.0
900–1,000	6	10.0
1,000+	6	10.0

on less than EC$700 per month, while 15 percent had a household budget of EC$700–$899 and an equal proportion of 10 percent were run on an income of EC$900–$1,000 and EC$1,000+. The average size of households sampled was five. During the months of the field research April to July, EC$700 was the bare minimum to support the basic needs of a family of five (Consumer Price Index, June to August 1994). Table 6.8, which compares household income by occupational status, suggest an association between low income and low status occupation.

The data below suggest that the majority of households with low status occupations operate on a household budget of less than EC$700, while the majority of households with intermediate status occupations operate on household budgets of EC$700 upwards. While the findings may sugggest a link between income status of households and support from relatives abroad, this link is not definitive. For instance, while 34 percent or one-third of low status households received remittances – 12 percent

Table 6.8   Household Income, by Occupational Status

Income	Low Status	Intermediate	High
100–299	27	-	-
300–499	18	4	-
500–699	8	2	-
700–899	8	8	-
900–1,000	8	4	-
1,000+	2	8	2
Total	71	27	2

Table 6.9   Support, by Occupation and Income Status
             (n=49)

Status	Regular	Sometimes	None
Low	12	22	35
Intermediate	4	9	16
High	1	-	-
Total	17	31	51

"regularly" or 22 percent "sometimes", almost the same one-third proportion or 35 percent received none. In contrast, while 13 percent of "intermediate" households received remittances either 4 percent "regularly" or 9 percent sometimes, 16 percent received none. For the high income households, 1 percent received remittances regularly from abroad. Forty-nine or 82 percent of the 60 heads of households admitted to having relatives abroad.

Summary

The findings discussed above strongly suggest that the two settlements of Mon Tout and Darbeau are socioeconomically poor but not depressed communities. There is relative but very little evidence of absolute poverty. The respondents all come, more or less, from the same socioeconomic background and there is a high degree of status consistency or, as Lenski (1954) called it "status crystallization". The definition applicable here is that argued by Jackson (1962: 469) who wrote that: ". . . status consistency can be understood as the degree to which individuals rank positions on important societal status hierarchies are at a comparable level".

Measured crudely using criteria such as ethnicity, land tenure, religion, type of housing, marital status, education, occupation, and income to rank the respondents, we have established that 68 percent are rural migrants, 90 percent are the landless poor, 87 percent are of African origin, 68 percent are either Roman Catholic or Spiritual Baptist, 68 percent are not married; 65 percent lived in wooden houses, 51 percent of these houses have two bedrooms; 90 percent of the respondents have acquired only primary education, 60 percent are engaged in low status occupations and 85 percent run their household on less than EC$700.

It should not be assumed, however, that social ranking is absent within the communities. This ranking is based on the perception and criteria of the community itself. Within the communities households are distinguished on the basis of marital status, type of housing, level of education and occupational status. Race, ethnicity and colour do not feature prominently or at all – at least the research was unable to detect these at work. In Grenada the dynamics of ethnicity and colour that are in operation in daily social interaction are very subtle, but ethnicity and colour do have socioeconomic and cultural significance and symbolic meanings.

What is clearer from the findings is the dynamics of gender inequality. Although the highest level of education – primary education – is the same for both sexes, female-headed households in those communities are poorer. Earlier, it was established that whereas 74 percent of married households were headed by males, of those households headed by women 77 percent were either single or engaged in visiting relationships (100 percent of all respondents who admitted to this type of arrangement). Most of the occupations that women engaged in fall within the low status category – housewife, cook, cleaner, domestic helper, charcoal burner, drinks vendor and food vendor. Sixty-seven percent of the unemployed respondents were women. It is evident from Table 6.10 below that the incomes of female-headed households are much lower than those of male-headed households. Of the 31 female heads who disclosed their household incomes, 75 percent operated their households on less than EC$700 as opposed to 46 percent of the 26 male heads who disclosed theirs. Fifty-four percent of male-headed households operated on EC$700+ per month as opposed to only 22 percent for women.

The implications of these gender related inequalities are clear: women's livelihood strategies and choices may differ from those of men.

Table 6.10   Income, by Sex

Income	Male	Female
100–299	4	11
300–499	4	10
500–699	4	3
700–899	6	3
900–1,000	3	3
1,000+	5	1
Total (n)	(26)	(31)

Choice enlargening and livelihood strategies

The choice enlargening and livelihood strategies discussed below are by no means exhaustive. They are the main strategies respondents admitted to. Further research and probing may yield additional strategies created and employed by the poor. The ones discussed here, however, are sufficient to illustrate the impact of the spatially polarized structure of the Grenada economy and "urban bias" upon the livelihood strategies of rural migrants/urban squatters and their ability to make choices that could improve their life chances and that of their children.

Squatting: The findings of this study support Perlman's (1986) observation that, far from being the "losers of rural societies" as they are sometimes misconceived, rural migrants to urban squatter settlements are usually the more highly motivated members of rural society who have a vision of the greater opportunities available to them in the urban area. The following two testimonies exemplify the thinking of some of the respondents on this issue of rural to urban migration:

If I had land in the country, I woulda stay and work it. My wife love to plant.

Actually I have a [house] spot in the country. In the country you could live a little better if you not working. But you can't just sit down in the country and do nothing. You have to come to town and look for work.

Actually, 50 percent of the rural migrants would have remained in their villages if they had lands or good paying jobs in the country. Forty-one percent of those from the rural parishes would have moved to town whether they had land or not, since they no longer perceive agriculture as profitable and employment and income generating activities outside of agriculture are limited in the rural parishes. The collapse of agriculture and the fall in prices of the traditional agricultural export crops were the most compelling reasons cited. The following testimonies express the manner in which it was felt and articulated:

The country [rural area] have nothing. Long time days, plenty estates. Estates used to offer work. These days crops have no demand: cocoa right down, nutmeg right down.

The estates close down. Those that not abandon cannot afford to give workers enough employment. Workers can't survive on the two or three days they get.

All estates sell and agriculture not as profitable as before.

It is evident from the above testimonies that many of the rural and other migrants to the urban squatter settlements are there because they make conscious and rational decisions calculated to enlarge their choices.

Many of the respondents chose to migrate and squat as a livelihood and goal achievement strategy. Many began by staying in the town during the week, returning to their rural village on weekends:

People from Sauteurs and Gouyave come down for carnival or to look for work and never return. Some used to go up on weekends. Now they don't go up at all.

I was working in Town. I couldn' see the way paying bus every day. I decided to get a spot here.

The communities of Mon Tout and Darbeau possessed most of the strategic functions of such settlements identified and described by Perlman (1986), strategic functions of which the respondents were not only aware but fully utilized as livelihood and choice enlarging strategies. The communities provide the space for people to establish their own rent-free housing and many are encouraged by the example of squatting:

We was renting in many places. Rent high. It was difficult for us. We see other people squatting here so we ask permission from the government.

I was renting at Grand Anse and then bought a little shack here. This was thirteen years ago. I never like renting.

Sixty-seven percent of the respondents chose the settlements because they disliked renting and never rented or used to rent, but endeavoured to avoid high rents. Forty-five percent had saved up enough to build their own homes as one of their goals in life but either they could find no alternative affordable house spot or decided that a better strategy would be to squat on state land and use their limited savings to build a shelter on the space taken and available.

The settlements also function as a space in which the individual could remain a permanent resident in the capital. They provide individuals with the strategic space in which they could minimize resource expenditure in providing themselves with their own shelter, and at the same time maximize other values such as capital investments, education of children, improvement in their lifestyles and enjoyment of the advantages of proximity to their jobs through locating themselves in the town. Conscious of the advantages of the space they occupy, 92 percent of the respondents would prefer to remain permanently in the settlements or at least in the capital. In addition to the advantages discussed above, there are other considerations which included investments, the proximity and love for the area. These considerations are supported by Table 6.11 on page 206.

Table 6.11 Choice of Space and Reasons for Preference

Reasons	Present Space (%)	Elsewhere (%)
No alternative	33	-
Investments	37	-
Proximity	13	-
Love area	9	-
Problems	-	3
Congestion	-	5

It should be noted that for 33 percent of them there is no alternative which they would prefer, whilst 37 percent cited the fact that they have invested everything in those settlements.

There is enough evidence to suggest that the respondents generally perceive an 'urban bias' in the development process, and consider the structure of the Grenada economy as spatially polarized. This understanding magnifies the advantages of urban squatting, which is evident in some of their testimonies below:

Everything centralized in town. If there was a greater spread, people from the country wouldn' be coming to town to look for work.

More factories and business places and better transportation in town.

It have more opportunities in town and that is the reason why people leave the country and come to town and squat.

In fact, 88 percent of all respondents – 87 percent in Mon Tout; 90 percent in Darbeau; 91percent of the females and 85 percent of the males – considered that comparatively, more opportunities for earning a living, broadening choices and improving their standard of living existed in St George's than in the rural areas. This is illustrated in Table 6.12.

Table 6.12 Reasons for Greater Opportunities in Town (%)

Reasons	Town	Country	Overseas
More jobs in town	53	-	-
More land in country	7	3	-
High income in town	3	-	-
More opportunity overseas	-	-	5
Quicker money in town	15	-	-
More developed	7	-	-
Fall of agriculture	5	-	-

Of the 92 percent who preferred to remain in the space acquired, the majority felt that there were more jobs in St George's. It is interesting to note that the second most compelling reason – related to the first – was not so much a perception of higher income to be earned in St George's, but that the capital provided an opportunity to earn quicker money.

Chain-migration: To a certain extent, the responses suggest that migration to the capital for many is a step in a chain migration that ultimately ends in emigration to a destination overseas, currently North America. While only 8 percent of the respondents planned to migrate eventually and reside permanently abroad, 47 percent regarded emigration as a viable livelihood and choice enlarging strategy. This tendency suggests that the culture of migration which Pool (1989) described in her study on emigration in Grenada is still strong. Eighty-two percent of the respondents have relatives abroad mainly in the USA and Canada. Employment and the improvement in their quality of life were the main reasons advanced for migrating. Many of those who regard emigration as a livelihood and choice enlarging strategy are nevertheless encumbered by obstacles in the way of their aspirations, which included the lack of sponsorship. The respondents were well aware of the importance of sponsorship, in the form of relatives and friends abroad who would invite the prospective emigrant over, help with travel expenses, provide accommodation, help in finding employment and generally help the emigree to adjust and adapt. In the absence of these types of contacts, emigration is a difficult endeavour. Other obstacles include the cost of travel, the non-possession of necessary documents, parental responsibilities and insecurity.

The information suggests that, to a certain extent, many of the people who migrate from the rural parishes to St George's are those who, for some of the above reasons, find it difficult to migrate. This conclusion is possible if one agrees with Pool's (1989) notion of a "culture of migration" and Herbert Blaize's assertion that "It is the normal pattern of behavior". It may even suggest the merits of the cynical question Tobias (1979; 1980) posed in his thesis about the noneconomic factors of Grenadian Emigration.

On the other hand, one needs to consider seriously the fact that many of the respondents had no desire to emigrate. Much has happened since the above views were expressed. If the fact that 53 percent of the respondents had no desire to travel is not too significant, given the small size of the sample, their responses and feelings about emigration needs serious consideration. The changes in immigration policies of overseas destinations which make it increasingly difficult for Grenadian would-be emigrants, information obtained from returnees and relatives residing in North America, and awareness of the present socioeconomic conditions that exist in other traditional destinations of Grenadian emigrants – Trinidad, Venezuela, Aruba, for example – have made many Grenadians more realistic about political and socioeconomic conditions and opportunities 'overseas'. These places are evidently not being perceived as the 'bed of roses' they once were as people's expectations have become more realistic. In addition, there is even a suggestion of patriotism as revealed in the following remarks:

If we learn to use what we have we could make it right here with the little that we have. I prefer to die in Grenada.

In the case of these two last quoted respondents and others of their persuasion, migration as a livelihood and choice enlarging strategy does not go beyond rural to urban migration.

Remittances: Remittances may be defined as "the homeward transfer of cash and kind sent back to Caribbean societies by emigrants who have left to live, study, invest or work abroad" (Conway, 1984). The kind of remittances familiar to the respondents include cash, money orders, parcels and barrels typically containing clothing, foodstuffs, toiletries, stationary and toys. Respondents were aware that remittances allow resources to be maximized for other purposes, and therefore regarded it as an important livelihood and choice enlarging strategy. Eighty-two percent of the respondents claimed to have relatives abroad and 75 percent agreed that it was helpful to have relatives abroad. Nevertheless, not all of those who had relatives abroad and thought it was helpful to have relatives abroad, actually receive assistance from them in the form of remittances. In fact, 49 percent received no remittances whatsoever from their relatives abroad while 51 percent were recipients, 21 percent on a regular basis, 30 percent on an irregular basis. Regular was estimated at an average of once a month for cash and money orders, and at least three times a year for barrels and parcels.

The extent to which remittances are perceived to be crucial to livelihood and choice enlarging strategies is evident in the complaints of the following respondents:

My relatives abroad, especially me sister in England does send something [money order] regular and I get a barrel now and then from me uncle in America. It does go a long way. Now government taxing barrel too high. How they expect poor people to survive?

Me two sons in St Thomas [USVI] send a help and it go a long way but right now things hard with them up there. I don't know how I go make out.

Some family not nice; they wouldn' stretch out a hand.

Some family know what it like in Grenada; they could help out the situation by sending a little something now and then.

The barrel does help out with the cost of living. But the cost of clearing it too high. They charge you a flat price and charge you extra for contents. This present government started it.

Maintenance of wide options

The findings of the study support Chambers' (1989) observation that the livelihood strategies of the poor vary by region, community, social group, household, gender, age and other variables. Although some of the respondents seek a single source of support, generally, strategies were complex and diverse. Through their ability to do different things, in different places at different times, most of the respondents sought to reduce risks, increase adaptability and seek autonomy through maintaining wider options, as illustrated below:

Can't afford to be unemployed. I is a mason, mechanic, carpenter – all these things. When things slow on one side, I do something else. I repair second hand bikes and sell them at a reasonable price. My wife does crochet, make doilies.

The 'Mister' provide an allowance. I sell drinks in the park, 'specially round sports time. Is a good thing. It bring in all three to four hundred dollars.

After retirement I decide to occupy meself doing something [shoemaking]; can't survive on a meagre pension.

Self-employment: Self-employment is a crucial livelihood and choice enlarging strategy of a fairly large section of the respondents. Thirty-five percent of the respondents were self-employed, four as small shopkeepers and the majority in the informal economy as craftsmen, beach vendors, drink and food vendors. Invariably, however, the 18 percent employed with the government and the 32 percent employed with the private sector – including domestic helpers and gardeners were also engaged part-time in the informal economy. For the Mon Tout respondents, the Sugar Mill Night Club located at the southern entrance to the community provided an opportunity to do thriving business on weekends from the back of cars and vans, from trays, and from 4 x 4 box-like booths scattered about the vicinity of the club, located ideally at a busy roundabout. Even among the 15 percent unemployed, the dream is to become self-employed, especially in the informal economy. Self-employment was the most popular future plan of 26 percent of the 49 respondents who disclosed their future plans. Table 6.13 shows the relationship between future plans and marital status based on a total of 49 respondents.

The desire to be self-employed was especially strong amongst heads of households in visiting relationships. Earlier it was shown that heads of households in visiting relationships were all women and amongst the poorest. Consistent with this observation, Table 6.13 reveals that of the 49 heads who disclosed their future plans, by far the most respondents who desired to be self-employed were females – 10 out of 13. In fact, amongst the 27 females who responded 37 percent planned to be self-employed. Reasons for wanting to be self-employed, for the 23 who gave a reason, ranged from loss of job to retirement.

Whilst 44 percent chose self-employment because of loss of jobs, an equal percentage chose self-employment and involvement in the informal sector out of a wish to be their own boss and a need to supplement their incomes. One respondent, a married female of Mon Tout, is head of her household. She is self-employed in the formal private sector as a small shopkeeper and her husband is engaged in the informal sector as a beach vendor. She feels that self-employment brings in a higher income to the

Table 6.13 Future Plans, by Marital Status

Plans	M	C/L	V	S
Go abroad	2	-	2	2
Move back	-	-	-	2
Self-employment	-	10	12	4
Better job	2	4	4	-
Build/Rep. house	14	2	-	2
Acq. land title	2	2	-	6
Expand business	10	4	-	-
No plans	-	2	-	-

Key: M- Married; V- Visiting; C/L- Common-law; S- Single

household, and allows them the independence and flexibility she cherishes. Others share the same sentiments.

The responses suggest that as a livelihood strategy individuals choose self-employment and participation in the informal sector because of the flexibility and often higher earning it offers, among other advantages, whilst others were simply unemployed and could not afford to sit down and do nothing.

Mutual support networking: Mutual support networking is another livelihood and choice enlarging strategy in which respondents engaged. It involved the creation and maintenance of contacts, and mostly reciprocal assistance in the day to day struggle to survive and make progress in life. The evidence of this mutual support networking is apparent in the testimonies below:

I and the children father couldn' get along so a friend get a place for me here.

I was renting in Belmont, wanted to build [a house], couldn' find nowhere else but here. I got a spot from family who living here already.

Mutual networking took different forms. These included accommodating relatives from the rural areas either working or schooling in St George's, and giving relatives a spot upon which to erect a house on the piece of squatted land. The pattern of settlement as observed by this researcher was generally one in which extended families, relatives, friends and people from the same parish tended to cluster. This clustering provides security to the members, mutual support and dependence, the possibility of sharing utilities and accommodation, and cooperating in economic ventures. The 'lend hand' and marun or Maroon characteristic of reciprocal assistance and communal labour sharing arrangements practised in the rural villages are transferred to the urban squatter settlement.

Household management: An important livelihood strategy is the manner in which household income is pooled and managed. Respondents were asked whether each working individual in the household spent his or her income separately to maintain him or her self and children, or whether each employed person contributed to the income necessary to run the household. This management also related to the allocation of roles and the division of labour within the household, particularly between mates. The terms 'segregated roles' and 'joint roles' to distinguish households in which sharing occurred from those in which the head of the household carried the burden alone, were borrowed from Botts (1971) in her study of families in London. They are used in this study as social indicators of the level of dependency on the heads of households and, consequently, as an indicator of the ability of the head to realize the livelihood and other goals of the household. It is assumed that joint-role households place less dependency stress on the head of the household and allocate to each mate more time and resources to fulfil goals.

In the case of the sample from Darbeau and Mon Tout, the heads of households were asked questions about financial decisions and divisions of labour relating to the household, in relation to other working members, particularly mates. The responses were categorized as either 'segregated' or 'joint'. Sixty-six percent were 'segregated' compared to 34 percent 'joint' out of a total of 58 that responded (Table 6.14).

It is noteworthy that all 34 percent of the households characterized as 'joint' were households in which the mates lived together – 17 percent married, 17 percent common law. All single households and visiting unions were classified as 'segregated'. Even so the dependency burden does not all fall upon the shoulders of the single mother. The current partner may help, though not necessarily consistently. Nevertheless, 16 percent of married households and 7 percent of those common law were also characterized as 'segregated'. These are households in which husbands and wives have precisely defined and differentiated roles.

Membership in savings and loans schemes: Membership in a credit and loan scheme, formal – credit union, insurance – or the informal susu, was a livelihood and choice enlarging strategy popular amongst respondents. Although the 33 percent who were actually members was less than half the total number of respondents, every respondent saw the strategic benefit of belonging to one.

Table 6.14 Household Management, by Marital Status (n= 58)

Marital Status	Segregated (%)	Joint
Married	16	17
Common-law	7	17
Divorced	3	-
Visiting	21	-
Single	19	-

Susu was the most popular of the three. It is called 'partner' in Jamaica, 'sobs' in Dominica (Lefranc 1993) and 'meeting turn' in Barbados. In Guyana it is called 'box hand' and in Belize, 'syndicate'. In Ghana, West Africa, it is called susu (Ayittey 1990), as it is in Trinidad and Tobago and Grenada. Susu is a traditional savings and loan scheme that is part of the cultural heritage of the folk and permeates almost all levels of the Grenadian society. There is a susu at almost every workplace and no village is without its susu. Brought over from West Africa, susu survived the vicissitudes of slavery and colonialism. Generations of poor families have depended on susu to build or repair houses, educate children, meet funeral expenses and so on. Five of the respondents, four of them women, were bankers. These were the organizers of susu 'hands'. A 'hand' is the amount of deposit agreed upon. The agreed deposit or the size of the 'hand' is dependent on the ability of the members to afford it. Susu 'hands' vary from as low as $20.00 to as high as $200.00 and a 'hand' may be drawn from as often as once every week to once every month. A 'hand' is drawn by turn and the member receives, in turn, the pool of all deposits handed in. Of the 33 respondents who claimed membership in such financial institutions, 85 percent had membership only in susu, while only 1 male and 1 female or 6 percent had membership in a credit union, and 2 males and 1 female or 9 percent were members of an insurance company. Table 6.15 shows the comparison between the sexes in relationship to membership.

Of the 33 respondents who were members of some financial institution, 39 percent were male, while 61 percent were female. Fifty-five percent of the women participated in susu as opposed to only 30 percent of the men. This is not surprising. Generally, susu in Grenada is controlled by females. The reasons for membership were invariably linked to the advantages of financial security, and the savings and loans that these institutions offer.

Table 6.15 Membership in Credit Union/Loan Scheme, by Sex

Membership	Male	Female (%)
Credit Union	3	6
Susu	30	55
Insurance	6	6
Total	39	61

Several plausible explanations can be advanced for the popularity of Susu in comparison to the relatively low popularity of the more formal institutions like insurance and credit unions. On the one hand, respondents reported having distrust for, and a lack of confidence in, these formal institutions which are linked to problems experienced in obtaining money from them and perceptions of corruption. On the other hand, the greater confidence in susu may be related to the fact that susu is an indigenous grass roots institution over which the poor exert total control. They know intimately the banker and the character of the other members who have a hand in the susu. These persons are usually their neighbours or work mates. Most importantly, the popularity of susu amongst the poor or the low income is related to the fact that susu offers loans without collateral, without interest, and on a short-term basis – a hand could be drawn every week or every fortnight. Moreover, every individual could join a susu on the basis of affordability and share in all of its benefits.

Investment in children's future: There is no question that caring for children and preparing them for the future are seen as strategies not only for the expansion of the choices and opportunities of the said children but also for the social and economic advancement of the family. As a Mon Tout woman puts it: "I don't want my children to go through what I go through: that's why I working so hard. I want to own the piece of land to leave it for them". Fifty-six percent of respondents wanted higher education for their children. Eleven percent want their children to get into one of the professions, 4 percent wanted them to acquire a trade, and another 4 percent wanted them to go overseas to seek their fortune or to acquire training, while 25 percent would do everything to help their children, but left all choices up to them. The rationale was based on traditional wisdom. Nevertheless, the tendency to do all in their power to "give the child a start in life" was universal. As one respondent expressed it: "I have no land to leave for them. I would like to be in a position to give them as much education as they could take".

Conclusion

The findings here generally suggest that respondents choose to adopt particular livelihood and choice enlarging strategies. They indicate, also, that respondents choices are based on rational considerations and decisions. The findings also suggest that, to a large extent, the polarized spatial structure of the Grenadian economy and 'urban bias' in the development process place limits on rural people's choices, provoke rural to urban migration and influence the organization of geographic as well as social and economic space.

Respondents do perceive an 'urban bias' in the development process. They interpret this bias in terms of an overconcentration of employment generating activities in and around the capital, thus forcing their migration to St George's in search of jobs and other opportunities. The concentration of tourism and the hotel industry, the industrial park and most other employment generating industries and activities in and around St George's act as a pull factor attracting rural migrants to the capital in search of a livelihood. The collapse or near collapse of the estate system and the agricultural economy is a rural push factor complementary to the urban pull factor. The lack of opportunities in the rural areas outside of agriculture, as well as landlessness, leave many people with little or no choice but to migrate in order to enlarge their choices. This helps to explain the rise in urban squatting as the relatively recent phenomenon that it is, in its present scale.

Migration to the capital is itself a livelihood strategy of respondents. This migration, in its turn, has forced them to create livelihood strategies in addition to those which they previously practised. Squatting is the most dramatic example of this new and additional livelihood strategy for many of them. Squatting enables the squatter to minimize resource expenditure for shelter and maximize other capital investments, proximity to jobs, education, improvement in their standard of living and the quality of their lives.

The findings show respondents resorting to a large range of choice enlarging and livelihood strategies. These include squatting, out-migration, remittances, maintenance of wide options, mutual support networking, indigenous credit and loans schemes, and investment in children's future. Nevertheless, a combination of insecurity of tenure, inadequate infrastructure, unemployment, and low incomes thwart the livelihood strategies both actual and planned of the respondents. Despite these disincentives, the respondents were, generally, highly motivated individuals and exhibited a spirit of resilience and optimism.

The communities are not merely loose aggregations of socially marginal people from disparate backgrounds. Far from that, they are well organized and cohesive communities, adapted to their environment. They have learned to use the urban space they have created for themselves to capitalize on the urban milieu and institutions for their self-improvement and the upliftment of their communities. For example, respondents were quick to point out that most of the infrastructure in Mon Tout were community self-help efforts organized by leaders within the community in conjunction with political representatives who helped mobilize the materials.

These communities are not the visual symbols of poverty and actual or potentially criminal areas as some might see them. An official of the Criminal Investigation Department (CID) of the Grenada Police Force gives credence to this suggestion when he remarked:

Mon Tout as a whole is not really crime prone per se . . . not much crime in Darbeau. The people in those communities are ambitious. They are seeking an opportunity to better their lives. Lands are getting scarce and people will grab at any opportunity to own a spot and put down a house.

This was supported further by the following report in the *Grenada Informer* of 1 July 1994:

For a while now the people of Darbeau and surrounding areas, have engaged in various self-help programs so as to better themselves and the Community in general. Some time ago the Darbeau Development Committee (DDC) came together with the required materials and constructed for themselves a garbage dump, using concrete blocks. They have also formulated the idea of constructing a Post Office in the area. [They] have done themselves proud in making the washing situation much better of the women, by recently installing two washing sinks . . . They have also paved and concreted the entire laundry area, alleviating the public washing area of mud.

There is little evidence of marginalization in those two communities. Respondents considered themselves well integrated in the rest of the urban and suburban society. Eighty-six percent of them feel that their lives have improved, their choices broadened, since migrating to the capital and resorting to squatting. Members of the communities are generally hard working as individuals and as a collective. They build their own houses in addition to much of the overall community infrastructure. In this way communities such as these contribute to the development of the urban infrastructure and are not simply a strain on it.

The communities themselves serve as a reception for immigrants. There is much evidence of networking and clustering in those communities. Migrants tend to cluster according to areas of origin and location of the community in relation to the direction from which they came. The emergence of clusters of migrants of the same rural origin suggest a type of migration – chain migration – that connects areas of origin and destination. It also suggests the kind of networking that would occur. This is mainly because the rural push is felt by all members of a community. This explains why Darbeau contains clusters of people from St Patrick's, St Mark's, St John's, and the northwest constituency of St George's while Mon Tout contains clusters of people mainly from St David's, Grand Anse and Calliste within the parish of St George's. People from the same community or parish, friends and relatives, band together, occupy space together, cooperate in constructing each other's houses or adding rooms to existing ones in order to accommodate more people. These linkages are in themselves livelihood strategies. For these and other reasons, including improvements in lifestyles and the enlargening of choices, migration for most of the respondents is permanent.

The findings also suggest that rural to urban migration may be motivated by perceived rather than actual better opportunities and a higher quality of life in the capital. The quality of life – in terms of housing, health, education, income, employment status and other indicators – has not improved for all of the respondents. Nevertheless, there is a strong suggestion that in the popular value system the urban culture is perceived as being somewhat superior to that of the rural. This is reinforced by a tendency of the urban folk to regard rural folk as backward and as 'country bumpkin come to town'. Thus, there are cultural as well as economic reasons for rural to urban migration and the reluctance of migrants to return to their rural villages, even if subjective gains of rural to urban migration may not be significant.

Finally, the study suggests the manner in which these communities are affected by government policies and politics. Politically, both Mon Tout and Darbeau are captive pools of votes that could be decisive in any election result. There is a feeling that the government and the politicians would not give willingly to any of the communities unless they are assured of their votes. And anything the communities want from any government would require the application of pressure on the government to get it. Through pressure and defiance they got the government to survey and allot the land and give the opportunity to purchase title to them. They are aware of their importance to politicians wanting their votes and are generally system supportive so long as the system is perceived as benefiting them. It is part of their livelihood strategy. They are clear about the kind of government assistance the community wants. These are listed as provision of public utilities, particularly roads and water (50 percent), provision of small loans (22 percent), creation of employment (20 percent), and housing assistance (9 percent) in that order.

Several policy implications follow from the findings of this study. These are outlined below:

1. Planned development

In a situation such as that of Grenada where human needs are hard to meet, resources of all kinds are limited, unemployment high, and rural to urban migration is on the increase, it is essential that policy be put in place to ensure that development takes place in a planned and orderly manner. Not only must such planning be concerned with the macroeconomics of development, it must integrate the spatial, social and equity aspects of planning as well.

2. Need for agrarian reform

There is a definite need for agrarian reform in Grenada. The fact that 90 percent of respondents cited landlessness as one of the most compelling reasons for squatting, and the fall in prices of the traditional export crops and consequent loss of livelihood as precipitating their migration to the capital is significant. They point to land reform and crop diversification as two of the most important aspects of agrarian reform that should be given priority. A successful land reform and crop diversification program will make land, particularly private ownership, available to the rural masses, while a change to nontraditional agricultural produce for which external markets could be found will serve to break the dependence on the traditional cocoa, nutmeg and banana crops.

3. Undertake systematic analysis of the rural-urban contradiction

It is evident that government and nongovernment agencies as well as national development planners must undertake a systematic analysis of the rural to urban contradiction in order to create linkages between rural and urban economies that would foster rural to urban area integration as a major strategy of national development. This is in recognition of the fact that rural development interventions and initiatives by themselves can only have a limited impact on the rural-urban dichotomy, and would be more effective if integrated within a comprehensive spatial planning and sustainable national development strategy. Such a development strategy should be holistic, involving qualitative changes in the political, social, economic and cultural lives of the people; it should be people centred, integral and transformative.

4. Broad-based, simultaneous operations at different levels

The feedback from respondents strongly suggests that policymakers in their attempts to intervene into their communities need to consider the following characteristics common to them. These include high levels of unemployment; low skills and educational attainment; an overrepresentation of young people; a high level of one parent families; a concentration of poor and cheap housing; and poor physical infrastructure. The fact that these problems are interdependent and mutually reinforcing necessitates a broad-based, integrated, multiobjective policy that would simultaneously operate at different levels. Single objective operations such as the surveying of the land by the government and offering the people legal title to their plots upon purchase, cannot work effectively unless programmes to enhance residents employability and income earning capacities are implemented. Many of the respondents complained that although they are offered the plots at fairly reasonable prices, they were either unemployed or their incomes were too low to allow them to purchase their lots.

In addition, as far as possible, policymakers must adopt the principle of public participation in policy design, implementation and evaluation. This may involve the public assessment of the problems of space organization and their alternative solution to those identified by professionals. This will ensure that the spatial and environmental perceptions of the people most likely to be affected by the policies are given due recognition in the policy making process. Moreover, it is one way of harnessing the initiatives of the people to complement the innovations of the professional planners.

5. Role for NGOs

All the respondents agree that NGOs have done nothing for the two communities studied. Nevertheless, the findings suggest that there are crucial roles that NGOs could play in these communities.

NGOs have and can continue to play a significant role in the empowerment of the rural and urban poor. Empowerment here refers to the ability of the poor to live fuller lives and have power over their destinies (Seragaldin 1991). My reference here is to the empowerment that comes through initiatives taken at the grass roots level by the poor themselves and through their collaborative efforts to acquire the skills and the means that would enable them to enlarge their choices and transform their lives.

NGOs have also played invaluable roles in developing countries in ensuring that development policies undertaken both by government and themselves reflect a concern for redistribution, social equality and popular participation in decision making.

6. Capitalize on self-help

Policies designed to help improve the quality of life in those communities – laying down infrastructure, providing public services like garbage collection bins and so on – could take advantage of the willingness of the residents to provide voluntary labour. The findings suggest, however, that such community self-help should not be abused. Self-help is a survival strategy of the poor to allocate scarce time and resources in accomplishing their own livelihood goals. It is not a way to relieve governments of the cost of labour in laying down the infrastructure and providing the services which the people of these communities, as tax payers, deserve. In middle class residential areas governments lay down infrastructure and provide amenities without expecting or calling upon residents to do it themselves. Many of the respondents pointed out this contradiction and identified it as social injustice and class bias.

7. Financial assistance

Many of the respondents, particularly the women, aspire to create their own employment. They are would-be entrepreneurs whose only hindrance is the necessary capital to launch their enterprises. They identified loans assistance as the second most popular government assistance they require after government employment creation. Policy should be put in place to identify or establish small loans schemes designed specifically to assist those in need without encumbrances that could discourage them. Such policies would have to take into account the fact that the poor usually choose between poverty and vulnerability, and in cases where debt may increase vulnerability they will not take the risk of going into debt. It is this choice and consideration that, to a large extent, explain the popularity of the Susu – it keeps no record, demands no collateral and requires only total trust. Any loans scheme must factor into its consideration this observation. Perhaps innovative ways could be devised to build upon the small man's own indigenous savings and loan institution – the susu. In many of the developing countries, governments have helped to set up special banks whose main objective is to make banking facilities accessible to the economically disadvantaged. These banks such as the People's Bank of Nigeria (PBN) (Taimiyu 1994) offer short term loan to the rural and urban poor who have no access or limited access to loans from conventional banks. They are usually targeted at those amongst the underprivileged who lack physical collateral, need a small loan and cannot afford to pay the high interests rates for the loans. The PBN, for example, use social collateral as security (Taimiyu 1994). The possibilities that lending arrangements such as these offer could be further explored and, if feasible, adopted.

8. Need for proper problem identification

Although government's decision to survey the lands and offer residents the opportunity to purchase titles to their lots was welcomed, the cutting up of the land itself and the politicians' need to please everyone, have resulted in physical and social problems. Some of these problems include congestion, as already small plots were subdivided by the surveyors to create space for other squatters. The social dynamics and local politics of the communities were completely ignored by those responsible for surveying the lands.

The policy implications are clear: rather than implement quintessentially political decisions, in future, the problems must be carefully identified through appropriate systematic studies before policies are implemented, although the government may argue that it has neither the money nor the personnel to conduct such studies.

Note

1.   Of mixed African/East Indian descent.

7

Putting up a
New Resistance

The Owtu and the Emergence
of an Open, Plural and Democratic
Left in Trinidad and Tobago

Kirk Meighoo

Introduction

The current crisis of development, unemployment, poverty, violence, sovereignty and social vision continues to cut deep into Trinidad and Tobago. And subaltern Trinbagonians,[1] though long used to struggling in extreme situations, are finding themselves in a particularly challenging situation where traditional modes of organized resistance are seeming more and more impotent in the face of the new realities of structural adjustment to a neoliberal global order.

Resistance to oppression in Trinidad and Tobago has traditionally been organized by the Left – trade unionists, Marxists, radical religious persons and intellectuals. After securing political independence in 1962, the ideological Left in Trinidad and Tobago became increasingly dominated by labour-centric understandings, informed theoretically by Marxisms and practically by the importance of the trade unions in transforming the country.

But as the power of global financial capital binds sovereign countries, tears down working livelihoods, and pulls in wealth, opportunity, and usefulness to a tiny centre, the Left needs to reorganize, rethink, redefine, and allow to flourish Trinbagonians' daily attempts to affirm their dignity and worth. To realize this, a new vibrant Left must emerge – one that is plural, open, and democratic. This is neither an idle nor idealist wish; important ingredients of a plural, open, and democratic left are lying about Trinidad and Tobago on the threshold of realization, and a historical leader of popular resistance, the Oilfields Workers' Trade Union (OWTU), has the potential to emerge as one of the leading centres of this 'new' Left.

How such a proposition was arrived at is important, for these concerns colour the approach to this study. A reading of recent (post 1989) Jamaican experience is that the masses of subaltern Jamaicans have rejected middle class leadership and public politics in favour of carving out their own social, cultural, and economic spaces – for instance, in the dancehall and the informal economy. Thus although Prime Minister Patterson raised the General Consumption Tax to 12 percent in 1993 and privatized the sugar industry in 1994, leaving thousands of workers jobless, there was no public protest.

In Trinidad and Tobago, however, a different situation emerged. Struggles in the public spaces of wider politics have been maintained. People are still resisting in front of the government's face. Every week, it seems, one group or other is marching around the Parliament building (Red House) – the police, electricity workers, nurses, nongovernmental organizations – or at least protesting somewhere else. Why has this been? An initial explanation was that the existence of the OWTU – a radical, non-party trade union – was instrumental in the creation of a popular, 'radical democratic' culture in Trinidad and Tobago subverting a middle class 'populist authoritarian' culture which contrasted with present-day Jamaican public politics (Compare Gray 1991; Stone 1980). By radical democratic culture is meant the flourishing of independent social movements within a hegemony of emancipatory goals. The major research questions were: (a) what has been the relationship between the OWTU and other social movements in terms of struggle in Trinidad to democracy and (b) how can public resistances to oppressions be further developed in Trinidad and Tobago?

Methodology

This study is of an exploratory, historical theoretical nature, informed by Jamesian and post-Marxist ideas. In addition, it is based on qualitative, as opposed to quantitative methods. The former involved the use of elite interviews with 24 purposively selected individuals, documents and the life history method, albeit applied to an organization.

The broader philosophical debates that have self- consciously intruded into methodology – questioning, for example, the appropriateness of a natural sciences model to studying people (Bryman 1988:3) or even natural science (Feyeraband 1975) transformed the terms 'qualitative' and 'quantitative' to symbolize two philosophically opposed, warring camps. Quantitative methods represent the scientific method, empiricism, and hypothesis testing, while qualitative methods, on the other hand, symbolize seeing through the eyes of the subjects, thick description, contextualization, process, and meaning (Bryman 1988: 62–71).

Though this study uses qualitative modes – elite interviewing, (organizational) life history, the researcher as the main research and analysis instrument – and shares much of the philosophical bases associated with them – phenomenology, naturalism, ethogenics, symbolic interactionism, and *verstehen* (Bryman 1988: 50) – it does not primarily seek to 'see through the eyes of the subject' or to reveal to the reader an insider's 'meaning'. Indeed, this is perhaps not a realizable task, for all presentation is selective, including insiders', and meanings are plural and unstable.

Rather – in violation of the tenets of the qualitative caricature – an attempt is made to piece together a potential and possibly desirable development in the Trinidadian Left using fragments revealed during interviews. This puts the study roughly in the mold of what Hakim (1987: 3–5) has labelled policy research (as opposed to theoretical research which is more disciplined by academic boundaries). She characterizes policy research as having an "emphasis on substantive or practical importance of research results rather than merely 'statistically significant' findings, and . . . a multidisciplinary approach which in turn leads to the eclectic and catholic use of any and all research designs which might prove helpful in answering the questions posed" (Hakim 1987: 172).

From another perspective, the study is informed by the 'advocate research' model of field work. This model seeks "to help improve the position of those individuals who are studied" (Burgess 1984: 20), although this study is not as self-righteous. No final answers nor definitive explanations are proposed – answers and explanations must be constantly negotiated and renegotiated.

The choice to my focus on the OWTU limited the exploration of the broader issues surrounding social movements, radical democracy, and rethinking the Left – especially how the Trinbagonian social movements relate to the New Social Movements and their postmodernity, about which so much has been recently written (eg, Laclau and Mouffe 1985; Pieterse 1992; Wignaraja 1992). Much research still needs to be done in this area.

Conceptual Framework

There has been no analysis of the postcolonial Trinidadian Left, *per se*. Close is Khafra Kambon's *For Bread, Justice and Freedom* (1988) – a political biography of George Weekes, the president general of the OWTU from 1962 to 1987. Indeed, the lens of Weekes' career captures virtually all significant movements of the postcolonial Trinidadian Left. However, despite Kambon's detail, his focus on Weekes precludes sustained analysis of the Left as a theoretical and practical phenomenon. Also, Franklyn Harvey's (1974) is a good reading of the period 1919 to 1970, but it broadly theorizes rather than closely documents the movements of post-colonial Trinidad and Tobago.

More commonly, works can be found on individual events or movements. The Black Power Revolution of 1970, for example, has inspired works by Craig (1982), Pantin (1991), and Meeks (1976), to mention three of the more important analyses; the birth of the United Labour Front has been favourably assessed by Baptiste (1976) and less so by Ryan (1989); and the events surrounding the 1990 attempted coup have been analyzed again by Ryan (1991). Each of these studies reads the Left from the perspective of the events of interest, rather than interesting itself in the Left as 'the Left'.

While the present study does have that interest in the Left *per se*, it by no means presents itself as a definitive statement on the Left. Rather, as mentioned before, it is concerned with the future of the Trinidadian Left, for the organized Left remains unsure and has been weakened by aggressive and dizzying rushes in both national and global currents. Serious efforts are needed thus to revive organized resistance.

Rethinking the left and democracy

In making a critical synthesis of the Left and democracy, it is first necessary to deal with Marxism – arguably the most severely attacked of the Left's

positions. As Mills (1991) argues, Marxism in the region has been dominated by a dogmatic, formulaic, vanguardist Marxist-Leninism and has
been unable to address adequately problems of race, gender, and envi-
ronmentalism within its class-centric epistemology. In the present situation, the heavy blows dealt by the degeneration of the Grenadian
Revolution in 1983 and the collapse of the USSR in 1991, in the context
of a brutal global restructuring of politics, production, and society have
put the Left in a severe crisis, fighting for its very existence. But in one
sense, the crisis is nothing new. For throughout its histories, Marxism and
the Left have faced a series of crises locally, regionally, and globally. In
fact, much of the rethinking prompted by earlier crises remain vitally
important in the present context.

An important starting point is the vast body of theory of the late C. L. R.
James. In the recently published book, *American Civilization* (1993), written
as notes in 1950, James argues for a radical Marxist rethinking of the Left
in the United States. That period in which James wrote has many parallels
with the present. The United States had just emerged victorious from
World War II and international political and production relations were
radically metamorphosing. The McCarthyist emergence of the Right,
which was to later victimize James had not yet begun, and the country
was rocked by aggressive industrial action at both national and local
levels. The organized Left was in disarray.

James argued that to 'Bolshevize America' the entire history of the
nation needed to be recognized as a revolutionary movement, not by a
few enlightened leaders in a limited circle of society, but by the American
people as a whole, with all their peculiar characteristics. Thus in James'
analysis, the pioneer history, the Abolitionist movement, the Civil War,
the labour movement, and the emerging mass popular culture, were all
given revolutionary significance. And, indeed, the Civil Rights struggle,
the Women's movement, and the New Left were foreshadowed a decade
or so before they started in earnest.

The labour movement, ardent Leninists, and revolutionists who
consciously labeled themselves socialists or Marxists were not privileged in James' analysis. For James, the lifelong Marxist, socialism was
the result of specific, culture-bound struggles of ordinary men and
women against oppression, not stale universal formulae written by
Marx, Lenin, Trotsky, and so on. It was humanity's creative and
unpredictable moves to direct democracy (Look Lai 1992). Marxism

was the method by which intellectuals and others were to understand the movement of the masses of people.

On the other hand, postmodern and post-Marxist political theories, with their emphasis on new social movements (eg, ecology, feminism, peace, antiracism) see Marxism as a historical phenomenon of the previous era of modernity – the age of total, rationalist, universalist theory. The New Social Movements, they maintain, have generated new practices and theorizing, much of which has not filtered through to social theory (Pieterse 1992b: 5). Trying to capture these, Laclau and Mouffe (1985: 1–2) argue that the new social movements

imply an extension of social conflictuality to a wide range of areas, which creates the potential . . . for an advance towards more free, democratic and egalitarian societies . . . What is now in crisis is a whole conception of socialism which rests upon the ontological centrality of the working class, upon the role of Revolution, with a capital 'r', as the founding moment in the transition from one type of society to another, and upon the illusory prospect of a perfectly unitary and homogeneous collective will that will render pointless the moment of politics. The plural and multifarious character of contemporary social struggles has finally dissolved the last foundation for that political imaginary. Peopled with 'universal' subjects and conceptually built around History in the singular, it has postulated 'society' as an intelligible structure that could be intellectually mastered on the basis of certain class positions and reconstituted, as a rational, transparent order, through a founding act of a political character. Today, the Left is witnessing the final act of the dissolution of that Jacobin imaginary.

Theoretically, Laclau and Mouffe challenge Marxism with postmodern insights. Discourse is a key concept, referring to an ordering of relationships among elements, thus creating identities. But because of the possibility of alternative elemental relationships, however, all discourses are subverted by others and can never close. Relatively stable identities, however, are created by overdetermination – that is, the convergence of many discourses affirming the identity of an element. However, these convergences are not perfectly congruent – for all identities are unstable. Closure is impossible. Indeed, antagonism, they argue, is the result of this potential negation of identity through the power of other discourses (eg, a serf is the servant of his or her master, but both serf and master are equal children of God, or a master can take away a serf's plot). Antagonism is the limit of objectivity. It is the possibility of an alternative relationship. These theoretical keys unlock the stability and permanence of identities and relationships.

From this perspective, postmodernists contend that "state and civil society today increasingly compete with capital and class" due to the "shifts in the form and rationale of maintaining and creating 'order' on the one hand and the focal point for efforts at preserving or enlarging social 'space' on the other" (Doornbos 1992: 1). Indeed, the goals of the New Social Movements are "more subtle, multiple and modest than the 'modern' views. It's a matter of progress against the backdrop of pragmatism and emancipation in the no-nonsense era" (Pieterse 1992b: 5).

What both the Jamesian and post-Marxist critiques do is to decentre the Left by contextualizing Marxism. For both, Marxism was a demand internal to the democratic revolution (Laclau and Mouffe 1985: 156; Worcester 1992). However, the post-Marxists base themselves on the argument that there are no universal and necessary privileged points of resistance in contemporary capitalist society – these points are determined historically in an active non-necessary way. On the other hand, James' focus is on the creative unpredictability of existential subjects – with an absolute surety of their resistance to oppression. For him, it is whatever the masses of people *do* – watch lots of violent movies, march on Washington, consistently subvert management's orders – that is important.

This brings us to the question of democracy, for if as James insists, the masses are creative and unpredictable, and as the post-Marxists assert discourse is never closed, fixing final ends is a totalitarian impossibility, like the Soviet Union. Democracy, then, is important for its openness and allowance of plurality. Indeed, in a recent struggle within the Trinbagonian Left upon which James had a significant impact, it has been argued that "Marxism without Democratic Participation by the people (especially those who survive under capitalist exploitation) is not Marxism" (Paul 1990a). In fact, the perspective of Schumpeter (1976: 242) is absolutely crucial when he remarks that, "Democracy is a political *method* ... incapable of being an end in itself, irrespective of what decision it will produce under given historical conditions. And this must be the starting point of any attempt at defining it". Central to this is the absolute necessity of the right to dissent, free expression, and argument. Theoretically, this is based on the instability of all discourse. This right to dissent taken up by the New Social Movements, such as the NGOs, has been used to expand democracy into the sacred nonpolitical and private areas defined by liberal democracy, such as the 'technical' area of development

(Clark 1990: 14). Indeed, the "social movements of the 1960s were regarded as an 'excess of democracy' resulting in the 'ungovernability' of Western societies . . . In like manner, the 'revolution of rising expectations' and consequent large-scale mobilization in developing countries were viewed negatively" (Pieterse 1992b: 7). Seemingly "everything" was politicized (Reddock 1991: 6–7).

Many postmodern and post-Marxist theorists emphasizing their rejection of the idea that identities are single, closed and constant (eg, a person is, at base, working class) have focused their political activity, therefore, on the realization of a radical democracy – one "without foundations" (Keane 1992). As Keane (1992: 25) observes, modernist democracy historically had a substantive grounding principle – for Mazzini, the growth of democracy was a Law of History; for George Forster and Tom Paine, democracy was grounded in the natural right of citizens; for Jeremy Bentham democracy was an implied condition of the principle of utility; for Theodore Parker, it was the form of government based on the principle of eternal God-given justice; and for Marx, it depended on the world-historic struggle of the proletariat.

Postmodernists, on the other hand, assert that foundations are ultimately untenable, that all meaning and identity is unstable and plural. For Keane (1992: 125), then, "democracy is best understood as an implied condition and practical consequence of philosophical and political pluralism". This is the political implication of their reading that New Social Movements, for example, do not take the interests or the identities of actors as given (Pieterse 1992b: 21). We are in the era of postmodern politics.

My own position is both Jamesian and post-Marxist. I reject the possibility of closure. However, I do believe that subordinated peoples' perspectives on their oppression are the most important liberating discourses on those particular struggles. For instance I will automatically privilege a white working class man's perspective on wage labour. However, his view on women's oppression or antiblack racism will not be treated with the same automatism, for resistance and oppression are historically and culturally defined and carried out by specific peoples, each with their own characteristics to draw upon.

Implicit in this argument is that oppressed people know what is best for them. The opposite argument is put forward by forms of elitist theory. Charles Mills (1988), in his analysis of elitism in Marxist theory, traces back to Plato's allegory of the cave the idea that enlightened elites have the right to rule. This perspective maintains that only a select few are able to know the true interests of society. The mass of people, although they may think they know their true interests, are dominated by "false consciousness". This is how many Marxists, for example, explain the unashamed and willing involvement of the working class in capitalism, the source of their oppression.

In direct challenge to this view, however, I firmly stand on the side of James C. Scott (1990) and his arguments against "false consciousness". His thesis is based on the idea that there exist public and hidden transcripts, ie that people participate in different discourses depending on their relation of power with their audience. For example, a slave may likely speak differently to his/her master than he/she would to her companions or to his/her lover. Scott (1990: xi) convincingly asserts that "every subordinate group creates, out of its ordeal, a 'hidden' transcript that represents a critique of power spoken behind the back of the dominant". Conversely, the 'public transcript' acts as a necessary shield, hiding acts of material and symbolic resistance (eg, pilfering, nonpayment of tax, laziness). "False consciousness", he maintains, is merely the subordinates' public discourse. Indeed, when more open alternatives are judged as less favourable by the subordinates, defending their shield (their 'commitment' to the status quo) is a necessity for continued resistance. So if workers do not demonstrate in an OWTU-led rally against privatization, rather than scolding the workers for being duped by management I would look to see why, "in their wisdom", as Glen Ramjag (1994b) puts it, they had not joined. Like feminist Naomi Wolf (1993), I reject the idea of subordinate people as primarily victims. Rather I see them as people waging a daily struggle for survival and, eventually, victory over their conditions. Domination is never complete. Democracy then is the condition where resistance is public, implying less unequal power.

By not rejecting Marxism, but by contextualizing it – by seeing it as a specific historical and cultural expression of resistance to oppression, the Left can more easily accommodate new and different discourses of liberation. But to do so, the closed Marxist definition of the Left, for example, that it must necessarily be against private property or profit, must be opened, allowing for other historical, culture-bound resistances to express themselves. The Left must therefore be plural, open, and democratic – plural to accommodate different struggles, open to allow new struggles to be expressed, and democratic to ensure that the subordinate end their own subordination in their own ways.

The OWTU and the Left in Trinidad and Tobago

Struggle has been central to the history of Trinidad and Tobago, and the OWTU has been a most important weight in the subaltern press against power. It has never been only concerned with traditional trade union issues and neither has it been afraid of politics (Ramsaroop 1990: 5). The OWTU was born out of a raging fire when in the 1930s, Tubal Uriah 'Buzz' Butler led oil workers in a series of powerful tumults against the British colonial government. In the 1940s and 1950s, the new legalized labour movement (made more 'responsible' by expelling leaders like Butler), in tandem with social work organizations, ethnic nationalist movements, youth groups, socialists, and home rule agitators struggled in the islands to gain independence from the British Empire (Reddock 1984b). However, after Independence was finally secured in 1962, the new government – the People's National Movement who emerged as the leader of the nationalist movement in the previous decade – found itself fiercely opposed by the increasingly (re)radicalized labour movement, of which the OWTU was a leading part. Oppression and resistance had been transformed in postcolonial Trinidad and Tobago.

The structure of the OWTU

The OWTU was founded in 1937 and, as would be expected, has had various modes of organization throughout its history. Today's organizational structure, however, can be traced back to the takeover in 1962 by the 'Rebel' faction, under which the union has remained to the present day. In *Rules of the OWTU* (OWTU 1989a: 2) it states, *inter alia*:

The objects of the Union shall be as follows:

1. To secure the complete organization in the Union of all workers who wish to join the Union, notwithstanding that such workers are not employed in the Oil Industry.

2. To obtain and maintain just and proper rates of wages, hours of work and other conditions of labour and generally to protect the interest of its members . . .

16. To do all other lawful things such as are incidental or conducive to the attainment of the above objects or any of them.

Importantly, Object 16 sanctions the creative and potentially subversive pursuit of its relatively tamer and more conventional objects listed above it.

The supreme body of authority in the OWTU is the Annual Conference of Delegates, with one representative for every fifty financial members. Subordinate to this is the general council, consisting of the president, the secretary, and a delegate from each branch, and the presidents of the district committees, meeting every month. This structure institutes more popular representation to check the more traditionally hierarchical structure below it. Occasionally, too, a Conference of Shop Stewards and Branch Officers (COSSABO) or a mass membership meeting (MMM) is called – very directly democratic decision-making fora.

The Executive Committee is next in the line of authority, meeting monthly, between General Council meetings. Below this are the Branch authorities, with their executives and management committees meeting every week. Next are the local district committees whose executives and committees meet every two weeks (OWTU 1994a). Additionally there was the now dormant Women's Auxiliary Group, who for reasons of membership commitment and organization no longer meet. Important too is the Education and Research Department, which performs several functions relating to regional and international relations, research and publications, education and training, sport, culture and the community.

Membership in the OWTU has risen and fallen dramatically throughout its history. In the beginning almost every oil worker was on its membership rolls (OWTU 1977). Numbers sharply dropped after Butler was expelled in 1939 and it was only in the early 1950s that it picked up. Membership rose from about 5,000 in 1951 to 8,700 in 1953. After dropping by 1,700 between 1961 and 1963, membership climbed again to a peak of 10,500 in 1967. After 1967, however, non-oil workers were allowed to join the union (Ramsaran 1990: 81) and membership skyrocketed to 20,000 by 1976 (OWTU 1977: 57). From the mid-1980s, however, through retrenchment and other union-busting techniques in the era of structural adjustment, membership has drastically reduced with no sure end in sight. In 1987 the OWTU had 13,400 members (Ramsaran 1990: 206) and the official membership figure for 31 March 1994 is 11,200 (OWTU 1994a).

Despite these fluctuations, the OWTU membership base has consistently expanded throughout its history, macrophagically moving from the representation of semi and unskilled workers to include skilled workers, white collar junior and senior staff, and workers in non-petroleum industries. Today, though smaller than it was at the beginning of the 1980s, the union still represents workers from the petroleum, chemical, construction, utilities, and food processing industries (OWTU 1994a).

The OWTU is also involved in other areas. For instance the organization also owns nonadministrative property including a recreation club, a printery, an agricultural estate and a farm. Additionally, as intimated above, the union is involved in activities not traditionally associated with trade unions. Some of these include for example, organizing national dialogues where national issues are debated, the Caribbean People's Book Fair, a steelband competition in South Trinidad, sports and competitions for special children, an annual school quiz, and participation in various academic and cultural events (OWTU 1994a). The OWTU, then, by itself, represents a large section of Trinidad and Tobago, organized democratically, and involved in a wide array of activities.

From independence to black power

In 1962, just before Trinidad and Tobago's formal independence, the 'Rebels' faction in the OWTU succeeded in their fight for 'one man (sic) one vote' in the union and the militant George Weekes was elected as president general. One month earlier, the Transport and Industrial Workers' Union (TIWU), breaking away from the Amalgamated Workers' Union (AWU), was also founded on the basis of full electoral democracy, with another militant, Joe Young, elected as its leader (Young 1994). This movement towards greater democracy, along with the election of militant leaders, revitalized workers' struggles against capitalist exploitation. Indeed, between 1960 and 1965, there were some 237 strikes involving some 82,000 workers and resulting in almost a million person-days lost (Henry 1988: 48).

George Weekes, leader of both the OWTU and the National Trade Union Congress (NTUC), had emerged as a national champion of workers' struggles. This was stormily evident in 1965 when, after their union leader Bhadase Sagan Maharaj, who also was the major national Indian religious and political leader, broke their strike by bringing in scab labour and gangster force, sugar workers, who are mainly Indian, approached the NTUC for help (Weekes 1965). George Weekes took up and encouraged the sugar workers' struggle against its leadership, stirring up strong reactions on all sides. This sometimes violent showdown, occurring at the same time as strikes by lock joint workers in the sewer network, workers of Federation Chemicals (FedChem), and threats by the Civil Servants Association (Als 1965: 41), prompted then Prime Minister Dr Eric Williams to call in the Defense Force and declare a State of Emergency in the sugar belt, specifically barring OWTU members (Ramsaran, 1990: 80). Soon after the state of emergency, the government released the anticommunist Mbafeno report on subversive activists and passed the infamous Industrial Stabilisation Act, which, among other things, took away unions' right to strike – substituting an industrial court system – and effectively prevented the sugar workers from joining with the oil workers.

Weekes was determined to fight this piece of antiworker legislation. As he argued (Weekes 1967:1), "Trade Unionism is essentially the organizing of workers for the purpose of striking". But many leaders in the NTUC were not willing to fight the PNM government. Weekes resigned from the post of NTUC President and the OWTU and other sympathetic unions left the grouping. Indeed, the OWTU, National Union of Government Employees (NUGE), National Union of Food, Hotel, Beverage and Allied Workers (NUFHB&AW) and TIWU organized a campaign against the ISA that would eventually find success only after years of national struggle (The Concerned Trade Unions, 1986).

In 1965 during the state of emergency, C. L. R. James had returned to Trinidad and was immediately placed under house arrest in the suburban community of Barataria, a non-sugar growing area brought under the emergency for this very reason. James, who was invited by Williams to edit the official newspaper of the PNM, *The Nation*, in 1958 only to resign amidst party intrigue and controversy in 1961, decided to start the Workers and Farmers Party (WFP) in 1965. Although the party fared dismally at the polls, it threw up important political activists including George Weekes, Basdeo Panday, Joe Young, and John Humphrey (Burnett 1989: 57). The OWTU had a strong presence in the party, and indeed, provided its printing services.

In 1968, however, the TIWU was engaged in an illegal, in the context of the ISA, defiant bus strike that was to boil over furiously into mass struggle and resistance. This action, along with marches, radical university organizations, the inspiration of Black Power struggles in the United

States, and bitter industrial action against British Petroleum and Texaco by the OWTU were fueling a violently dancing national fire.

Black Power to bloody Tuesday

By 1970, the Black Power Revolution had begun. The university based National Joint Action Committee (NJAC), a national coalition of socialist, black nationalist, trade union, unemployed, and other radical groupings, emerged as the leaders of this mass uprising. The Black Power Revolution can be said to have started with the Sir George Williams University Affair in Montréal, Canada where five West Indian students were charged with destroying university computers in a response to racism. NJAC organized a march around the capital Port of Spain in February 1970 singling out foreign and local white-controlled business places in a cry for Black Power. The leaders were taken to court, and after their release on bail the next day, they set about mobilization throughout the country in lectures, demonstrations, and marches including a historic march from Port of Spain to Caroni in order to symbolize and encourage the common struggle of Africans and Indians (Riviere 1972). As the intensity and purpose of the mass actions were growing, including plans for a joint May Day between NJAC and the labour movement (OWTU 1970: 55), the PNM called a state of emergency on 21 April 1970. In further rebellion, young soldiers in the army refused to carry out the Emergency orders that day. This 'mutiny', however, was soon contained.

The state of emergency allowed the government to use its full force to crush the rebellion and its leading organizations such as NJAC (Kromah 1987: 23). The OWTU was victimized through the incarceration of Weekes and three other Union members, attempts to burn down its printery, the union headquarters, and its recreation club, the confiscation of books and records, and the attacking of their business places (OWTU 1970: 55). It was at this time that the COSSABO and the MMM were introduced, to radically deal with the aggressive attacks by the establishment (Kambon 1988: 238). In addition, the OWTU played a leading part – in conjunction with NJAC and other unions – organizing jerseys, posters, leaflets, streamers and indoor meetings to defeat the repressive Public Order Bill introduced on 7 August 1970 – all this done during the state of emergency, while the leadership of both the OWTU and NJAC were in prison (Kambon 1988: 237–38).

After the emergency was lifted later that year, the unions floutingly engaged in numerous strike actions, effectively defeating the 1965 ISA. The general election in May was boycotted by all the major political opposition parties; the NJAC-OWTU political axis was most significant at this time (Kambon 1988: 259). In response, the governing PNM called another state of emergency in 1971 and passed the Industrial Relations Act (IRA) to replace the destroyed ISA.

Despite the PNM's efforts to localize the economy and create a people's sector, mass unrest continued with numerous small groups coming and going like bubbles in a furious boil. Included in these groups was the National Union of Freedom Fighters, a guerrilla group, brutally outgunned by the state. The prime minister threatened to resign in 1973 but later reversed his decision. At about the same time, the formation of Organization of Petroleum Exporting Countries (OPEC) and the ensuing rise in oil prices dramatically changed the fate of the country as it was to experience its biggest economic boom ever.

Despite the economic growth, however, ordinary people were still suffering. After the death of Bhadase Maharaj, the leader of sugar workers, OWTU lawyer Basdeo Panday had been invited to lead the workers in the warring sugar industry (Ramsaran 1990: 103). By 1975, in the midst of intense labour struggles in the cane fields, the sugar estates, and the oil fields Committee for Labour Solidarity ([CLS] 1981: 5), a United Labour Front (ULF) was convened in San Fernando. It brought together 25 to 40,000 people from quite mainstream to quite radical backgrounds under the leadership of the All Trinidad Sugar and General Workers Union (ATSGWU), the OWTU, TIWU, and the newly formed Islandwide Cane Farmers Trade Union (ICTU) led by Raffique Shah, a leader of the army mutiny in 1970. By this time NJAC had spaded out its socialist members who were active in trade union struggles and transformed itself into a cultural nationalist organization (Udika 1993: 16).

On 18 March 1976, after the police brutally attacked a 10,000-strong march for "Bread, Peace and Justice", the ULF was transformed into a political party, becoming the official opposition in 1976. Importantly, the campaigning of the ULF gave the OWTU greater credibility in the East/West corridor of Trinidad expanding its influence from its base in South Trinidad (Ramsaroop, 1990: 36). Many of the newer leaders of the OWTU, such as David Abdulah, Gerald Kangalee, Cecil Paul, Winston Edwards, Ian Belgrave, Doodnath Maharaj, Winston Dass, and (now president general) Errol McLeod – who was elected MP for Oropouche – were important members of the ULF.

However, after two years in the seat of political opposition, leadership struggles caused a significant portion of the more socialist oriented and African members to leave the party including three of the four founding leaders – Raffique Shah, George Weekes, and Joe Young. One of the arguments advanced for the failure of the ULF to win the 1976 general election was that the party was seen as 'too Indian'. This was to be the last large mass movement in Trinidad and Tobago.

By 1977, however, due to "pressure from the OWTU and other world progressive forces" Shell Oil, Tesoro, the sugar industry, transport, communications, television, radio, and television, printing and packaging, and meat processing industries had all been nationalized (OWTU 1977: 4-5). Additionally, through wage increases secured from the multinationals by the OWTU (followed by increased demands by other workers), a significant increase of money had been retained for use in the domestic economy. And the Cost of Living Allowance (COLA) won in 1945, shift bonuses, high quality housing plans, pension plans won in 1965, and compensation for dangerous work due to heat, rain, or height which were first won by the OWTU, also spread to other workers (OWTU 1977).

The end of the oil boom, structural adjustment and the *coup d'etat*

Unrest continued in the society, as new groups, including the Housewives Association of Trinidad and Tobago (HATT) emerged along with the labour movement articulating popular protest. By 1980 and 1981 a tidal wave of protest – including strikes by teachers, nurses, doctors, FedChem workers, and sugar workers – was rocking the island and the PNM was put under great pressure (Abdulah 1994b). Nineteen eighty-one, however, saw the death of Prime Minister Dr Eric Williams, who despite all the enemies he made, earned respect from a great majority of Trinbagonians for his work to liberate Trinidad and Tobago. Elections were held that year, prompting the formation of the radical Committee for Labour Solidarity (CLS)[2] whose mission was to build a critical working class political consciousness and unity that would later be able to root in a future party (CLS 1981: 1). In the elections, however, the PNM was re-elected under the leadership of George Chambers.

By 1984, the oil boom was over. Importantly, structural adjustment was beginning cautiously and slowly in both the private and public sectors

(Kangalee 1994). With its fierce attack on unionism, the labour-centric forms of resistance that were ideologically and practically developing in the 1970s were losing much of their material basis. Between January 1984 and July 1986 there were twenty instances of employers locking out their employees (JTUM 1986). During these lockouts, watered-down individual contracts were used to replace collective agreements. On the other hand, there were only six strikes during the period and these were either to prevent wage freezes or the taking back of benefits especially COLA (JTUM 1986). Employers were becoming increasingly aggressive and attacked the unions ferociously. Indeed, between 1982 and 1986 50,000 workers were retrenched (JTUM, 1986). But the unions fought back. Much of the struggle against this heightened employer aggression was concentrated in industries along the East-West corridor, with some of the most important strikes occurring at Lever Brothers, Bermudez, McEnearney, Brewery Workers, Tractors and Machinery, Neal & Massey, and Metal Box. Spirited struggles in the South at Texaco, Dunlop, and FedChem and in Tobago at Crown Reef and Crown Point Hotels dealt with similar issues (OWTU 1986).

In addition, workers of the Development and Environmental Works Division (DEWD) were demonstrating on the streets in 1984-85, nurses were protesting, dockworkers and Caroni workers were publicly remonstrating in 1985–86, as were the pig and foodcrop farmers. Marches were held in San Fernando, Cedros, and Arima in May and August 1984. In January 1984, at the decision of an innovative joint Trade Union COSSABO, thousands picketed around the Red House, pre-empting harsher budget measures. The OWTU called the other unions to discuss these burning issues resulting in a Statement on Retrenchment and another picket around the Red House in September 1985. A joint COSSABO of nine major unions was later called and on 23 October 1985 a Day of Sacrifice was called. One hundred thousand people representing 15 unions rallied in Woodford Square in the largest working day demonstration of workers since 1975 (The Concerned Trade Unions 1986). Also important was the intense struggle by the Women's Movement against the government over the Sexual Offences Bill in 1986.

These actions, combined with the unifying of four major opposition parties – ULF, Tapia House Movement, the Organization for National Reconstruction, and Democratic Action Congress – into the National Alliance for Reconstruction (NAR) with its euphoric 'One Love' campaign, defeated the PNM in 1986. It was the first defeat for the latter since 1958.

Under the NAR, however, structural adjustment policies further intensified – even while George Weekes became a senator, and the OWTU received the honour of being the only Union having a stamp issue devoted to it. Retrenchments, wage cuts and freezes, privatization, and the dismembering of the public sector evoked strong reaction from the population. In 1988, with the signing of an IMF agreement and the expulsion of the ULF elements from the NAR, structural adjustment proceeded at an even faster pace. That year, in October, a massive antigovernment rally was organized in the capital by the trade union movement (OWTU 1990: 73). Also, the OWTU responded to the swift autocratism of the NAR by initiating a National Dialogue series, calling on trade unions, small and medium businesses, the churches, cultural organizations, progressive intellectuals, political parties and organizations, women's groups, co-operative societies, state enterprises, community organizations, university-based organizations and individuals, and concerned citizens (OWTU 1988: 72). It also spearheaded "Community Media for Development" that year so that the media would "reflect all views and in particular the views, concerns, and interests of the majority of people – the working people" (OWTU 1988).

Aggressive resistance was resurfacing, with the Meat Processors workers engaged in a struggle against one of the first privatizations in the country, occupying the plant for two and a half years. Furthermore, a Joint Trade Union Movement (JTUM) had been formed to bring about trade union unity and militancy, while community and newly formed nongovernmental organizations intensified protest. On 6 March 1989, the country responded to a call by the labour movement to take the day off from work, shutting down the entire country in a Day of Resistance. That month, too, workers at the Crown Reef Hotel in Tobago occupied the building to protest the retrenchment of 100 workers. In addition, in 1990, the Summit of People's Organizations (SOPO) – with significant organization by the OWTU leadership – was created to unite the various struggles against the policies of the NAR.

In the midst of mass protest, on 27 July 1990, a small group of men from the Jamaat-al-Muslimeen violently deposed the government for a period of ten days while mass burning and looting occurred in Port of Spain. A state of emergency was called and the government tried to silence opposition and control the country. Resistance was not crushed however. Importantly, after years of intensive and creative efforts, led by many OWTU Officers, the trade union movement unified under the National Trade Union Centre (NATUC) in 199 – with OWTU President-General, Errol McLeod, as its president. In the 1991 general elections, the NAR was wholly discredited and the PNM was re-elected. But far from discontinuing the policies of structural adjustment, the PNM continued them, notwithstanding its populist rhetoric while in opposition.

Entry Points to an Open, Plural, and Democratic Left

The struggle for democracy has been central to popular struggle in Trinidad and Tobago. Indeed, through intense battles, the country has had universal adult suffrage since 1946, more than two decades before many of the 'advanced' countries in the North. And certainly, the Commonwealth Caribbean as a whole stands out in the post-World War II world for its democratic longevity and stability (Rueschemeyer, et al. 1992: 226). In contrast, however, other commentators, such as Jones (cited in Ramsaroop 1990: 7–10), argue that the Caribbean has been bequeathed an undemocratic and authoritarian heritage. He argues that the prevailing nonbargaining culture had to be broken by violence and agitation through nonconstitutional means: crimes, absenteeism from plantations, strikes, riots, and demonstrations. These were in turn met by official reformism, paternalism, and co-optation used to wither away the groups – strategies commonly employed today. As evidence of this heritage, Jones points to the culture of individual self-enhancement, the official hostility to intellectualism displayed by the prominence of nongovernment schools, the white supremacist discourse, the limited universe of pressure groups, and the mutual interest of both Government and the official Opposition in maintaining the status quo (Ramsaroop 1990, 7–10).

Due to its relatively late settlement Trinidad has been referred to as a "frontier society" (Rohlehr 1990: 19; Lewis 1968: 197) with many religions, diverse ethnic identities, and an immigrant fibre characterizing the country. This has heightened concerns of autonomy, difference and identity, and contributed to its high valuation of freedom – very similar to James' (1993) argument about the USA. Indeed, in June of 1994, out-going US Ambassador to Trinidad, Sally Cowal, noted the similarity between the two countries' love for freedom and democracy. These traits are a distinctive part of a Trinidadian personality, which both Look Loy (1994), a political activist, and Kangalee (1994), OWTU Education Officer, substantiated. This very West Indian trait, historically engaged with a relatively open pluralism as opposed to a closed authoritarianism, gives it its Trinidadian character. Besides 'character', Christopher Laird (1994) argues that Trinidad's population has been better educated politically due to the smaller size of the country, and the wider education system.

Democratic discourse in Trinidad and Tobago

In addition to its plural history, it is argued that the liberal democratic system of government in Trinidad and Tobago has given the society a public political transcript based on (liberal) democratic ideals – liberty and equality. Even when defending the interests of the powerful, the local media, for example, couches the defense in terms of democracy (*Express*, 15 December 1970).

More progressively, the Tapia House Movement, a political party coming out of the influential University based New World Group of the 1960s, provided some interesting contributions to the expansion of democracy in the 1970s. This was done through their publications and analyses of the Trinbagonian political structure, calls for decentralization, and their obsessive struggle for constitutional reform which included the establishment of a large "Macco Senate" open to all national community groups (Duncan 1977: 14).

A particularly hopeful time surrounded the coalition that created the NAR in 1985. Indeed, a collection of papers from a major conference entitled *Forging a New Democracy* (Sebastien 1985) was an early contribution, prodding the political boundaries of change in Trinidad and Tobago. And in respect of the political form that the NAR should take, Lloyd Best (1986), also of Tapia, advocated that:

The party [the NAR] must remain a coalition of interests; it must remain a coalition party, which is not the same thing as a coalition government. Its virtue is precisely that it is not monolithic and right now I believe we are selling our party [the NAR] the wrong way by stressing that it is unitary.

Indeed, during the time of the split in the NAR, the principal leaders of the ULF faction Basdeo Panday, John Humphrey, and Trevor Sudama complained of "authoritarianism", "schoolmasterism", and "dictatorial mentality", respectively (Baptiste 1988; *Express* 1988; Mahabir 1988).

Within more recent times, Hulsie Bhaggan of the United National Congress, the former official opposition led by Basdeo Panday, created a national stir by voting against her party's position in Parliament. She opened up the issue of "conscience voting" on certain issues, and questioned the process "where the personal views of some form the basis of the party line" (*Sunday Guardian*, 10 July 1994).

But despite its importance, the Left, as feminist lawyer Roberta Clarke (1994) argues, has not grappled with the issue of democracy sufficiently. The degeneration of the Grenadian Revolution of 1979–83, ending in the murder of Maurice Bishop and a US invasion, placed a post squarely in their path. But the issue of democracy was bypassed. As Mills (1988: 13) laments: "The left has spectacularly discredited itself, and will be on the defensive for years to come".

Recently, however, spurred on by the international crisis of the Left following the revolutions in Eastern Europe, there has been a sharpened debate over democracy within the Left in Trinidad and Tobago. Indeed, the OWTU leadership has been at the centre of the two major debates. The first debate centred around the political party called the Movement for Social Transformation (MOTION), and the second surrounded the 1994 OWTU elections.

MOTION

The political leader of MOTION, David Abdulah (1994a), recounts that when the Committee for Labour Solidarity was formed in 1981, it was based on a new vision of democracy. The vanguardist Leninist ideologies, which were popular in the late 1960s and early 1970s, had lost prominence in Left circles as that new generation of leadership gained experience with organizing Trinbagonians especially through the ULF and the OWTU. The CLS, in fact, was very much like a modern day version of the Political Action Committee (PAC) of 1964–65, in which C. L . R. James was involved (Burnett 1989:4). The PAC was a "workers' nonpartisan watchdog" which later transformed into the Workers' and Farmers' Party (Hackshaw 1991: 11).

The CLS committed itself to struggle against elitism – "an elitism that begins on the premise that a few people, or worse yet a leader, can decide for the people what is best for them" (MOTION, 1989: 1). Its immediate goals were to demand consistently the democratic rights and freedoms to march, assemble freely and bargain collectively, strike, and join the union of one's choice (CLS 1981:15). One of their first acts was to distribute a critical, class-based analysis of the political parties running for the 1981 elections (Ramsaroop 1990: 42).

After 7 years of nonpartisan activity, a convocation was held at the OWTU headquarters "attended by over 1,200 patriots of Trinidad and Tobago". Following up on a mandate given at this meeting, for a period of ten months, the CLS enthusiastically set about mobilizing the masses locally and regionally (MOTION 1989: 2).

On Saturday 10 September 1989, on the crest of a momentous wave, the Founding Congress of the Movement for Social Transformation was held in Port of Spain with three or four thousand in attendance. But trouble was brewing. A section of the leadership was critical of the party's practice of democracy. According to a former executive member of MOTION:

Essentially . . . the split revolved around the question of whether in fact we should have a plural, democratic left, with a plural, democratic vision, or whether we should have – to be theoretical or dogmatic, I suppose – democratic centralism. That was the essence of the split. [And three of us at the leadership level] came down firmly on the side of a plural, democratic left, in which the membership of the party could make decisions, of which the leadership would have to abide by and respect. And there were others who believed that the leadership should have veto power and should make decisions for the membership – I could not abide by that.

Indeed, during the first years of the party, executive member Cecil Paul (1990b), for example, raised the issues of the relationship between the Leftist party and democracy. The issues raised were of more than theoretic and programmatic interest, however. Freedom of popular expression was a major issue. Thus the charge that "a clique operated within the CLS and subverted democratic decision making to the extent that opposition and new ideas are treated with hostility, contempt and abuse". One of the events which helped to finalize the break surrounded the changing of the economic programme in March 1990. At a meeting where three quarters of the membership were absent, a split vote was broken by the chairperson's deciding vote. An indignant executive member argued:

I am not prepared to be in any party that will not allow a 'minority' view to continue to exist and for those with opposing view to peacefully exercise their rights to get others to accept their view . . . The problem with MOTION is some of the leaders and their political culture of arrogance, disrespect and contempt for not only the members and activists of the Party, but for the grass roots people of this country. Unless that culture is defeated, MOTION will continue to be plagued with internal conflicts and will remain a small insignificant left wing group. One understands why the workers have not related to the party.

Finally, on 24 April 1991, six persons – Keith Look Loy, Raffique Shah, Paul Harrison, Alva Allen, Cecil Paul, and Sylvester Ramquar – resigned from the 12-member executive council. The split, so soon after its founding, immobilized the party like the leadership warned, leaving it 'motionless', as is popularly said. One commentator noted that 70 percent of the activists had stopped participating and executive and activist council meetings were discontinued. What did remain in motion, however, was the drive for increased democracy in the Left.

The 1993 OWTU elections

In 1993, Cecil Paul and Sylvester Ramquar in many ways re-enacted the MOTION split by contesting the election for the positions of president general and first vice-president of the OWTU, leading a team of 'New Rebels' against the 'old' Rebels. Cecil Paul and Sylvester Ramquar resigned from the OWTU executive in April 1992 "because of dictatorship and abuse of Union Funds, inefficiency, and lack of concern for workers by president-general" Errol McLeod (New Rebels Movement 1993a: 1). After attempts at reconciliation failed – formalized by the appearance of Sylvester Ramquar on national television (New Rebels Movement, 1993a: 1–3) – the campaign became particularly vicious. While concerned with many issues such as the mishandling of the finances, extravagance, nonopenness and nonaccountability, a central concern of the New Rebels' campaign was "democracy in the union". They were viciously harsh and critical of President General Errol McLeod for his supposed affluent lifestyle, reckless statements, national unpopularity, lack of and hostility to new ideas, inability to mobilize and undemocratic leadership – attacking and victimizing of members, ad hoc decisions such as the naming of the C. L. R James Centre, denying voting privileges to the almost 1000 retirees and life members (New Rebels Movement 1993b: 2). They deplored that officers were "not allowed to criticize reports at conferences" and complain that the OWTU has been used to fund MOTION – in particular the expenses of the Caribbean Bookfair and the Caribbean People's Assembly, while MOTION colleagues have been given unlimited powers. George Weekes, they argue, though involved in two political parties never allowed that to happen (New Rebels Movement 1993b: 4). The Movement alleged further that the president-general had picked members for the 1990 executive who would be loyal betraying the Rebels original democratic principles, and condemned the placing of the president-general's image in General Council Reports, in offices, on the *Vanguard* front page over the last year, and even on scrap pads.

In response, Errol McLeod (OWTU 1994a), in an open letter to George Weekes, who in fact declared his support for Cecil Paul, flatly denied charges of being undemocratic. Indeed, he cites instances of actually stretching rules to give time to speakers, etc., and instead charges that these accusations are, in fact, subversive distractions. He reminds Weekes that Weekes himself was similarly accused of being undemocratic, ruthless to opponents, politically interfering, and being "bosom buddies" with one-time PNM minister Errol Mahabir. The charges of being undemocratic were also refuted by David Abdulah (1994a), who accused their opponents of trying "to destabalize the OWTU".

The Rebel Team, led by Errol McLeod, responded by calling for their members to "think about the real issues" (Rebel Team 1993). They asked workers to "Think about the need to strengthen and preserve the unity of our union; that unity which is so necessary if we are to successfully tackle the problems that we face". Their message was that popular unity rather than creative plurality was paramount. It was even suggested that New Rebels were linked to the Central Intelligence Agency (CIA), and it was further noted that the media and the ruling PNM even referred to the upcoming elections, implying that people were watching (OWTU 1993).

However, McLeod and the Rebel Team won the elections easily, but the victory was not clear cut. The New Rebels (1993a: 1) overshot their expected target by 7 percent. The results of the elections are shown in Table 7.1.

Table 7.1 1993 OWTU Election Results

	South	Total	North	Total		Total
McLeod	3,309	(81%)	697	(38%)	4,006	(68%)
Paul	761	(19%)	1,140	(62%)	1,901	(32%)
Total	4,070	(100%)	1,837	(100%)	5,907	(100%)

Note: Total not voting: 3,100 (34%)

The results show a clear split between Paul's base in the North and McLeod's base in the South. OWTU Education Officer, Gerry Kangalee (1994), notes that this was the first split since 1971 when the then executive tried to take away Weekes' leadership while he was incarcerated. Indeed, the present split has, according to some observers, heavily demoralized the union.

Regardless of the intent of the 'Paul faction' in both OWTU and MOTION, important issues have been stormily opened up for all future Left formations. Breathing holes of ideological plurality and absolute freedom of mass expressions have started to be cut. These arguments surrounding the consolidation and expansion of democratic practice are indispensable in creating a new and revitalized plural, open, and democratic Left.

There have been many efforts at bringing marginalized social groups together throughout Trinbagonian postcolonial history. Prominent among these was the formation of NJAC in 1969–70 and the ULF in 1975. However, these groupings revolved around political ideologies – in particular, black nationalist and working class, respectively.

While these types of coalitions remain important, they differ from the newer coalitions which are of interest here. The older coalitions may have been plural and democratic, but I argue that they were not particularly open. That is to say, there were wrong ideas, strategies, goals, directions etc. that could be judged as being wrong on *pre-given* measures – sometimes substantial edifices of thought. This often reduced plurality by excluding or sidelining interests because they were based differently. On the other hand, in an *open* collaboration, ideally, *appropriateness* would be debated on *particular situations*. In my scheme, however, there would be one pre-given criteria: the parties should not be dissatisfied with their degree of input in decisions. This restriction, however, theoretically widens the boundaries of participation and indeed encourages plurality.

I maintain that attempts to construct a plural, open, and democratic Left through this type of open collaboration have been made already in Trinidad and Tobago – practical attempts which actually preceded the theoretical battles above. There have been three important ones – the struggle against the establishment of Export Processing Zones (EPZs) in 1988, the Summit of Peoples Organizations (SOPO) in 1990–91, which is perhaps the most important one, and the present effort at organizing an Assembly of Caribbean Peoples.

The EPZ struggle

The 1988 campaign against the creation of Export Processing Zones organized by Working women marshaled over thirty women's organizations – including the Democratic Women's Association, Trinidad and Tobago Women's NGO Network, the Caribbean Association for Feminist Research and Action (CAFRA), church-based Mothers' Unions – plus the Bank and General Workers' Union and the OWTU into an Action Committee against Free Trade Zones, inspired by the successful action two years earlier carried out by a similar Sexual Offenses Bill Action Committee (Ross-Frankson, et al. 1990; Reddock 1990: 25). In their efforts to halt the NAR government's plans, the committee primarily engaged in an education and media campaign but were also engaged in working up interested people, communities, action groups, and the trade unions to discuss alternatives (Reddock 1990: 23).

But, like other single-issue groupings, the Action Committee Against Free Trade Zones, of course, dissolved after the issue was held off. However, these issue oriented groupings were creating an open type of politics that influenced the broader-focused groupings that were to emerge. Ideology was not a requirement. Struggle was. Discourses of emancipation were free to overlap and subvert. Indeed, this sort of politics developed and dominated the important SOPO in 1990.

The rise and fall of the SOPO

SOPO was formed in February 1990 and dissolved in October of that same year. This grouping emerged in a particularly turbulent time in Trinidad and Tobago's history. The NAR government, the first non-PNM government, was steadily losing popularity. The party had radically split in 1988, with the mainly ULF dissenters forming the United National Congress (UNC) under the leadership of the popular Basdeo Panday. That year, despite the numerous economic alternatives offered by the labour movement and others, the NAR signed an IMF agreement and formally committed Trinidad and Tobago to structural adjustment policies and IMF conditionalities. Thus the 1989 budget of the NAR instituted a series of measures which included a 10 percent cut in public sector worker's salary, the refusal to implement the COLA awards of the Industrial Court, the removal of items from the protective list to local manufacturing, removal of price controls on many basic items, privatization of the state sector, and large-scale retrenchment in both private and public sectors, furthering its unpopularity (CPTU 1991: 43).

In resistance, rank and file workers came together in a massive COSSABO meeting. The COSSABO decided to expand the old Joint Trade Union Group to become the Joint Trade Union Movement (JTUM). It also resolved to withdraw all Labour's participation in the various planning bodies in which they were involved (CPTU 1991: 43). The action especially startled the government because of the resistance by the traditionally conservative unions.

The JTUM further consolidated its organizational structure, holding worksite meetings, media conferences, and mass public meetings. The build up was for a general strike and on 6 March 1989, the Day of Resistance was called. On that day workers stayed home and shut down virtually all large, small, public, private, union, and nonunion workplaces throughout the country – from supermarkets to public transportation to the protective services to owners of businesses. The unemployed even blocked the roads, calling for "revolutionary action" (CPTU 1991: 43).

The government was now forced to listen to the citizenry. The education minister, in fact, resigned because of the resistance. The NAR responded with a National Consultation at Chaguaramas on 2 May 1989 involving business, government, and abour. The labour movement, however, despite the attempts at unity through the successful venture in JTUM, was split along its traditional division between the conservative Trinidad and Tobago Labour Congress (TTLC) and the radical Council of Progressive Trade Unions (CPTU). The Labour Congress was, in fact, intimidated through the closing of the Workers' Bank, the location of their members' savings and their headquarters, and worked with the government in joint technical teams while the CPTU organized a hunger march on 22 April. The movement was split.

Individual unions, however, such as the OWTU, the Steel Workers' Union (SWU), the National Union of Government and Federated Workers (NUGFW), Transport and Industrial Workers' Union, the Public Service Association, Trinidad and Tobago Unified Teachers Association, nurses, and others, took action into their own hands. Key areas of the economy like oil, transport, education, health, and public service were used by the workers to defeat wage freezes and COLA cutbacks, while securing pensions and other benefits (CPTU 1991: 44).

In December 1989, the NAR introduced its 1990 budget with even more extreme measures than the budget of the previous year. Included were the introduction of the regressive and hugely unpopular Value Added Tax, and nonpayment of wage awards to its employees. It was a war. In a demonstration of the workers' resolution at the time, another COSSABO was convened on 16 January 1990 and out of this came the decision to form a grouping of all the different concerned groups in the society. As a consequence, the Leadership of the JTUM set about to assemble such a grouping.

Nine days later, the first meeting to effect this demand was held. By 8 February 1990, a 'Summit of National Leaders' was convened, embracing an impressive sweep of people's organizations – 17 trade unions, 5 farmer's associations, 5 political parties, 1 religious organization, 3 religious leaders in an individual capacity, 1 women's organization, 1 community organization, and 2 youth organizations (*Summit* 1990). An editorial in the *Trinidad Guardian* of 19 February 1990 dismissed SOPO as a "Strange Summit" (*Trinidad Guardian* 1990) noting its "unusual composition" with "such diverse units" who "normally have very little to do with one another", styling it as another Errol McLeod threat.

However, SOPO's membership was to expand from its original base as more women's groups, NGOs, sports and culture clubs, rate payers unions, squatters, youth groups, rural organizations, writers associations, political organizations, and credit unions joined the grouping (SOPO 1990:4). However, on 12 May 1990 a National People's Assembly was called with a disappointing 168 people signing the attendance list. This was a crucial problem of SOPO – it did not focus on physically mobilizing mass support; it remained a leadership affair. There it was proposed, however, that a directly democratic national referendum on the economy be called. SOPO was in the process of struggling to establish its existence and to create its identity in a moment of extreme possibility. This process was further complicated with the attempted *coup d'état* in July 1990, which was carried out by one of the member groupings of SOPO.

Indeed, the coup forced SOPO to take a stand on a highly sensitive issue. Its position was arrived at after much debate. For example, from the minutes of a SOPO meeting, the Writers' Association expressed the view that SOPO "should not say we disagree [with the Muslimeen] even if we do. [We] should help our faithful brothers". Others were disappointed with SOPO's delayed reaction with one member stating, "Why

SOPO did not meet at the 1st weekend. We should [have] acted then and failed at a crisis moment . . . We need to reassess ourselves. We did not act at the right time! At the crisis moment SOPO was nothing". The OWTU, a leading member of SOPO, in fact condemned the coup emphasizing its own commitment to democracy and democratic change (Partap 1990). The political parties stopped their involvement altogether and this precipitated its demise.

In its *Statement on the Events of July 27th*, SOPO militantly stated:

The SOPO is deeply concerned about the political climate in Trinidad and Tobago. It is our view that a repressive clique is in control of our society and that our Government has not learnt any fundamental lesson from the events of July 27th 1990. Instead the authorities have moved to consolidate their very weak position (SOPO 1990).

Both the NAR and the St George Council (Alexander 1990) officially condemned SOPO on 27 October for failing to condemn the 27 July attack on Parliament. PNM member Lenny Saith was harangued by Clevon Raphael of the *Trinidad Guardian* for his links to SOPO, and the Guardian expressed horror at SOPOs influence in the newsroom of Trinidad and Tobago Television (TTT). On the other hand, in the sympathetic *TnT Mirror*, Lennox Brown hyperbolically suggested that SOPO was Trinidad's answer to the Green Movement sweeping Europe. He praised it as an advance over Tapia – effective political thinking and organization without being a purely intellectual group: "SOPO has a direct political hotline to the streets: It is a Tapia House of the streets". And the streets were where the power was.

Indeed, despite the attempts to discredit it and the restrictions imposed by the state of emergency, SOPO struggled to remain active after the coup. But, by the end of 1990, it had effectively disintegrated.

Reflections on SOPO and openness

Even though it may have 'failed', SOPO represented an important challenge to previous organized resistance. For despite its lack of physical mass support, it was theoretically expansive. An important tension existed in SOPO over whether it should be open or closed. Others complained in hindsight that SOPOs problem was that it had no philosophical or principled base. It was simply against the NAR and Structural Adjustment which allowed, for example, an opportunistic, unlikely and unethical alliance with the PNM.

However, despite the desire for closure, SOPO practised an openness that would never let it shut. All the interest groups continuously brought their struggles in for SOPO to carry forward, from the National Service issue to shortages in education funding to squatter's problems. Knolly Clarke (1994) noted thus that "each group had its own agenda".

Openness did have its price however. SOPO members have argued, in fact, that this lack of definite direction allowed Abu Bakr to work out his agenda of violent overthrow of the state. It has also been forwarded that the discredited PNM was able to retake state power because of the renewed legitimacy it received in SOPO. It has been suggested also that different persons involved in SOPO had "designs" to use it as a vehicle for political power – in particular, Cecil Paul, Knolly Clarke, and David Abdulah. And it has been widely intimated that the political parties deliberately held back SOPO's development to prevent themselves from being overshadowed and bypassed by SOPO.

While these reservations are valid, it could be argued that it was not *voluntary* openness that allowed political opportunism, but the openness of existence itself. For as all identities require, SOPO did attempt some partial closures. And one of these closures was attempted whenever it explicitly stated that it was not a political party seeking state power. It saw transformation transcending the state. Thus in a letter to the NAR Government, it stated: "We do not seek political power. What we seek is the removal of the policies of structural adjustment. But if you do not remove them we will have to remove you". But whatever the strength of the desire, the closure of the question of state power is a theoretical impossibility – political 'opportunists' can always slip through, especially when confronting the state.

Alternatively, most SOPO members experienced this openness in a particularly positive way. For example, all but one of the participants in SOPO informed me that the integrity of their struggles was respected and not subordinated to a union agenda. Indeed, many people who would not have joined with the unions against structural adjustment felt comfortable participating in SOPO (Ramjag 1994b). In fact, the respect and autonomy that did exist was integral to the identity of the project itself. Thus SOPO, though dying an infant death, showed great possibility for organizing resistance and redefining the Left along plural, open, and democratic lines in Trinidad and Tobago. Indeed, it is my contention that future large-scale attempts at resistance that downplay the experience and insight offered by SOPO do so to their great detriment.

The Assembly of Caribbean Peoples

The Assembly of Caribbean Peoples is a present initiative of the OWTU Executive for a Caribbean wide forum for developing "an Agenda for the Sovereignty of the Caribbean and improvement of the lives of Caribbean people . . . " by offering an alternative to the present economic and social policies being pursued internationally and locally (ACP 1992: 1).

The assembly's call to a whole range of social, economic, political, labour, cultural and sporting groupings to "a process of deeply participatory dialogue" (ACP 1994b) has been encouraged, I contend, by the possibilities of openness and plurality that SOPO offered. This inspiration is very direct, for Chairperson Errol McLeod and Secretary David Abdulah were actively involved in SOPO. However, Abdulah (1994b) emphasizes that:

With the Assembly we are trying to . . . *avoid* the mistakes of SOPO insofar that SOPO was this very big, high-profile, and so on but a lot of fundamentals had not been worked out and therefore it allowed the Muslimeen to find the space that they had to do what they had to do . . . They de-railed the mass movement . . .

With the Assembly – we're not trying to give the impression that it is a monolithic organization by any means – we have *limited* objectives but to facilitate people working together and so on, so that basically we are trying to build the bridges.

As a primary illustration of their approach, local preparatory committee meetings – set up to guarantee and stimulate more genuine grass roots level control and participation – constitute the base units of the Assembly. Indeed, at a Trinidadian committee meeting in November 1993 three of the five non-secretariat people in attendance were women. But there are critics of course. For instance, one OWTU Officer comments that he can't see why West Indian cricket is left out of the assembly – "they're not progressive? not left? They can't be serious!" And Rawwida Baksh-Soodeen (1994), steering committee member of CAFRA, argues that the respect and equality given to them in the assembly is a negotiated one. She feels their presence is token – a concession to the power of the women's movement.

The assembly, furthermore, has run into organizational problems. Because of low finances, running behind schedule, late arrival of materials and poor attendance at meetings, the steering committee decided in

January 1994 to have the Assembly on a smaller scale with less ambitious goals. The Assembly, though struggling, represents the latest attempt to revitalize the Left along open, plural, and democratic lines.

Extra-labour social movements

One of the main reasons why I argue for a plural, open, and democratic Left is that a plurality of resistances in Trinidad and Tobago has produced a wide range of movements. Indeed, other social movements, such as women's groups, farmers' organizations, cultural movements, youth groups, religious movements, and community development organizations, have long been in active existence in Trinidad and Tobago. In fact, as Selena Tapper (1992: 4) has argued, these were the founders of the trade unions and political movements which eventually took power in the 1960s in most postcolonial English-speaking Caribbean countries, marginalizing the 'original' groups. However, since the coming of international aid and structural adjustment in the 1980s, their disempowered descendants have increased their importance and prominence through reformation into nongovernmental organizations (NGOs).

But furthermore, as many argue, their rise in the 1980s contains a new dimension, rejecting the solutions of the past (Tapper 1992: 4). Despite their undoubted roots in the long tradition of social welfare and volunteerism in the Caribbean (Anderson 1992: 7), many have placed Caribbean NGOs within the framework of "New Social Movements" (NSMs) (Baksh-Soodeen 1993). Indeed, these NSMs have been identified as institutional openings to a new type of resistance (Wignaraja 1992; Pieterse 1992), very much in line with my concerns of a new, open, and democratic Left.

The NSMs, it is argued, are based on a loss of faith in the ability of the conventional politics of transformation to deal with new crises of the military-industrial complex, nuclear weapons, and the environment, for example (Baksh-Soodeen 1993: 13). They stand in contrast to the labour movement, which is argued to be too implicated in the structures, institutions, and dilemmas of the past, defending old interests and social relations. They reject the siting of power solely in capital, the focusing on the worker/capitalist relationship, the primary setting of the struggle in the workplace, and the privileging of the worker as the transformative actor. Instead power is seen as more diffuse and processual, as opposed to a fixed goal able to be captured (Baksh-Soodeen 1993: 13–14, 18). NSMs include the interests and agency of a range of marginalized groups and constituencies. They have challenged older goals and ideas, forms of struggle and organization.

Caribbean NGOs have as their centre various marginalized groups, not necessarily workers. They have characteristically resisted governmental cooptation, bureaucratization, hierarchy, centralization, vanguardism, and the divisions between leaders/intellectuals and the masses/people that have been associated with much of the older movements. As part of their outlook, they have held a commitment to "a liberal democratic variant of pluralism and the importance of the 'civic culture' " (Anderson 1992: 9) placing themselves as "links between the state and the citizen, for the promotion of the interests of the various strata and sectors" (Tapper 1992: 5). Indeed, as Anderson (1992: 10) argues, they seem to follow a general Gramscian strategy – building hegemony, gaining widespread consent and seeing democratization as the practice of politics. Anderson (1992: 10) also notes their strong emphasis on "the idea of democracy as an organically global system – economic, political, social, cultural and ecological".

Historically, Anderson (1992: 7–8) has noted several stimuli for the distinctive, new bursting forth of NGO formation in the 1980s. These include resource availability, political disillusionment/activist orientation of founding members; high levels of skill and experience in social sector programming and community work, the existence of nascent community-based structures, a minimally receptive political culture, the absence of culturally specific avenues for popular expression that were supported by research, management, and promotion, the devastation of natural disasters, the spirit of the Grenadian revolution and the establishment of the OECS. NGOs were late in coming to Trinidad and Tobago, but I emphasize that structural adjustment, with its attacks on social services and the state sector, has multiplied the struggles in Trinidad and Tobago and extended political discourses into new areas.

The political stance of the NGOs, too, has been historically located by Anderson (1992: 9). The disinclination to accept government leadership and authority, she argues, comes from the middle class orientation of the leadership and a generalized sense of belonging to the political Left. Also, NGOs' emphasis on autonomy, she forwards, is the fall-out from the tragic collapse of the Grenadian revolution and the subsequent implosion of the radical Caribbean Left. This pushed the NGOs to develop philosophically rigorous groundings and move away from alliances based on sectors and 'operating styles' towards more issue defined mobilization as with SOPO, the EPZ struggle, and the assembly).

Their practical work with alternative people-based development has given NGOs a wealth of valuable practical and organizational experience and authority. Because of their richness, I maintain that their emergence and importance are a vitally essential part of any movement to a plural, open, and democratic Left. Their ideological, organizational, and constituent differences and innovations reflect a plurality, autonomy, novelty, and authenticity necessary to realize that vision of resistance for which I argue.

The women's movement

The most powerful of these extra-labour groups is the women's movement. It has been a most important movement in Trinidad and Tobago, rivaling the centrality of the labour movement at times. Indeed, Rhoda Reddock has asserted that the "the women's movement today is stronger than the left" (*Sunday Express*, 26 April 1987). She continued, "The only remnant of the 1960s-1970s radicalism still alive today is the women's movement . . . The rape violence question, above all, permits a perception that, on issues directly touching women, a certain radicalized consensus has quietly developed". She has described feminism as "the critical consciousness and awareness of women's subordinated and or exploited position in society and the commitment to do something to change it" (Reddock 1984a:1). In her doctoral thesis, Reddock (1984b) surveys women's involvement in struggle from 1898 to 1960. There she notes that with the creation of 'responsible' trade unionism in the 1940s came new distinctions that were to spade women out of the movement. A man/woman dichotomy was equated with distinctions between responsibility/irresponsibility, wage/nonwage, formal/informal, economy/politics, production/consumption, and exclusive/ inclusive, while industries became the membership basis for individual unions (Reddock 1984b: 621–22). Indeed, as part of this purge, Trinidadian women were largely "housewifized". Subsequently, their support and action were no longer actively sought by men (Reddock 1984b: 652). Women then organized themselves in mainly charity, social work and other service-centered organizations.

A 'second wave' of feminism emerged in the 1970s, and surrounded by the UN Decade for Women, the upsurge of feminist literature from the North, the critical experience of women in the Black Power and New Left movements of the 1960s, and the increased feminist consciousness in popular expression, the Housewives Association of Trinidad and Tobago (HATT) was founded in 1975 (Mohammed 1989:41; Reddock 1990: 8). In addition, that year a National Commission on the Status of Women was established by the government, giving state legitimacy to a new wave of feminist perspectives and research (Mohammed 1989: 41).

HATT dissolved in the late 1970s and was followed in 1980 by the establishment of Concerned Women for Progress (CWP), described by Shepherd, et al. (1987: i) as the first new 'progressive' feminist group to emerge in Trinidad. They organized battles surrounding the Legal Status of Children and the Succession Bill, and held Trinidad and Tobago's first public forum on rape in 1982 (Mohammed, 1989: 42–43). By 1983, however, CWP had expired, replaced by the more woman-centred and less traditionally socialist organization, the Group (Mohammed, 1989: 43). This refocusing was very important, as it represented a clear ideological break from many of the members' earlier socialist positions, signaling a more radical pluralization of the Trinidadian Left.

In 1985, through the activity of the Group and others, the real introduction into public discourse of the issue of rape occurred through intensive use of television, newspapers, theatre and other public fora. In 1984–85, too, a Rape Crisis Centre was established followed by the setting up of a halfway house for battered women (Mohammed 1989: 44). Also in 1985, there was the formation of the Caribbean Association of Feminists for Research and Action (CAFRA) in Barbados with members from Antigua, Barbados, Belize, Curacao, Guyana, Jamaica, Martinique, St Vincent and the Grenadines, Suriname and Trinidad and Tobago. Notably, in that first year, only Trinidad and Tobago could mobilize a CAFRA National Meeting, attesting to the relative strength of the Trinbagonian women's movement. And in this same year, Women Working for Social Progress (Workingwomen) emerged out of this grouping to become the most influential women's group in Trinidad and Tobago.

Working women were to play a leading role in several struggles which included the passage of the Sexual Offences Bill in 1986, agitation against the establishment of EPZs in 1988 and the passage of the Domestic Violence Act in 1991. In addition they also staged seminars/workshops to address the problems of women and organized the First National Women's Economic Conference in 1993.

This history attests to the fact that the women's movement has led some of the most important struggles in Trinidad and Tobago since the 1980s, many with wide connections to other social groups and organizations. In addition, on a much smaller scale, ongoing work has been carried out. But the organizations mentioned above have not been the only important women's groups. Others include the Women and Development Studies Group, the National Organization for Women, NGOs for the Advancement of Women, the National Union of Domestic Employees/Wages for Housework Campaign, Hindu Women's Organization, the Democratic Women's Association, Church Women United, the National Women's Caucus, and the Women's Resource and Outreach Centre.

The farmers' movement

The farmers' organizations in Trinidad and Tobago are another important grouping. Their discourses of oppression and liberation are sited in a different ecological-economic setting from the urban-based discourses, having a long history and deep rootedness, further pluralizing Left discourse.

The farmers' organizations which are the focus here are national-based as opposed to the many community-focused service or charity organizations. In fact, there is a vast network of community groups in Trinidad and Tobago such as village and community councils, women's groups, farmers' organizations and cooperatives engaged in a variety of work. Indeed, some 400 community councils are affiliated with the National Association of Village and Community Councils and some 136 farmers' organizations exist throughout Trinidad (CNIRD 1989: 27).

Within this universe, according to a survey by the Caribbean Network for Integrated Rural Development (CNIRD 1989), there are three nationally based farmers' associations in the country. They are not involved in actual production in farming communities, but rather are bodies that represent farmers in their dealings with government agencies. All see their main objective as that of advocacy on behalf of their membership (CNIRD 1989: 4–5).

The National Farmers and Workers Union (NFWU) was formed in 1973 as the Islandwide Canefarmers Trade Union under the leadership of

Raffique Shah as a response to farmers' request for strong leadership and representation. In 1989, there were approximately 4,000 registered members. They have represented farmers' interests to Caroni Ltd, the government, and insurance companies for land, marketing and pricing issues, competitive insurance rates and policies, and have organized a marketing cooperative and a credit union. They obtain material assistance from TIWU and OWTU.

The CNIRD (1989: 32) lists among its achievements the removal of the Cess Act in 1965, the formation of the Federation of Farmers in collaboration with other farmers' organizations, active work for the unity of farmers, and effective representation of cane farmers with Caroni Ltd. Indeed, Raffique Shah, as the leader of the Islandwide Cane Farmers Trade Union (ICFTU), took it through numerous, vigorous battles in the mid 1970s. Coming out of these struggles was the uniting of sugar and oil workers to form the historic United Labour Front, making NFWU an integral part of the history of the Left in Trinidad and Tobago (Rajack n.d.: 79-80).

The Trinidad Islandwide Cane Farmers Association (TICFA) was established in 1947 but has been under the process of revitalization, in competition with NFWU as it was in 1973. Its presence has been less noticeable than the other two organizations.

The remaining farmers' group is the National Foodcrop Farmers' Association (NFFA). The NFFA was established in 1974 when, because of a tremendous glut of produce on the market – resulting in low prices – farmers staged a no sell campaign to induce some measure of price controls (CNIRD 1989: 38). This was a successful campaign fought in midst of enormous national unrest and popular upsurge. Leadership conflicts halted the organization for a while and membership dropped. However from 1979–81 severe flooding and loss of crops re-energized the organization to take action. Vigorous protests and demonstrations secured their representation on government boards to ensure the execution of agricultural policy (Rajack n.d.: 90–91). In 1989 there were 15 branches of NFFA spread over Trinidad. There are approximately 2,000 farmers registered as members, the majority of whom are small farmers. The majority of members are men, and they are in the main squatters on state and private lands (CNIRD, 1989: 38). One of their principal aims has been to keep the suburban community of Aranguez as a vegetable producing area. This has brought them into extensive contact with the community extending its involvement to include infrastructural, cultural, and educational issues. The farmers, suspicious of government and other nongovernmental organizations see the NFFA as a 'watch dog', trade-union type organization and as assistants in bringing new information to them (Rajack n.d.: 92–93). Furthermore, the NFFA have participated and built links with the various workers' and Mass organizations in the country such as the CPTU and SOPO (Ramjag 1994a).

The labour movement

Although we must recognize the great importance of other movements, it cannot be denied that the labour movement has been an undoubted leader of resistance in Trinidad and Tobago and continues to play this role despite recent setbacks. The latter pertain particularly to the impact that structural adjustment policies have had on its membership, stability, and its moral authority.

The labour movement under structural adjustment

Over the last few years unions have been heavily clouted ideologically and organizationally. This has been done largely through the policies of structural adjustment and liberalization adopted in Trinidad and Tobago in the 1980s.

One major strategy of this 'economic recovery' programme is to reduce the workforce – 'down-' or 'right-sizing'. Through 'voluntary' schemes of retirement and separation, and outright retrenchment of workers, numbers have declined drastically in Trinidad and Tobago. Indeed, from 1983 to 1993, the labour movement has lost about one half of its membership (Diptee 1993). This has not only lessened the physical importance of labour in particular firms – it has financially retarded their unions since membership dues are often the main sources of finance.

Unions have been viciously attacked in other ways as well. For example, these attacks include the reversing of Industrial Court orders on previously negotiated benefits and the freezing of wages through the Court of Appeal, or if an appeal could not be granted, through shutting down the company; replacing collective agreements by locking out employees and re-admitting persons only after they signed weakened individual contracts in which previous agreements have been deleted; restricting union recognition and jurisdiction through amendments to regulations and requirements; taking away the right to union representation from certain categories of workers; illegally withholding union dues or suggesting that no dues should be paid between agreements; creating dummy companies or constantly changing the names of companies to by-pass labour legislation; increased use of scab labour, the regulation of picketing eg how often, how far, who is allowed; hiring contractor labour to deny employees work and taking petty legal action to drain unions of their finances (JTUM 1986).

But the assaults on unions described above have not only been material. They have been ideological as well. In this respect, the OWTU president general (OWTU 1994a) stated during the tenure of the PNM government:

> Never before, not since the rough periods (1930s–1950s) of colonial rule have such brazen efforts been made to eliminate Unions and organized labour as are now being witnessed under the neo colonial rule of the Patrick Manning administration . . . The crisis is not just economic. It is also moral, social and psychological. It is a crisis of relationships – of leadership, political and community – a crisis of confidence.

Moral authority

Whereas in the 1970s it was possible to argue that the labour movement was in a leadership position of popular resistance and struggle, today after its beating during structural adjustment, its authority has diminished. For example, unions are said to be lazy and inefficient, too powerful an interest group, working for their own interest against the national interest, ineffectively confrontational, and their ideas and visions are old, outmoded, and not in keeping with the times.

Indeed, recently, the labour movement has been unable to mobilize even its own workers. For example in the PSA, only 15,000 out of 45,000 are unionized (*Sunday Guardian*, 20 June 1993). And the call to a Day of Resistance II in April 1994 was only half-heartedly received. Indeed, both the government and the labour movement were claiming victory on that day (*Express*, 26 April 1994). Division has certainly demoralized the OWTU in particular, especially considering the viciousness with which the elections were fought.

While the impact of the external threats are important, the fortress mentality that it engenders is a threat to democracy, plurality, openness, and, ultimately survival. My counter to this tension between democracy and security is that the best defense against subversion is a freely and fiercely committed population – not a forced unity. Indeed, in their best moments, both the United States and Cuba illustrate this point. It seems unthinkable that an invasion in either of those two countries would meet a cowed population. Both peoples are intensely committed to their democracies. It is therefore on internal questions such as, 'why is the population not fiercely committed?' that we must focus.

One major problem of the labour movement is the overwhelming male bias of the unions. Rhoda Reddock (1984b) has documented the history of how women were rooted out of the labour movement in the 1940s, as the Trinbagonian Trade Unions were being beaten into the likeness of the responsible British unions. Since then, the unions have not been re-imaged.

Presently, on the NATUC 21–member executive there are no women. As Thelma Henderson (1994) has chided, it is "embarrassing and a shame". In another critique, Indar Sahadeo (1986) has commented that the Trade Union Movement has not achieved a "comparative advantage" over management or government. He identifies as a source of major problems the inability of the Trade Union to adapt to changing circum-stances structurally, organizationally, administratively as much as other organizations have done, the inadequacy in human development, and short-sightedness – the lack of adequate resources for efficient research and development.

There are many creative ideas in the labour movement but these have been thwarted by either the employers or labour leaders who feel their leadership threatened. Outside of the labour movement, too, there have been suggestions. For example, Sabrina Mowlah-Baksh (1994) of the Caribbean Conference of Churches for Ecumenical Planning and Action in the Caribbean Network (CEPAC) has suggested:

I sort of perceive Unions to be exclusive to Union workers and the interests of the workers. And I don't feel that has changed although I see some headways being made in terms of them now trying to reach out, in terms of them establishing the CLR James Centre and I think there's a pre-school now . . . Although that is what they are about, you know, they're representing their workers and thing, and of course now you will hear their voice on the whole structural adjustment issue. But I feel they need to get more involved and try to assist those not only in the Unions. You see, Labour has always played an important part in this country. And I don't feel, if you have that gift, if you have that . . . potential to help it shouldn't be limited to those who . . . pay you to do it . . .

I feel they should get involved in the community level as well. You know, the labour movement, the unions have money – at least I think they have – because of the amount of buildings they have, some of the buildings they have just wasting, doing nothing, picking up dust. And I feel that especially at the level of educating, or maybe do some more funding, offer some more scholarships at the community level, that kind of thing. I feel that the Union have the potential to get more *intimately* involved at the community level.

As shown earlier, however, the OWTU has been involved in various ways with the national community and continue to be involved. Thus Alva Allen (1994) of the OWTU, for example, remains hopeful and faithful arguing that "at times we are like the sun, with overcast clouds, struggling to shine. But shine we will".

The labour movement and wider struggle

The labour movement, and the leadership of the OWTU in particular, has been committed to fighting structural adjustment and organizing resistance in new ways. Indeed, this has been a historical characteristic of the labour movement, beginning as it did in the 1930s with its threat of anti-British 'irresponsibility' (Cardinez 1986: 16), and its related role in the nationalist movement, generally (Ramasaran 1990: 13).

This commitment to wider struggle was not just in showing the wider benefits of the union's collective agreements. As George Weekes affirmed, "the role of the trade union movement in a capitalist society is [not just] to go around the bargaining table every three years" (OWTU 1977: 51). Indeed, out of the labour struggles of the 1960s and 1970s came nationalization, the ending of racism in employment, the creation of a peoples sector cooperatives and the Workers' Bank, the institutionalization of social welfare, an unemployment levy, and unemployment relief programmes (Paul 1987).

However, in today's new and challenging environment, concrete results have yet to be seen. But in his first presidential address, the successor to George Weekes, Errol McLeod (1987) announced:

One of our first steps forward is to recognize and internalize that the old institutions never did and never will serve us. We have to forge and establish new peoples' institutions. Each and every one of us must do our part. We must all get involved in our trade unions and keep them independent of all (and I say all) the bourgeois/capitalist boardroom-controlled political parties. I dare say we must keep them independent of even the so-called labour parties if and when they are formed or emerge again . . .

Experiences in Barbados, England, and currently in Jamaica advise us as much. We must get involved in community and other organizations and begin the work of transforming them into instruments of power geared towards fundamental change in the society . . . We must continue in the fine tradition of Butler, Rienzi, and Weekes, attempting to unite the workers as a class. We must develop our consciousness to guard against being divided by reasons of race – Indian or African, or by politics PNM or NAR, or by religion – Hindu or Christian. We must work towards a transformed economy and a new democracy expressive of all sections of our national community.

Though less effective, the commitment to mass struggle obviously remains, for as Lex Lovell, president of the Steel Workers of Trinidad and Tobago (SWUTT) asserts:

If the labour movement does not take up the plights of the poor people and the workers to get benefits and what not, society won't exist. Because it is the labour movement who gets social benefits and fringe benefits for the human being. No businessman or government comes and gives you hand-outs (Lovell and Mowlah-Baksh 1994).

The democratic tradition of labour

Apart from the critical leadership role it plays, what makes the labour movement a potential entry point to a new plural, open, and democratic Left is its historic commitment to democracy. In this respect, a former executive member of MOTION commented:

Some trade unions and the workers labour organizations have been the unofficial Opposition since the beginning of this century. One remembers the call and struggle for nationalization, Independence (Home Rule), the Right to Vote, the ISA, the IRA, the Public Order Act, etc.

These struggles and victories could only have resulted from a Trade Union that had its independence from the political parties. The workers were allowed to pick their leaders and not the party leadership doing it for them. The workers were allowed to struggle for ideas, not based on party instruction, but on what is best for the country.

Workers were allowed to decide their struggles and the battleground. This was not decided by the Central Committee.

In 1962, TIWU became the first union to institute a one person-one vote (as opposed to a delegate) system for the election of executives. The OWTU followed one month later. Other unions, however, did not win this type of democracy until much later. For example, the All Trinidad Sugar Estate and Factory Workers Trade Union's first one person-one vote executive elections were held in 1977, three years after Basdeo Panday assumed leadership of the union (Ramsaran 1990:164). As Weekes commented on the struggle in 1965 (cited in Als 1965: 20):

And the one way in which our discredited or backward leadership could cling to power was by clogging or circumventing the normal democratic processes and claiming some sort of divine right on the basis of past services rendered and divine wisdom to do so. This was the case of Rojas in the OWTU who in 1962 refused to carry out the democratic decision of the annual conference to pursue strike action against retrenchment at BP; of Drayton in SWWTU who ordered his union members back to work and resigned when he was disobeyed; of Alexander in the FWTU who was voted out of office while attending an ILO Conference in Geneva, for neglecting his union and members; of the leaders of congress retired by a no-confidence resolution of the General Council in 1963.

Internally, for example, democracy is a major foundation and ambition of much of the movement. Democratic methods seep through it. For example, in May 1994 an OWTU Officers and Shop Stewards Training Seminar listed as its first objective, "To generate a consensus amongst the second rank leadership of the Union on the key issues confronting the Union and what our objectives should be" Indeed the OWTU have innovated directly democratic forms such as COSSABOs for all second rank leadership and MMMs for all members. This democratic orientation has been extended also to the wider society. For instance, traditionally, the union has been often called the 'bulwark of democracy' or the 'watchdog of democracy'.

Unfortunately, democracy has been spread in the movement like a sloppy paint job. In fact, John Hackshaw (1994: 26), a veteran trade unionist, claims:

Over the years, what has been taking place in the trade union movement is the weakening of the democratic process by some trade union leaders rather than strengthening it. They use manipulative procedures to achieve their own ambitions and personal desires without concern for the moral or ethical consequences.

On the other hand, however, the debates on democracy in arguably the most democratic Union in the country, the OWTU, provide the potential for a strong push in a more democratic direction, maintaining the radical spirit of the older principles, eg, one person-one vote in executive elections while going beyond them.

And, as was the case with the Steel Workers' Union of Trinidad and Tobago, the entry of experienced workers from the oil and sugar industry, bringing their union experiences with them, radicalized and democratized the Union (Lovell and Mowlah-Baksh 1994). Also, participation in the Joint trade union COSSABOs was (for many unions) a new, inspiring experience in broad, direct democracy (Paul 1987). Lastly, the institutionalization of NATUC has as its founding principles ideological plurality, independence from political partisanship, internal democracy, and collective activity, thus keeping up the democratic push (The Concerned Trade Unions 1986).

Trade union democracy is seen as a model by many. Indeed, it has been argued that all political parities in the country should adopt the "supposedly hyper-democratic OWTU-style" elections to increase accountability and representativeness (*Sunday Guardian,* 28 May 1989).

In the debates over democracy and centralism in MOTION, Cecil Paul (1990b) argued, "Fortunately for some of us we are exposed to the progressive trade unions and its broad democratic practices. Centralism in MOTION was in contradiction to democracy in our trade unions". Indeed, Labour's organization of a mass, democratic national COSSABO to form the innovative SOPO clearly illustrates the potential for labour to push the Left in new, radically democratic directions.

As Michael Rustin (1989) argues, the 'old' movements, such as the labour movement, should not be written off in organizing contemporary resistance. These organizations must not be treated in such an essentialist and ahistorical fashion as some NSM theorists treat them. Their histories of struggle can often link with or provide a substantial social foundation for the 'new' movements. In Trinidad and Tobago, the labour movement, in particular the OWTU, with its rich history and involvement in leading and uniting the trade union movement and in being bloodily involved in some of the most important mobilizations in the country's history, surely has a central role to play – one that must certainly be argued and worked out – in bringing about a plural, open, and democratic Left. Indeed, its actual moves to do so, by leading the organization of SOPO and the Assembly of Caribbean Peoples, attest to this radical potential.

Conclusion: The OWTU and New Leadership

The argument presented in this paper is that the ingredients of a plural, open, and democratic Left are indeed lying about Trinidad and Tobago, and that the OWTU is in a strong historical position that allows it to become a leader of this new Left.

My hopefulness and optimism, however, stand in sharp contrast to many of my interviewees' assessments. Their readings may come from a closeness to the situation which I do not have, but I also believe that they come from different theoretical lenses through which they view Trinbagonian society. Comments that the present state of apathy, individualism, resignation, fatigue, and necessity for mere survival make irrelevant – or more pessimistically, have finally defeated – the Left are common. This reading, I believe, may be true for the *older* projects of the Left. But I argue that the myriad of ways the oppressed 'merely' survive should be included in a renewed Leftist project not excluding the more traditional strategies of the organized Left. The traditional Leftist insistence that resistance must follow certain lines, be 'pure' and 'consistent', represents a certain repression that is not only undesirable but ineffective as well.

But further adding to many of my interviewees' skepticism of my thesis is the importance I attach to the OWTU. Many comment that the OWTU is bankrupt – ideologically, morally, and organizationally – and should not – indeed, could not – lead any extra-labour resistance in Trinidad and Tobago today. My reading, however, is slightly different. While not denying the problems, I think that the OWTU remains centrally important in Trinbagonian resistance. For one, the OWTU's history of collaboration in both large-scale projects – such as SOPO, National Dialogues, and the Assembly of Caribbean peoples – and various small-scale activity has given OWTU an impressive historical access to a wide variety of associations. In this regard, both Abdulah (1994a) and Mowlah-Baksh (1994) of CEPAC opine similarly.

Interestingly, the expanded definition of the OWTU as an NGO, illustrating the positive aspects of the instability of identity, has allowed it considerable latitude of action. Added to this, the important debates on expanding democracy in the union make the OWTU a very likely site of change to this new open, plural and democratic Left.

However, a further commitment to democracy is needed to mobilize the membership of the OWTU, especially the encouragement of a plurality of opinions. Indeed, the recent militant and victorious T&TEC strike for pension security and struggles in the southern oil industry (*Vanguard*, 15 July 1994) have outlined a resurgent radicalism, escalating in some cases to the point of physical assaults on management. How the union leadership handles these cases may be very important. For example, are the instances of violence going to be covered up as an embarrassment or will they be staunchly and openly defended as a sign and expression of the workers' desperation? That is a question of democracy and free self-expression. From another perspective, Ramsaroop (1990:17) in looking at the OWTU's influence on the politics of Trinidad and Tobago, has commented that the organization "believes that it holds the key to the elimination of gross disenchantment on the part of the masses". Relatedly, the OWTU president general (OWTU 1994a) stated:

The second challenge we face is to develop and build a powerful unity of workers and the poor and oppressed in this country ie a new national movement. But this can only be done if we can find new ways of doing public education, if we can reach out to and work with the other sections of the national community.

The third challenge is to build a political vehicle that will confront the issue of power. The absence of a cohesive and coherent political mechanism to take the workers forward and with individual unions and persons doing their own thing, a level of cynicism and apathy has also developed among workers and the poor.

This implied idea of a unified front, though similar to my idea of a plural, open, and democratic Left, is as Baksh-Soodeen (1993:56) argues a left-over from traditional, centralist Marxism. The major theoretical difference between the two conceptions is the acceptance of the impossibility of closure – ideologically, organizationally, strategically, etc. Plurality is heightened and encouraged. While all identities require some balance between closure and openness what Laclau and Mouffe (1985) term "hegemonic articulation", the focus of my ideal Left is shifted from attempting closure to embracing and managing openness. In many ways, it may be like the old idea of seeing a glass half empty or half full – in reality it is the same glass. But living in history makes a difference. For seeing a glass as half empty assumes that one knows how tall the glass is and what its shape is like. But no one can claim with surety what heights and shapes the future may bring. Indeed, in the words of veteran trade union hero Joe Young (1994), "That is as unpredictable as tomorrow's hairstyle".

The vision of a united plurality no longer seems appealing. Henderson (1994) has argued that the splitting up of the ULF in 1977 and the NAR in 1988 have made the population suspicious and cynical towards these united fronts which are seen as motivated by individual selfishness and opportunism. In any case, alliances in this era of union decline and NGO upsurge seems to have the balance of power altered somewhat, and in keeping with the thesis of power and democracy by Rueschemeyer, *et al* (1992) and Thomas (1984), this points towards Left coalitions that are more polycentric, plural and democratic.

The Left will have to change and move constantly, just like the bourgeoisie and just like the workers. Extensive use of fun, style, entertainment, and public image, often looked down upon by the Left, I see as important components in helping oppressed peoples fulfil themselves. Is this not an integral part of what people desire of struggle? People know what they want. And they have been rejecting the traditional Left. The organized Left must grow and meet the challenges accordingly.

Notes

1. 'Trinbagonian' is the nonformal adjective form of the proper noun, 'Trinidad and Tobago'. It originated with the Left (along with the non-formal proper nouns, 'Trinago' and 'Trinbago'), but has been increasingly accepted in more formal circles within Trinidad and Tobago.
2. This grouping was formed by the 'Shah faction' of the split in the United Labour Front, and members of the OWTU played a leading role.

Bibliography

Abdulah, David. 1994a. Personal interview. 30 May.

Abdullah, David. 1994b. Personal interview. 11 June.

Abrams, N., 1959. *The Teenage Consumer*. London: Routledge and Kegan Paul.

ACP. 1994a. A message of urgency: call to the Assembly of Caribbean Peoples. Trinidad and Tobago: OWTU.

ACP. 1994b. *Towards a People's Agenda for the Sovereignty of the Region and the Welfare of Our People*. Trinidad and Tobago: OWTU.

ACP. 1992. *Background Paper*. Trinidad and Tobago: OWTU.

Afari, Yassus. 1994. Defend the culture. *Sistren* 16, nos. 1 & 2.

Aimey, Rawle. 1994. Personal interview. 7 July.

Allen, Alva. 1994. Personal interview. 27 May.

Allen, John. 1993. Development in a community under stress. *Development Journal* 28, no. 2.

Alexander, Gail. 1990. St George council condemns SOPO. *Trinidad Guardian*, 27 October.

Als, Michael. 1965. *Is Slavery Again!* Trinidad: Cacique Publishers.

Amin, Samir. 1993. Social movements at the periphery. In *New Social Movements in the South*, edited by P. Wignaraja. New Delhi: Sage.

Anderson, M. Alison. 1992. *The Political Basis of NGOs: Philosophy, Ideology & Modus Operandi*. Trinidad and Tobago: CNIRD.

Anderson, P., and D. Gordon. 1989. Labour mobility patterns. In *Development in Suspense*, edited by Norman Girvan and George Beckford. Kingston: FES.

Aptheker, Bettina. 1989. *Tapestries of Life*. Amherst: University of Massachussets.

Armstrong, James K. L. 1990. *Overview Report of Human Settlements Sectors in the OECS*. Prepared for OECS/UNCHS/ UNDP, Castries.

Ayittey, George B. N. 1990. Let's stop neglecting Africa's small savers. *World Development* (May).

Baksh, Ishmael J. 1986. Education and equality of opportunity in Trinidad and Tobago. *Caribbean Journal of Education* 13, nos. 1 & 2 .

Baksh-Soodeen, Rawwida. 1993. Gender planning or feminist development theory/practice: a conceptual framework for analyzing male bias in the programmes and structures of 6 Caribbean NGDOs. MSc thesis, ISS, The Hague.

Baksh-Soodeen, Rawwida. 1994. Personal interview. 17 May.

Baptiste, Jennifer. 1994. Personal interview. 1 July.

Baptiste, Owen. 1988. What is Panday really up to? *Express*, 10 February.

Baptiste, Owen, ed.1976. *Crisis*. Trinidad and Tobago: Inprint.

Barbados Family Planning Association. 1990. *President's Report*. Bridgetown: Barbados Family Planning Association.

Barkley-Brown, Elsa. 1992. What has happened here: the politics of difference in women's history and feminist politics. *Feminist Studies* 18, no. 2.

Barriteau-Foster, Eudine. 1992. The construct of a post-modernist feminist theory for Caribbean Social Science research. *Social and Economic Studies* 41, no. 2.

Barthes, R. 1976. *Elements of Semiology*. London: Jonathan Cape.

Bates, Robert. 1981. *Markets and States in Tropical Africa*. Berkeley: University of California Press.

Bates, Robert. 1993. Urban bias: a fresh look. *The Journal of Development Studies* 29, no. 4 (July).

Beck, Tony. 1993. Survival strategies and power amongst the poorest in a West Bengal village. *IDS Bulletin* 20, no. 4 (July).

Becker, Howard. 1963. *The Outsiders – Studies in the Sociology of Deviance*. New York: Free Press.

Beckles, Hilary. 1987. *Black Rebellion in Barbados*. Bridgetown: Caribbean Publishers.

Beckles, Hilary, and Verene Shepherd, eds. 1993. *Caribbean Freedom*. Kingston: Ian Randle Publishers.

Behar, Ruth. 1990. Rage and redemption: reading the life story of a Mexican market woman. *Feminist Studies* 16, no. 2.

Belle, George. 1993. The abortive revolution in Barbados. In *Caribbean Freedom*, edited by H. Beckles and V. Shepherd. Kingston: Ian Randle Publishers.

Berg, B. 1989. *Qualitative Research Methods for the Social Sciences*. Massachusetts: Allyn and Bacon.

Berger, B. 1963. Adolescence and beyond. *Social Problems* 10.

Best, David. 1982. Can creativity be taught? *British Journal of Educational Studies* 30, no. 3 (October).

Best, Lloyd. 1986. Why NAR must remain a coalition. *Sunday Express*, 9 March.

Brake, Michael. 1985. *Comparative Youth Culture*. London: Routledge and Kegan Paul.

Brandon, E. P. 1989. *The Deductive Logical Competence of Non-Graduate Caribbean Teachers*. Mimeographed.

Brathwaite, Farley. 1985. *Unemployment in Barbados: Preliminary Analysis of Selected Policy Programmes*. Pamphlet: UWI Main Library, Cave Hill Campus.

Brierley, John S. 1992. A study of land redistribution and the demise of Grenada's estate farming system 1940–1988. *Journal of Rural Studies* 8, no. 1.

Brody, Eugene B. 1981. *Sex, Contraceptives and Motherhood in Jamaica*. Massachusetts: Harvard University Press.

Bryman, Alan. 1988. *Quantity and Quality in Social Research*. Contemporary Social Research Series 18, edited by Martin Bulmer. London: Unwin Hyman.

Buchanan, Paul. 1992. *Community Development in the 'Ranking' Economy*. 2nd. edition. Kingston: College of Arts Science and Technology.

Burdan, R., and S. Taylor. 1975. *Introduction to Qualitative Research Methods*. Toronto: John Wiley & Sons.

Burgess, Robert G. 1984. *In the Field: An Introduction to Field Research*. Contemporary Social Research Series 8, edited by Martin Bulmer. London: Allen & Unwin.

Burnett, Keith. 1989. The rise and decline of the Workers and Farmers Party: a historical study. Undergraduate thesis, University of the West Indies, St Augustine.

Campbell, Peter. 1994. Dictatorship in the UNC charges Bhaggan. *Sunday Guardian*, 10 July.

Cardinez, Teresa Ann-Marie. 1986. The factors influencing mass political conscious-ness in Trinidad 1946–56. MSc thesis, University of the West Indies St Augustine.

Caribbean Eye. 1994. Trinidad and Tobago: Banyan.

Carter, Richard C. 1992. Crime in Barbados: a sociological analysis. *The New Bajan* (April/May).

Census Summary Report. 1991. Statistical Department, Ministry of Finance, St George's, Grenada

CEPAC. 1992. *Annual Report*. San Fernando: CEPAC.

CEPAC. 1990. *An overview of CEPAC*. San Fernando: CEPAC.

Chadwick, Bruce *et al*. 1984. *Social Science Research Methods*. Englewood Cliffs: Prentice Hall.

Chambers, Robert. 1989. Editorial. *IDS Bulletin* 20, no. 2 (April).

Chambers, R., and G.R. Conway. 1992. *Sustainable Rural Livelihoods: Practical Concepts for the 21st Century*. Brighton: Institute of Development Studies Discussion Paper 296.

Clark, John. 1990. *Democratizing Development: The Role of Voluntary Organizations*. Connecticut: Kumarian Press.

Clarke, Colin G. 1983. Dependency and marginality in Kingston, Jamaica. *Journal of Geography* 82, no. 5.

Clarke, Edith. 1957. *My Mother Who Fathered Me*. London: George Allen & Unwin.

Clarke, Knolly. 1994. Personal interview. 24 May.

Clarke, Roberta. 1994. Personal interview. 25 May.

CLS. 1981. *Fight Back With Solidarity: A Statement of Intent*. San Fernando: Vanguard.

CNIRD. 1989. *Profile of Rural Development Agencies/Groups in Trinidad and Tobago*. Trinidad and Tobago: CNIRD.

Cohen, A. K. 1955. *Delinquent Boys – the Subculture of the Gang*. London: Collier-Macmillan.

Cohen, Phil. 1972. *Subcultural Conflict and Working Class Community*. Birmingham: University of Birmingham.

Colburn, Forrest D. 1993. Exceptions to urban bias in Latin America: Cuba and Costa Rica. *Journal of Development Studies* 29, no. 4 (July).

Comacho, D. 1993. Latin America: a society in motion. In *New Social Movements in the South*, edited by P. Wignaraja. New Delhi: Sage.

Commonwealth Secretariat. 1991. *Change For The Better: Global Change and Economic Development*. London: Commonwealth Secretariat.

Commonwealth Youth Programme (Caribbean Centre). 1987a. *Report of a Regional workshop on Teenage Parenthood*. London: Commonwealth Secretariat.

Commonwealth Youth Programme (Caribbean Centre). 1987b. *Report on a Survey of Unemployment and Occupation Preferences of Youth in the Caribbean*. London: Commonwealth Secretariat.

The Concerned Trade Unions. 1986. *Towards United Trade Union Activity*. Paper presented to a special all day seminar of representatives of all trade unions.

Conway, D. 1981. Fact or opinion on uncontrolled peripheral settlement in Trinidad. *Ekistics*.

Conway. D. 1984. Potential and impact of remittances on micro-state development in the Caribbean. *Bulletin of Eastern Caribbean Affairs* 11, nos. 4 & 5.

Coombs, Donna. 1994. Personal interview. 7 June.

Cooper, Carolyn. 1988. That cunny jamma oman: female sensibility in the poetry of Louise Bennett. *Race and Class* 29, no. 4 (Spring).

Corbin, Alpheus. 1970. Has the NJAC precisely evaluated the real nature of the relevant needs of the country? *Express*, 15 December.

Coser, Lewis A. 1977. *Masters of Sociological Thought*. USA: Harcourt Brace Jovanovich.

Cotlear, David. 1989. The effects of education on farm productivity. *Journal of Development Planning*, no. 19.

CPTU. 1991. *Grand Council Report*. Paper presented to Special Convention on the Dissolution of the Council of Progressive Trade Unions. 11 October. Port of Spain: CPTU.

Craig, Dennis. 1971. *The Use of Language by 7-year-old Jamaican Children*. London: University of London.

Craig, Dennis R. 1983. Teaching standard English to non-standard speakers: some methodological issues. *Journal of Negro Education* 52, no.1.

Craig, Dennis R. 1986. Social class and the use of language: a case study of Jamaican children 1986. In *Varieties of English Around the World, Focus on the Caribbean*, edited by Gorlach, Manfred and Holm. London: John Benjamin.

Craig, Susan. 1982. Background to the 1970 confrontation in Trinidad and Tobago. In *Contemporary Caribbean: A Sociological Reader* 2, edited by Susan Craig, 385–424. Trinidad and Tobago: College Press.

Craton, Michael. 1993. Continuity not change: the incidence of unrest among ex-slaves in the British West Indies, 1838-1876. In *Caribbean Freedom*, edited by H. Beckles and V. Shepherd, 192–206. Kingston: Ian Randle Publishers.

Daily Gleaner. 1987. 2 November.

Daily Gleaner. 1993. 21 November.

Davis, Angela. 1981. *Woman, Race and Class*. London: The Woman's Press.

De Britto, Navarro. 1986. Reflections on education in Latin America. *La Educacion* 1, no. 99.

De Landsheere, Vivian. 1987. Minimum competency in secondary education. *Prospects* 17, no. 1.

De Saussure, F. 1974. *Course in General Linguistics*. London: Fontana.

Degazon-Johnson, Rolande. 1982. An investigation into home and school correlates of alienation among a sample of Jamaican youth. MA thesis, University of the West Indies, Mona.

Demas, William G. 1977. Employment strategies and youth movements in the Caribbean. *Caribbean Assembly of Youth Conference Paper*. Port-of-Spain.

Denzin, N. 1970. *Sociological Methods: A Sourcebook*. Chicago: Aldine.

Diptee, Judy. 1993. Trade unions losing members. *Express*, 24 May.

Dodd, David, and Michael Parris. 1976. *Socio-Cultural Aspects of Crime and Delinquency in Georgetown*. Mona: Institute of Social and Economic Studies.

Doornbos, Martin. 1992. Foreword. In *Development and Change* 23, no. 3.

Douglass, Lisa. 1992. *The Power of Sentiment: Hierarchy and the Jamaican Family Elite*. Boulder and San Francisco and Oxford: Westview Press.

Downes, D. 1966. *The Delinquent Solution*. London: Routledge and Kegan Paul.

Duke, Nicole. 1993. Unions facing 'retrenchment'. *Sunday Guardian*, 20 June.

Duncan, Carlos. 1977. Tapia and its politics. Undergraduate thesis, University of the West Indies, St Augustine.

DuToit, Brain, and Helen I. Safra. 1975. *Migration and Urbanization: Models and Adoptive Strategies*. The Hague: Mouton.

Economic Commission for Latin America and the Caribbean. 1992. *Education and Knowledge: Basic Pillars of Changing Production Patterns with Social Equity*. Santiago: ECLAC-UNESCO.

Edwards, Dennis J. 1981. Aspects of social and political Attitudes among youth in West Kingston. MSc thesis, University of the West Indies.

Eisenstadt, S.N. 1956. *From Generation to Generation*. Chicago: Chicago Free Press.

Eldermire, A. M. D. 1993. An epidemiological survey of the elderly in Jamaica. PhD thesis. UWI Mona: Department of Social and Preventitive Medicine.

Ellis, H., et al. 1990. A knowledge, attitude, belief and practices survey in relation to AIDS amongst children aged 11–16 in Barbados. *Bulletin of Eastern Caribbean Affairs* 16, nos. 1 & 2.

Ellis, Hayacinthe. 1991. *A Study of Socio-Economic and Socio-Demographic Contributions to Crimes in Jamaica*. 1950-1984. New York: Peter Lang Publishing House.

Emmanuel, Patrick A. M. 1993. *Governance and Democracy in the Commonwealth Caribbean: An Introduction*. Monograph Series no. 3. Barbados: ISER.

Emmanuel, Patrick. 1994. Voters survey and opinion poll for the 1994 general elections in Barbados. *Sunday Sun* 13–27 August; 5 September.

Ennis, Robert H. 1984. Problems in testing informal logic, critical thinking, reasoning ability. *Informal Logic 6*, no.1.

Express. 1988. Panday told he could do better. 9 February.

Eyre, L. Alan. 1984. Internal dynamics of shanty towns in Jamaica. *Caribbean Geography* 1, no. 4.

Eyre, Alan L. 1986. The effects of political terrorism on the residential location of the poor in the Kingston urban region. *Urban Geography* 7, no. 3.

Femia, J. 1981. *Gramsci's Political Thought*. Oxford: Clarendon Press.

Figueroa, P., and G. Persaud, eds. 1976. *Sociology of Education: A Caribbean Reader*. New York: Oxford University Press.

Fishman, Jacob, and Fredric Solomon. 1972. Youth and social action: an introduction. In *The Seeds of Politics: Youth and Politics in America*.

Frank, Andre Gunder. 1969. *Capitalism and Under-development in Latin America*. London: Monthly Review Press.

Freire, P., and D. Macedo. 1987. *Literacy: Reading the Word and the World*. South Hadley, MA: Bergin and Garvey.

Frith, Simon. 1984. *The Sociology of Youth*. Lancashire: Causeway Press.

Fung-Kee-Fung, Peter. 1985. We need a New National Movement. *Sunday Guardian*, 10 March.

Gee, James Paul. 1988. The legacies of literacy: from Plato to Freire through Harvey Graff. *Harvard Educational Review* 58, no. 2.

Getzels J. W., and P. W. Jackson. 1962. *Creativity and Intelligence*. New York: Wiley.

Gilroy, Paul. 1987. *There Ain't No Black in the Union Jack*. London: Hutchinson.

Girvan, Norman, *et al.* 1973. Unemployment in Jamaica. In *Readings in Political Economy of the Caribbean*, edited by Norman Girvan and Owen Jefferson Kingston: New World.

Goodridge, Sehon. 1986. Generation gap, fact or fallacy? Problem or opportunity? *Bulletin of Eastern Caribbean Affairs* 12, no. 5.

Gordon, Derek. 1987. *Class, Status and Social Mobility in Jamaica.* Mona, Jamaica: ISER.

Gordon, Shirley. 1974. *Reports and Repercussions.* London: Ginn & Co.

Gordon, Shirley. 1968. *Reports and Repercussions in West Indian Education, 1838-1933.* Jamaica: Caribbean University Press.

Government of Barbados (Ministry of Community Development and Culture). 1991. *Negative Factors Impacting on Youth in Barbados.* Bridgetown: Government Printing Office.

Government of Barbados (Ministry of Labour and Community Development). 1992. *Labour Market Information Report.* Bridgetown: Government Printing Office.

Government of Barbados (Ministry of Finance). 1992. *Towards the 21st Century, Barbados Development Plan, 1992–2000.* Bridgetown: Government Printing Office.

Government of Grenada. Census summary reports for 1981 and 1991. St George's, Grenada: Statistical Department, Ministry of Finance and Planning.

Government of Grenada. *Statistical Pocket Digest, 1991.* St Georges's, Grenada: Statistical Department, Ministry of Finance.

Government of Grenada. *Annual Economic Report, 1993.* St George's, Grenada: Ministry of Finance.

Government of Grenada. Consumer Price Index (CPI) summary sheet June–August, 1994. Grenada: Central Statistics Office.

Gramsci, Antonio. 1971. *Selections From the Prison Notebooks.* London: Lawrence & Wishart.

Grant, Lennox. 1987. The politics of gender. *Sunday Express*, 26 April.

Gray, Obika. 1991. *Radicalism and Social Change in Jamaica, 1960-1972.* Knoxville: University of Tennessee Press.

Grenada Handbook Directory. 1946. Barbados: The Advocate Co. Ltd.

Hackshaw, John Milton. 1991. *Trade Unions and Politics.* San Fernando: Vanguard.

Hackshaw, John Milton. 1994. *Democracy in Political Parties and the Labour Movement.* Trinidad and Tobago: John Milton.

Hakim, Catherine. 1987. *Research Design: Strategies and Choice in the Design of Social Research.* Contemporary Social Research Series 13, edited by Martin Bulmer. London: Unwin Hyman.

Hall, Douglas. 1982. *The Caribbean Experience: An Historical Survey, 1450–1960.* Kingston: Heinemann Educational Books (Caribbean) Ltd.

Hall, G. Stanley. 1904. *Adolescence and its Relations to Psychology, Anthropology, Sociology, Sex, Crime, Religion, and Education.* London: Appleton and Co.

Hall, Stuart, et al. 1978. *Policing the Crisis.* London: Macmillam.

Hall, S., and T. Jefferson, eds. 1976. *Resistance Through Ritual.* London: Harper Collins Academic.

Harding, Sandra. 1991. *Whose Science? Whose Knowledge? Thinking Women's Lives.* New York: Cornell University Press.

Harding, Sandra, ed. 1987. *Feminism and Methodology*. Indiana: Indiana University Press.

Harewood, Jack. 1966. Population growth in Grenada. *Social and Economic Studies* 15, no. 2.

Harris, Louis, et al. 1975. The myth and reality of aging in America. Study prepared for the National Council on the Aging.

Harry, George. 1989. Powers yes, but to which people? *Sunday Guardian*, 28 May.

Hart, Keith, ed. 1989. *Women and The Sexual Division of Labour*. Mona, Jamaica: Consortium Graduate School of the Social Sciences.

Harvey, Franklyn. 1974. *Rise and Fall of Party Politics in Trinidad and Tobago*. Toronto: New Beginning Movement.

Headley, Bernard. 1992. *Jamaican Crime and Violence at Home and Abroad*. Chicago, Illinois.

Heaton, Tim B., et al. 1982. Migration and the transformation of employment and household structures. *Singapore Journal of Tropical Geography* 3, no. 1 (June).

Hebdige, D. 1979. *Subculture – the Meaning of Style*. London: Methuen & Co.

Held, David. 1992a. Democracy: from city-state to a cosmopolitan order? In *Political Studies* 40. Kingston: FES.

Held, David, ed. 1992b. In *Political Studies* 40. Special Issue: Prospects for democracy. Kingston: FES.

Heitner, Keri, et al 1990. *What Do Workers Have to Say? Skills and Technological Change*. Springfield.

Henderson, Thelma. 1994. Personal interview. 13 July.

Henry, Paget, and Paul Buhle, eds. 1992. *C.L.R. James's Caribbean*. London: MacMillan.

Henry, Zin. 1988. Industrial relations and the development process. In *The Independence Experience: 1962–1987*, edited by Selwyn Ryan. St Augustine: ISER.

Hill-Collins, Patricia. 1991. *Black Feminist Thought: Knowledge, Consciousness and the Politics of Empowerment*. New York and London: Unwin Hyman.

Hodge, Merle. 1994. Personal interview. 11 July.

Hooks, Bell. 1981. *Ain't I A Woman: Black Women and Feminism*. Boston: South End Press.

Hooks, Bell. 1988. *Talking Back: Thinking Feminist, Thinking Black*. Canada: Between The Lines.

Humphreys, L. 1970. *Tearoom Trade*. Chicago: Aldine.

Institute of Social and Economic Research. 1992. *The National Survey on Youth*. Kingston, Jamaica: ISER.

International Labour Organisation. 1987. *Training and Retraining-Implications of Technological Change*. Geneva: ILO.

Isaacs, Ian. 1984. Problem solving in Jamaican high schools. Paper presented at ICMEV, University of Adelaide, Australia.

Jack, Jacqueline. 1994. Personal interview. 13 June.

Jackson, Elton F. 1962. Status consistency and symptoms of stress. *American Sociological Review* 27, no. 4.

Jagdeo, Tirbani. 1984. *Teenage Pregnancy in the Caribbean*. Antigua: Caribbean Family Planning Association.

James, C.L.R. 1993. *American Civilization*. London: Blackwell.

James-Bryan, Meryl. 1986. Youth in the Anglophone Caribbean: the high cost of dependent development. *CEPAL Review* 29.

Jones, Edwin. 1987. *Coalitions of the Oppressed*. Kingston, Jamaica: Institute of Social and Economic Research.

JTUM. 1989. *Towards a Peaceful Approach to Economic Recovery*. Trinidad and Tobago: JTUM.

JTUM. 1986. *Statement from the JTUM to the Working People, Farmers, Housewives, Youths, Unemployed of Trinidad and Tobago on the Economic Crisis*. Trinidad and Tobago: JTUM.

Jules, Didacus. 1987. Building a national movement: the Caribbean experience. In *Literacy in the Industrialised Countries: A Focus on Practice*, edited by Margaret Gayfer. Toronto: International Council for Adult Education.

Jules, Didacus. 1988. Planning functional literacy programmes in the Caribbean. *Prospect* 18, no. 3.

Kambon, Khafra. 1988. *For Bread, Justice and Freedom: A Political Biography of George Weekes*. London: New Beacon Books.

Kane, Robert, et al. eds. 1990. *Improving the Health of Older People: A World View*. Oxford: Oxford University Press.

Kangalee, Gerry. 1994. Personal interview. 8 June.

Keane, John. 1992. Democracy and the media – without foundations. In *Political Studies* 40.

Keniston, Kenneth. 1975. Youth as a stage of life. In *Youth*, edited by R. J. Haughurst and P.H. Dreger. Chicago: University of Chicago Press.

Kennedy, Coreen. 1989. Technical-vocational education and youth unemployment in Barbados. Dissertation, University of the West Indies, Cave Hill.

King, Ruby. 1987. The Jamaica Schools Commission and the development of secondary schooling. In *Education in the Caribbean, Historical Perspectives*, edited by Ruby King. Mona: Faculty of Education, UWI.

Kinsella, Kevin. 1988. *Aging in the Third World*. International Population Report Series no. 79, US Dept. of Commerce.

Kirby, P., et al. 1987. *Jobs For Young People*. London: Commonwealth Secretariat.

Kothari, R. 1993. Masses, classes and the state. In *New Social Movements in the South*, edited by P. Wignaraja. New Delhi: Sage.

Kromah, Jean. 1987. NJAC: change from extra-constitutional to constitutional politics in Trinidad and Tobago, 1970–1986. Undergraduate thesis, UWI St Augustine.

Laclau, Ernesto, and Chantal Mouffe. 1985. *Hegemony and Socialist Strategy: Towards a Radical Democratic Politics*. London: Verso.

Ladner, Joyce, ed. 1973. *The Death of White Sociology*. New York: Vintage Books.

Laguerre, Michael S. 1990. *Urban Poverty in the Caribbean*. New York: St Martin's Press.

Laird, Christoper. 1994. Personal interview. 18 May.

Lankshear, Colin. 1986. Humanizing functional literacy: beyond utilitarian necessity. *Educational Theory* 36, no. 4 (Fall).

Lau, Lawrence. 1990. *Models of Development*. San Francisco: ICS Press.

Learman, Paul. 1975. *Community Treatment and Social Control: A Critical Analysis of Juvenile Corrections*. Chicago: University of Chicago Press.

Lenski, Gerhard E. 1954. Status crystallization: a non-vertical dimension of social status. *American Sociological Review* 19, no.1.

Levi-Strauss, C. 1969. *Totemism*. New York: Penguin.

Lewis, Gordon. 1969. *The Growth of the Modern West Indies*. New York: Monthly Review Press.

Lewis, Gordon. 1993. The challenge of independence in the British Caribbean. In *Caribbean Freedom*, edited by H. Beckles and V. Shepherd. Kingston: Ian Randle Publishers.

Le Franc, Elsie. 1993. *Status Group Formation in Small Communities: A Case Study of a Dominican Small Farming Village*. Kingston: ISER.

Lipton, Michael. 1977. *Why Poor People Stay Poor: Urban Bias in World Development*. Cambridge: Harvard University Press.

Lipton, Michael. 1993. Urban bias: of consequences, classes and causality. *The Journal of Development Studies* 29, no. 4 (July).

Locher, H.C. 1980. *The Fate of Migrants in Urban Haiti*. Ann Arbor: University of Michigan Microfilm International.

Look Lai, Walton. 1992. C.L.R. James and Trinidadian nationalism. In *C.L.R. James' Caribbean*, edited by Paget Henry and Paul Buhle. London: MacMillan Press.

Look Loy, Keith. 1994. Personal interview. 15 June.

Lorde, Audre. 1984. *Sister Outsider: Essays and Speeches*. Trumansburg, New York: The Crossing Press Feminist Series.

Lovell, Lex, and Anthony Mowlah-Baksh. 1994. Personal interview. 14 June.

Mabogunje, Akon L. 1989. *The Development Process: A Spatial Perspective*. London: Unwin Hyman.

Macmillan, W.M. 1938. *Warning from the West Indies*. London: Penguin.

Mahabir, Mikey. 1988. Sudama: PM has no power to dismiss NAR members. *Express*. n.p; n.d.

Mamdani, M. 1993. Social movements and democracy in Africa. In *New Social Movements in the South*, edited by P. Wignaraja. New Delhi: Sage.

Mangalam, J. J., and Schwarzweller, Harry K. 1970. Some theoretical guidelines toward a sociology of migration. *International Migration Review* 4, no. 2 (Spring).

Marx, Karl, and Fredrich Engels. 1970. *The German Ideology*. London: Lawrence & Wishart.

Massiah, Joycelin, ed. 1986. Women in the Caribbean (Part 1). *Social and Economic Studies* 35, no. 2 (Special Number).

Massiah, Joycelin, ed. 1986. Women in the Caribbean (Part 2). *Social and Economic Studies* 35, no. 3 (Special Number).

Mathurin-Mair, Lucille. 1975. *The Rebel Woman in the British West Indies During Slavery*. Jamaica: Institute of Jamaica for the African-Caribbean Institute of Jamaica.

Matza, D. 1969. *Becoming Deviant*. Englewood Cliffs: Prentice Hall.

Max-Neef, M., et al. 1989. Human scale development. *Development Dialogue* 1.

McIntyre, Arnold. 1987. *Science and Technology Policy in Developing Countries: Some Implications for the Commonwealth Caribbean*. Mimeographed.

McLaren, Peter L. 1988. Culture or canon? Critical pedagogy and the politics of literacy. *Harvard Educational Review* 58, no.2.

McLeod, Errol. 1987. *Presidential Address to the 48th Annual Conference of Delegates*. San Fernando: Vanguard.

Meeks, Brian. 1976. The development of the 1970 revolution in Trinidad and Tobago. MSc thesis, University of the West Indies, St Augustine.

Meighoo, Kirk. 1992. History, class, ideology and empowerment: an examination of Ssrvol and development in Trinidad and Tobago. IDS Research Paper. University of Toronto: Scarborough.

Merton, R.K. 1938. Social structure and anomie. *American Sociological Review* 13.

Miller, Errol. 1969. Body image, physical beauty and colour among Jamaican adolescents. *Social and Economic Studies* 18, no. 1.

Miller, Errol. 1986. *Marginalization of the Black Male: Insights from the Development of the Teaching Profession*. Mona, Jamaica: ISER.

Miller, Errol. 1987. Academic upgrading of unqualified teachers in the Windward Islands by distance teaching: feasibility study. Study commissioner by the Organization for Cooperation in Overseas Development and the Canadian International Development Agency.

Miller, Errol 1990. *High Schooling in Jamaica*. UWI, Mona: ISER.

Miller, Errol. 1991. *Men At Risk*. Kingston, Jamaica: Jamaica Publishing House Ltd.

Miller, Errol. 1992. *Perspectives on Education For All*. Baltimore: Johns Hopkins University Press.

Miller, David. 1992. Deliberative democracy and social choice. In Political Studies 40.

Miller, W.B. 1958. Lower class culture as a generating milieu of gang delinquency. *Journal of Social Issues* 14.

Milliband, Ralph. 1969. *The State in Capitalist Society*. London: Quartet Books.

Mills, Charles. 1988. Getting out of the cave: tension between democracy and elitism in Marx's theory of cognitive liberation. Paper presented at Conference of Caribbean Studies Association, Guadeloupe.

Mills, Charles. 1991. Marxism and Caribbean development: a contribution to rethinking. In *Rethinking Development*, edited by Judith Wedderburn. Kingston: Consortium Graduate School.

Mohammed, Patricia. 1989. Women's response in the 70s and 80s in Trinidad: a country report. *Caribbean Quarterly* 35, no.12.

Mohammed, Patricia. 1991. Reflections on the women's movement in Trinidad: calypsos, changes and sexual violence. *Feminist Review* no. 38 (Summer).

Mohammed, Patricia. 1993. Gender, ethnicity and class in Trinidad. In *Trinidad Ethnicity*, edited by Kevin Yelvington. Knoxville, Tennessee: University of Tennessee Press.

Mohammed, Patricia. 1994. A social history of post-migrant Indians in Trinidad from 1917 to 1947: a gender perspective. PhD dissertation, Institute of Social Studies, The Hague.

Mohammed, Patricia. 1994. Nuancing the feminist discourse in the Caribbean. Paper presented at the 19th Annual Caribbean Studies Association Conference, Merida, Mexico, 23–28 May 1994.

Mohammed, Patricia, and Catherine Shepherd, eds. 1988. *Gender in Caribbean Development*. Mona, Jamaica: University of the West Indies.

Mohanty, Chandra Talpade, et al. 1991. *Third World Women and the Politics of Feminism*. Bloomington and Indianapolis: Indiana University Press.

Momsen, Janet H., ed. 1993. *Women and Change in the Caribbean: A Pan Caribbean Perspective.* Kingston, Jamaica: Ian Randle Publishers.

Moore, Mick. 1993. Economic structure and the politics of sectoral bias: East Asia and other cases. *Journal of Development Studies* 29, no. 4 (July).

Moraga, Cherrie, and Gloria Anzaldúa; eds. 1983. *This Bridge Called My Back: Writings By Radical Women of Colour.* New York: Kitchen Table Women of Colour Press.

Morris, David. 1993. United Nations Development Programme: Human Development Report 1991. *Economic Development and Cultural Change* 41, no. 4 (July).

MOTION. 1989. *Towards a New Democracy and the Road to Full Employment.* San Fernando: Classline Publications.

Mowlah-Baksh, Sabrina. 1994. Personal interview. 10 June.

National Committee on Excellence in Education. 1983. *Nation At Risk.* Washington: US Government Printing Office.

Nettleford, Rex. 1991. Education and society in the Commonwealth Caribbean, issues and problems. In *Education and Society in the Commonwealth Caribbean,* edited by Errol Miller. Mona: Institute of Social and Economic Research.

Newels, Roswitha, et al. 1990. *Integrated Macro-Economics Development Planning for Sustainable Development: Guideline for Island Developing Countries.* UNDP.

New Rebels Movement. 1993a. *Manifesto.* Trinidad and Tobago: New Rebels Movement.

New Rebels Movement. 1993b. *Manifesto of the New Rebels Movement: Highlights of Our Programme.* Trinidad and Tobago: New Rebels Movement.

Nickerson, Raymond, et al. *1985. The Teaching of Thinking.* Hillsdale: Lawrence Erlbaum.

Nolan, C.A., and E.P. Brandon. 1984. Conditional reasoning in Jamaica. Paper presented at the Conference on Thinking, Harvard. Mimeographed.

Nurse, Lawrence. 1986. Organised labour in the Commonwealth Caribbean. In *A Caribbean Reader on Development,* edited by Judith Wedderburn. Kingston: FES

O'Conner, James. 1989. Uneven and combined development and ecological crisis: a theoretical introduction. *Race and Class* 30, no. 3.

O'Donnell, Michael. 1985. *Age and Generation.* London: Tavistock Publishers.

OWTU. 1986. *General Council's Report.* San Fernando: OWTU and Vanguard.

OWTU. 1994a. *General Council's Report.* San Fernando: OWTU.

OWTU. 1994b. *The Case Against the Sell-Out of the National Interest.* San Fernando: Vanguard.

OWTU. 1994c. *What You Need to Know About Privatisation.* San Fernando: Vanguard.

OWTU. 1993. *General Council's Report.* San Fernando: OWTU.

OWTU. 1992. *General Council's Report.* San Fernando: OWTU.

OWTU. 1990. *General Council's Report.* San Fernando: OWTU

OWTU. 1990. *SOPO is Born!* San Fernando: OWTU

OWTU. 1989a. *General Council's Report.* San Fernando: OWTU.

OWTU. 1989b. *Rules of the OWTU.* San Fernando: Vanguard.

OWTU. 1988. *General Council's Report.* San Fernando: OWTU.

OWTU. 1970. *General Council's Report.* San Fernando: OWTU.

OWTU. 1977. *OWTU: July 1937–July 1977.* San Fernando: Vanguard

Bibliography

OWTU. 1969. *The OWTU: 1937–1969*. San Fernando: Vanguard.

Pantin, Raoul. 1988. *Black Power Day*. San Juan: Longman Trinidad.

Papadopoulus, George S. 1988. Education: the search for a new consensus. *The OECD Observer* 154 (October/November).

Parekh, Bhiku. 1992. The cultural peculiarity of liberal democracy. In *Political Studies* 40. Kingston: FES.

Parsons, Talcott. 1964. Age and sex roles in the United States. In *Essays in Sociological Theory*, edited by Talcott Parsons. Chicago: Chicago Free Press.

Partap, Harry. 1990. OWTU no lawless brigade. *Sunday Express*, 14 October.

Patterson, Orlando. 1967. *The Children of Sisyphus*. London: Longman.

Paul, Cecil. 1987. *Labour Unity Post – PNM*. Trinidad and Tobago: JTUM.

Paul, Cecil. 1990a. *Democracy and Centralism*. Trinidad and Tobago: MOTION.

Paul, Cecil. 1990b. *Developments in Eastern Europe and the Socialist World – The Crisis of Socialism*. Trinidad and Tobago: MOTION.

Paul, Cecil. 1994. Personal interview. 19 May.

Pavri, Francis. 1990. Technology and people: the importance of the human element in information technology. In *Technology and Singapore Society: Trends, Policies and Applications*, edited by Eddie Kuo, et al. Kent Ridge: Singapore University Press.

People's Forum. 1992. Trinidad and Tobago: SWUTT.

Perez, Carlota. 1985. Microelectronics, long waves and world structural change: new perspectives for developing countries. *World Development* 13, no.3.

Perlman, Janice. 1986. Six misconceptions about squatter settlements. *Development* 4.

Persaud, Narine. 1985. *The Development of Under-development in Grenada*. Ann Arbor: University of Michigan Microfilms International.

Phillips, Anne. 1992. Must feminists give up on liberal democracy? In *Political Studies* 40, edited by David Held. Kingston: FES.

Pick, Hella. 1964. Research on youth groups and youth leaders in developing countries: 1957–1964. *Department of State: External Research Staff Papers*. Washington: Department of State.

Pieterse, Jan Nederveen, ed. 1992a. *Development and Change* 23, no. 3. Special Issue: Emancipations: Modern and Postmodern.

Pieterse, Jan Nederveen. 1992b. Emancipations, modern and postmodern. In *Development and Change* 23, no. 3.

The Planning Institute of Jamaica. 1993. *Economic and Social Survey Jamaica 1992*. Kingston, Planning Institute of Jamaica.

Planning Institute of Jamaica. 1992. *Social and Economic Survey, 1991*. Kingston: Planning Institute of Jamaica.

Planning Institute of Jamaica. 1990. *Social and Economic Survey, 1989*. Kingston: Planning Institute of Jamaica.

Pool, Gail R. 1989. Shifts in Grenadian migration: an historical perspective. *International Migration Review* 23, no. 2 (Summer).

Porter, Robert B. 1984. Spatial perceptions and public involvement in Third World urban planning: the example of Barbados. *Singapore Journal of Tropical Geography* 5, no. 1.

Price, Richard. 1990. *Alabi's World*. Baltimore: Johns Hopkins University Press.

Psacharopoulos, George. 1984. Assessing priorities in developing countries: current practice and possible alternatives. *International Labour Review* 123, no. 5 (September/October).

Psacharopoulos, George, and Francis Steiner. 1988. Education and the labour market in Venezuela, 1975–1994. *Economics of Education Review* 8, no. 3.

Rajack T.A. (n.d.) *Small Farmer Organization for Small Farmer Development*. Trinidad and Tobago: CNIRD.

Ramjag, Glen. 1994a. Personal interview. 17 May.

Ramjag, Glen. (1994b). Personal interview. 27 June.

Ramsaran, Dave. 1990. Trade union organization: a comparative study of trade unionism in the oil and sugar sectors. MSc thesis, University of the West Indies, St Augustine.

Ramsaroop, Bidgawatee. 1990. The influence of the OWTU on the politics of Trinidad and Tobago from 1976 to the present. Undergraduate thesis, University of the West Indies, St Augustine.

Ramtahal, Mohan. 1982. The ONR – case study of the emergence of a mass political party. Undergraduate thesis, University of the West Indies, St Augustine.

Rebel Team. 1993. *United and Ready for Struggle*. San Fernando: OWTU.

Reddock, Rhoda. 1984a. *The Caribbean Feminist Tradition*. Trinidad and Tobago: CAFRA.

Reddock, Rhoda. 1984b. Women, labour and struggle in 20th century Trinidad and Tobago: 1989–1960. PhD dissertation, ISS, The Hague.

Reddock, Rhoda. 1990. *Women's Organizations and Movements in the Commonwealth Caribbean in the Context of the World Economic Crisis of the 1980s*. Trinidad and Tobago: CAFRA.

Reddock, Rhoda. 1991. Towards a framework for the study of women, gender and social movements in Africa. Paper presented for the CODESRIA Workshop on Gender Analysis and African Social Science, Dakar, 16-21 September.

Reddock, Rhoda. 1993. Primacy of gender in race and class. In *Race, Class and Gender in the Future of the Caribbean*, edited by J. Edward Greene. Mona, Jamaica: ISER.

Reddock, Rhoda. 1994. Women, labour and struggle in 20th century Trinidad and Tobago, 1898–1960. PhD dissertation, University of Amsterdam.

Resistance II: Gov't, Labour claim victory. 1994. *Express*, 26 April.

Richardson, A.G. 1982. The measurement of creativity and related personality inputs among a sample of Jamaican adolescents. PhD dissertation, University of the West Indies, Mona.

Riviere, Bill. 1972. *Black Power, NJAC, and the 1970 Confrontation in the Caribbean: An Historical Interpretation*. Mona: ISER.

Roach, Lawrence. 1986. Implementing community base policing in the London Metropolitan Police. In Loree, et al, eds. *Community Policing in The 1980s: Recent Advances in Police Programs*, edited by Ottawa.

Roberts, Kenneth. 1983. *Youth and Leisure*. London: George Allen & Unwin.

Robinson, Deanna, et al. 1991. *Music at the Margins*. California: Sage.

Rodney, Walter. 1993. The Ruimveldt Riots: Demerara, British Guiana, 1905. In *Caribbean Freedom*, edited by H. Beckles and V. Shepherd. Kingston: Ian Randle Publishers.

Rohlehr, Gordon. 1986. Images of men and women in the 1930s calypso. In *Gender in Caribbean Development*, edited by Patricia Mohammed and Catherine Shepherd, Mona, Jamaica: University of the West Indies.

Rohlehr, Gordon. 1990. *Calypso and Society in Pre-Independence Trinidad*. Port of Spain: Gordon Rohlehr.

Rojas, Don. 1988. One people, One Destiny: the Caribbean and Central America Today, edited by Don Rojas. New York: Pathfinder.

Roopsingh, Gangadaye. 1990. Black Power: attitude changes among Caroni residents 10 years later. Undergraduate thesis, University of the West Indies, St Augustine.

Ross-Frankson, Joan, et al.1990. Conversations about campaigns. *Woman Speak!* 26–27.

Rousseau, Gregory. 1994. Personal Interview. 3 June.

Rubin, Vera, and Marisa Zavalloni. 1969. *We Wished to be Looked Upon: A Study of the Aspirations of Youth in a Developing Society*. New York: Teachers College Press.

Rueschemeyer, Dietrich, et al.1992. *Capitalist Development and Democracy*. Cambridge: Polity Press.

Rumberger, Russell, and Henry Levin. 1989. Education, work and employment in developed countries, situation and future challenges. *Prospect* 19, no. 2.

Rush, Timothy. 1987. Writing, reading and reality. Paper presented at the Annual Meeting of the Wyoming Association of Teachers of English, Rock Springs, 3–4 October.

Rustin, Michael. 1989. The politics of post-Fordism, or the trouble with 'New Times'. *New Left Review* 175.

Ryan, Selwyn. 1991. *The Muslimeen Grab for Power*. Port of Spain: Inprint.

Ryan, Selwyn. 1989. *Revolution and Reaction: A Study of Parties and Politics in Trinidad and Tobago, 1970-1981*. St. Augustine: ISER.

Sahadeo, Indar. 1986. *The Development of the Trade Union Movement – Local, Regional, and International*. Trinidad and Tobago: Cipriani Labour College.

Savasdisara, Tongchai. 1984. The non-economic factors in rural-urban migration in Thailand. *Singapore Journal of Tropical Geography* 5, no. 2.

Sawyer, Ethel. 1973. The study of so-called deviant communities. In *The Death of White Sociology*, edited by Joyce Ladner. New York: Vintage Books.

Schumpeter, Joseph A. 1976. *Capitalism, Socialism and Democracy*. 5th ed. London: George Allen & Unwin Ltd.

Scott, James C. 1990. *Domination and the Arts of Resistance: Hidden Transcripts* New Haven and London: Yale University Press.

Sebastien, Raphael. 1985. *Forging a New Democracy*. Trinidad and Tobago: Office of the Leader of Opposition.

Senior, Olive. 1991. *Working Miracles: Women's Lives in the English Speaking Caribbean*. Cave Hill, Barbados: ISER.

Shaw, P. R. 1975. *Migration Theory and Facts: A Review and Bibliography of Current Literature*. Philadelphia: Regional Science Research Institute.

Shepherd, Cathy, et al. 1987. *The Group 1983-1987*. Trinidad and Tobago: The Group.

Shields, Vicki Rutlegde, and Brenda Derwin. 1993. Sense-making in feminist social science research: a call to enlarge the methodological options of feminist studies. *Women's International Forum*. 16, no. 1.

Sistren and Honor Ford Smith. 1987. *Lionheart Gal*. Ontario, Canada: Sister Vision Press.

Smith, M. G. 1965. *The Plural Society in the British West Indies*. Berkeley & Los Angeles: University of California Press.

Social Welfare Training Centre. 1980. Conference on the Elderly in Jamaica. UWI, Mona. 10–13 November.

SOPO. 1990. *Statement of the Events of 27 July 1990*. Trinidad and Tobago: OWTU.

Stoddart, K. 1986. The presentation of everyday life. *Urban Life* 15, no. 1.

Stokes, Blossom O'M. 1984. Correlates of alienation among selected Jamaican adolescents. PhD dissertation, University of the West Indies, Mona.

Stone, Carl. 1973. *Class, Race and Political Behaviour in Urban Jamaica*. Kingston, Jamaica: ISER.

Stone, Carl. 1980. *Democracy and Clientelism in Jamaica*. New Jersey: Transaction Books.

Stone, Carl. 1988. Crime and violence: socio political implications. In *Crime and Violence: Causes and Solutions* edited by P. Phillips and J. Wedderburn. Mona, Jamaica: Department of Government.

Stone, Carl. 1991. The role of the state in Third World development. In *Rethinking Development*, edited by Judith Wedderburn. Kingston: Consortium Graduate School of Social Sciences.

Streeten, Paul. 1984. Basic needs: some unsettled questions. *World Development* 12 no. 9.

Summit of National Leaders: Resolution. 1990. Trinidad and Tobago: OWTU.

Sutherland E.H., and D.R. Cressey. 1966. *Principles of Criminology*. Philadelphia: Lippincott.

T&TEC Workers Beat Back Pension Attack. 1994. *Vanguard* 15 July.

Talmon, J. L. 1952. *The Origins of Totalitarian Democracy*. Middlesex: Penguin Books Ltd.

Tandon, Yash. 1991. Political economy of struggles for democracy and human rights in Africa. *Economic and Political Weekly* 22 (June).

Tapper, Selena. 1992. *NGOs and Social Movements in the Commonwealth Caribbean*. Trinidad and Tobago: CNIRD.

Taylor, Burchel. 1992. "Free for all?"– A question of morality and community. Kingston: Grace Kennedy Foundation Lecture.

The Grenada Informer. 1994. 1 July.

The Statistical Institute of Jamaica. 1993. *Demographic Statistics 1992*. Kingston, Statistical Institute of Jamaica.

Thomas, Clive. 1974. *Dependence and Transformation*. New York: Monthly Review Press.

Thomas, Clive Y. 1984. *The Rise of the Authoritarian State in Peripheral Societies*. New York: Monthly Review Press.

Tobias, Peter M. 1976. *How You Gonna Keep Em Down in the Tropics Once They've Dreamed New York?: Some Aspects of Grenadian Migration*. Ann Arbor: University of Michigan Microfilm International.

Tobias, Peter. 1980. The social context of Grenadian migration. *Social and Economic Studies* 29, no. 1 (March).

Todaro, M.P. 1969. A model of labour migration and urban unemployment. *American Economic Review* 69.

Bibliography

Todaro, Michael P. 1985. *Economic Development in the Third World*. New York: Longman.

Toffler, Alvin. 1980. *The Third Wave*. USA: Bantam Books.

Townsend, Peter, and Dorothy Wedderburn. 1969. *The Aged in the Welfare State*. G. Bell and Sons Ltd.

Trinidad Guardian. 1990. Strange Summit. Editorial. *Trinidad Guardian*, 19 February.

Trotman, David. 1986. *Crime in Trinidad and Tobago, Conflict and Control in the Plantation Society: 1838–1900*. Knoxville: University of Tennessee Press.

Trotsky, Leon. 1978. *Leon Trotsky on Black Nationalism and Self Determination*. New York: Pathfinder.

Udika, Adisa Shabaka. 1993. The NJAC and the change from revolutionary to conventional politics. Undergraduate thesis, University of the West Indies, St Augustine.

UNICEF. 1990. *Draft Situation Analysis of Children and Women in Grenada*. Bridgetown: UNICEF Caribbean Area Office.

United Nations. 1989. *Health of the Elderly*. Report of a WHO Expert Committee. *Technical Report Series 779*. Geneva: World Health Organization.

United Nations. 1990. *Human Development Report 1990*. New York: Oxford University Press.

United Nations. 1991a. *Ageing and Urbanization*. Proceedings of the UN International Conference on Ageing Populations in the Context of Urbanization. Japan (12–16 September 1988). New York: United Nations.

United Nations. 1991b. *World Population Prospects 1990*. New York: United Nations.

United Nations. 1994a. *Ageing and the Family*. Proceedings of the United Nations International Conference on Ageing Populations in the context of the Family. Japan. (15-19 October 1990). New York: United Nations.

United Nations. 1994b. *Human Development Report 1994*. New York: Oxford University Press.

Unrest Brews in South. *Vanguard*. 15 July.

Vanguard View. 1994. *Vanguard*. 28 May.

Valentine, C.A. 1968. *Culture and Poverty*. Chicago: Chicago Free Press.

Wallerstein, Immanuel. 1984. *The Politics of the World-Economy*. Cambridge: Cambridge University Press.

Weekes, George. 1967. *The ISA*. San Fernando: Vanguard.

Wignaraja, Ponna, ed. 1992. *New Social Movements in the South: Empowering the People*. London: Zed Press.

Wignaraja, Ponna, ed. 1993. *New Social Movements in the South*. New Delhi: Sage.

Willis, Paul. 1978. *Profane Culture*. London: Routledge and Kegan Paul.

Wiltshire-Brodber, Rosina. 1988. Gender, race and class in the Caribbean. In *Gender in Caribbean Development*, edited by Patricia Mohammed and Catherine Shepherd. Mona, Jamaica: University of the West Indies.

Wolf, Naomi. 1993. Women as winners. *Glamour* (November).

Worcester, Kent. 1992. The question of the canon: CLR James and modern politics. In *C.L.R. James' Caribbean*, edited by Paget Henry and Paul Buhle. London: MacMillan.

Young, J. 1965. *High Treason: The TUC and the Sugar Workers' Strike: Why I Resigned*. San Fernando: Vanguard Publishing Company.

Young, J. 1971. *The Drug Takers*. London: Paladin.

Young, Joe. 1994. Personal interview. 16 June.

Index

Contributors

Deryck R. Brown is an MSc Social Sciences graduate of the Consortium Graduate School. He received his PhD in Development Studies, specializing in Development Administration and Management, from the University of Manchester. He is currently a Research Fellow at the Institute of Social and Economic Research, University of the West Indies, Cave Hill, Barbados.

Donneth Crooks is Lecturer in Sociology at the University of Technology, Jamaica.

David M. Franklyn is a Human Settlements Officer with the United Nations Centre for Human Settlements (Habitat), Nairobi, Kenya.

Guy Hewitt works at the Commonwealth Secretariat in London.

Oral Khan is a Major and the Assistant Staff Officer with the Jamaica Defence Force.

Sharon Kelly-Stair is a freelance education consultant.

Kirk Meighoo is a postgraduate student at the University of Hull, England.

Althea Perkins is a research assistant at the Mona Unit of the Centre for Gender and Development Studies, University of the West Indies, Mona, Jamaica.

www.ingramcontent.com/pod-product-compliance
Lightning Source LLC
Chambersburg PA
CBHW071840270326
41929CB00013B/2057